The History of Civilization

Edited by C. K. OGDEN, M.A.

The History of Music

The History of Civilization

Edited by C. K. Ogden, M.A.

Introduction and Pre-History

The Early Empires and Greece

Rome and Beyond the Roman Empire

Middle Ages to Modern Times

Historical Ethnology

Subject Histories

* An asterisk indicates that the volume does not form part of the French collection " L'Évolution de l'Humanité".

A full list of the SERIES will be found at the end of this volume.

The History of Music

By

CECIL GRAY

LONDON
KEGAN PAUL, TRENCH, TRUBNER & CO. LTD.
NEW YORK: ALFRED A. KNOPF

First published - - - May 1928
Second Edition (corrected and revised) June 1931
Reprinted - - - - February 1935
Reprinted - - - - May 1942
Reprinted - - - - January 1944

PRINTED IN GREAT BRITAIN BY
LUND HUMPHRIES
LONDON · BRADFORD

CONTENTS

PREFACE

HISTORIES of music generally belong to one or other of two definite categories : either they are elementary text-books primarily designed for educational purposes, or else they are so scientific in method and technical in language as to be virtually unintelligible to any one except a highly trained musician. So many reliable works of both kinds are already in existence that to add to their number would be a work of supererogation ; on the other hand, there would seem to be a distinct need for a survey of the entire field of musical history intended for the average, intelligent music-lover rather than for the student, and for the general, cultured reading public rather than for the professional musician. No apology then, is needed for the present modest attempt to supply this deficiency. It aims at striking a mean between the abstruse and the elementary, the scientific and the educational ; consequently musical illustrations have been dispensed with, technical terms are only employed when it proved impossible to avoid them, and biographical information, which occupies such a disproportionate amount of space in most works of this kind, has been entirely eliminated save for the occasional citation of relevant facts which help to shed light upon some particular aspect of a composer's work. At the same time, the reader is presumed to be already acquainted with the bare rudiments of music, and to have a rough general knowledge of the most important events and personalities in musical history. Finally an attempt has been made to study the art of music, not as a thing apart, but in relation to other human activities and to life generally, as befits a volume belonging to a series entitled *The History of Civilization.*

The criticism is often made that such an undertaking is beyond the scope of a single volume and cannot possibly be satisfactorily accomplished by a single writer, but this is only partially true. As Mr. G. K. Chesterton has said somewhere, even if one sets out to write the religious history of East

Rutlandshire in a large number of volumes, one will inevitably be compelled, sooner or later, to select one's material and to reject a great deal that seems to be of secondary importance ; similarly an absolutely complete and exhaustive history of music is no more possible in a hundred volumes than in one. It is equally true that no one man can hope to be acquainted with every piece of music that has been written, or even to be an authority on every period. The present writer, indeed, makes no claim to be regarded as an authority on any period whatsoever, but this is not necessarily altogether a disadvantage. In some ways it is even a positive advantage, for the period-specialist is notoriously unreliable and lacking in a sense of proportion when he comes to consider the part in relation to the whole, and his own particular period in relation to other periods.   He cannot see the wood for the trees, in fact, and the main defect of the many otherwise admirable histories of music in which a number of specialists on different subjects and epochs collaborate, consists in the fact that no clear conception of the whole emerges from the vast accumulations of data which they bring together.   For in the history of art as much as in any other branch of historical research, facts are meaningless until interpreted, and the function of the musical historian is, or should be, as different from that of the period-specialist as the function of the philosopher is from that of the chemists, physicists, biologists, anthropologists, and other scientists who provide him with his material.   His concern, in short, is not with the discovery of facts, but with their interpretation, and the revelation of their intrinsic significance. This is all that the present writer has attempted in the following pages, and if his conclusions should sometimes seem to differ strikingly from those arrived at by most historians, it will generally be found to be on points on which authoritative opinion is itself perplexed and divided, or where some purely æsthetic issue is involved.   There is no statement of fact in the following pages in support of which the opinion of at least one of the most eminent modern authorities cannot be adduced.

C.G.

London, *April*, 1928.

THE HISTORY OF MUSIC

INTRODUCTION

IF, in contradiction of the Preacher, there is anything on the earth of which it could be said, " See, this is new ", it is surely that which we are accustomed to call the historical sense. The ability to identify ourselves momentarily with some bygone or otherwise unfamiliar mode of thought, the swift, intuitive sympathy which ignores all temporal limitations, the magic carpet of the spirit which transcends all geographical and racial frontiers, is the Danaan gift of the twentieth century, unknown to any other, and perhaps its most valuable contribution to human thought and sensibility. In earlier times we invariably find a narrow and intolerant attitude towards any form of art or mode of life which differed widely from their own ; every age consistently regarded itself as the unalterable, procrustean standard by which everything must be judged and measured, and the art of all its predecessors had to be adapted, edited, restored, or otherwise defaced, before it could be accepted. To-day, on the contrary, our aim is rather to preserve the element of strangeness, unfamiliarity, and even uncouthness, of a primitive or exotic work of art ; indeed, it is often precisely this aspect of it that affords us the greatest pleasure. History and archæology are no longer ghoulish, necrophilistic activities, as formerly ; their object is not to analyse and dissect the past, but rather to make it live again. As Michelet wrote at the beginning of his monumental and epoch-making history of France, " l'histoire est une résurrection ".

In this, as in everything else, music lags a long way behind the other arts. While the student of literature, painting, sculpture, or architecture, is capable of deriving both pleasure and profit from the study of even the most ancient and primitive forms of his art, it is only quite recently that music written before the time of Bach has come to be regarded as possessing any interest whatever apart from its scientific and evolutionary significance. A piece of old music is still habitually regarded as a step towards something else rather than as anything in itself ; and until quite recently it was considered necessary to re-write it before it could be made tolerable to modern ears, as the saying is, in precisely the same way that the eighteenth century used to repaint and restore the pictures of early pre-Renaissance artists.

Happily this objectionable practice is now almost entirely a thing of the past ; certainly no modern editor of good repute would dare to tamper with old music in this arrogant and presumptuous manner. Instead, however, of trying to make it live again, we treat it as if it were a dead thing ; we no longer deck it out in inappropriate modern costume, but lay it out like a corpse, a fit subject for scientific analysis or dissection, but not for æsthetic appreciation ; scales and modes are studied, elaborate descriptions are given of obsolete instruments and methods of notation, and we are shown how one form developed or gave birth to another, how certain tendencies gradually manifested themselves, and how others gradually disappeared. Indeed, the whole history of the art is generally conceived as a collective and almost anonymous activity, in which individual genius is merely a secondary consideration in comparison with the formal and idiomatic development of musical language. In the words of the prophet Emerson, " the greatest genius is the most indebted man ", and a great work of art is primarily regarded as a synthesis of previously existing elements, the outcome of several centuries of evolution.

That there is such a thing as evolution of musical forms and idioms is a self-evident fact which needs no demonstration. But while it is unquestionably a study of the greatest interest and profit to the musician to trace the gradual development of his artistic language, seeing how each period and each composer have played their respective parts in shaping, modifying, extending, and perfecting the instrument at his disposal, rendering it more plastic and more readily responsive to every subtle inflection of his thought, it does not constitute the history of an expressive art such as music any more than a philological study of language could pass for a history of literature, or a description of a man's physiological development for a biography. As Flaubert has said somewhere, " on prend tout en considération sauf le talent ", and talent is ultimately the only thing that really matters. With the onward march of time the very aspect of a work may change ; colours fade, marbles crumble away, and the idioms of one generation are forgotten by the next. Genius alone is absolute ; everything else is relative, impermanent, unessential.

The almost exclusive preoccupation of musical historians with questions of formal and idiomatic evolution has had many dire results, and none more so than the habit it has engendered of regarding a whole school or period as leading up to one or two outstanding figures, in whom all the virtues and qualities of their predecessors are presumed to be contained. In this way all music up to about 1600 is popularly supposed to be summed up in Palestrina, that of the seventeenth century in Bach and Handel, that of the eighteenth century in Haydn and Mozart, while all other early composers are dismissed as being merely of historical interest, and their works regarded as mere antiques. It is certainly no exaggeration to say that in consequence for most people, for most cultured musicians even, the whole of music is represented by a bare handful of names, and our concert programmes are practically confined to the merest fraction of the world's masterpieces. Not one tenth of the greatest music is known to anyone except a few antiquarians, and this is largely a direct outcome of the evolutionary conception of musical history prevailing at the present time. Once we lay it aside, however, and consent to look at composers and works for what they are in themselves, and not simply for what they came from and what they led up to, a countless army of great composers arises, as if at the stroke of a magician's wand, from the arid and sterile field of musical history ; the three great regiments of the Netherlanders under Dufay, Okeghem and Josquin des Prés, the great Roman school of Palestrina, together with the Venetians under Gabrieli, the Spanish under Victoria, and the English under William Byrd : the second Venetian and Roman schools of the seventeenth century, side by side with the Neapolitan school of Alessandro Scarlatti, and many others—their work as alive now as the day it was composed, if we only care to exercise our sympathy and imagination a little.   It is as if it were written in a kind of invisible ink ; only the warm breath of imaginative enthusiasm is required to rekindle it into life.

The great obstacle that stands in the way of our understanding and appreciation of this old music consists in the problem of notation.   Notation, indeed, is the curse of music. Apart from the fact that the difficulty of fixing our fluid and unsubstantial thought in this hopelessly inadequate, artificial, and clumsy mould, results in the loss of at least one half of its potential beauty, it even then exists only in a partial and incomplete way ; it still requires the insight and understanding of executants before it can really be said to exist as other works of art do.   While the limestone bust of Amenophis IV in the Louvre remains as perfect to-day as at the time when it was carved, in spite of the ravages of time ; while the Last Supper of Leonardo on the calcined and peeling wall of the refectory in the convent of Santa Maria delle Grazie at Milan still retains, and will continue to retain until there is no longer any vestige of it left, a beauty and perfection which compel our reverent homage and love ; we unfortunate musicians have not got the work itself.   We have to content ourselves with a lifeless symbol, a hieroglyph, meaningless until interpreted, to which the key is often wanting.   The written poem, the carven statue, the painted wall or canvas, are the works themselves, and speak for themselves without any intermediary, but the musical score is not and cannot.

· This is to some extent true of all music, but more particularly is it true of old music.   To-day we have come more or less to regard the written note as absolute, the performance as only a reproduction or realization of the work as it exists on paper, and it is true that we can to a great extent imagine the effect in performance for ourselves.   In the older music it was very different ; the work-in-itself lay in its performance, the notation being only mnemonic, a convenient kind of shorthand.   It is not the music itself, but only its shadow or pale reflection. For us the ideal interpreter is almost a species of impersonal machine ; in the sixteenth and seventeenth centuries he was quite literally a part of the work.

There is a story to the effect that the Emperor Leopold I of Austria, a great lover of music, desired to possess a copy of the celebrated *Miserere* of Allegri, which he had heard sung in the

Sistine Chapel at Rome. The Pope granted permission for a copy to be made, which the Emperor took back with him to Vienna. But although he obtained the finest singers in the city in order to perform it, the result was quite different from what he had heard in Rome. Believing that the *maestro di cappella* of the Sistine Chapel had deceived him, and had substituted some other work for that of Allegri, the Emperor had him dismissed from his post. The unfortunate musician protested, and was eventually able to prove, that the work of which he had given a copy was indeed Allegri's *Miserere*, but that its beauty resulted in large measure from the way in which it was sung, and not so much from the actual notes themselves.

In other words, modern notation is explicit, ancient notation implicit. The dividing line between creation and interpretation was less sharply drawn in those days than it is now. The progressive encroachments of the modern composer over the line once held by the executive musician have gradually reduced the latter to the rank of a mere artisan or mechanical labourer ; in older times he was at least as important a figure as the composer himself, sometimes even more so. To realize the truth of this contention we have only to compare a modern score with an old one. The former bristles with indications of *tempo*, phrasing, accentuation, dynamic intensity, and expression ; the latter makes use of none of them. Their equivalent lay in the splendid executive traditions of the age, which are now wholly and irrevocably lost. In default of it, the task of bringing this old music to life again demands an effort such as that which we must make when we visit the Roman Forum. After the first unavoidable moments of bitter disappointment, it gradually awakens under the spell of imaginative enthusiasm, and takes life and shape once more. The dream becomes the reality, and even as we walk among the mouldering and disfigured mounds of brick and travertine, they are transmuted into the Temples of the Gods and the Golden House of Nero.

Musical history need not be the mortuary or charnel house that most writers have made of it. These old works are not corpses, but are full of potential life, and exist in a state of suspended animation. They lie there on the dusty shelves of our musical libraries like mummies embalmed in their cere-clothes, on their breasts the scarab, symbol of resurrection, awaiting only our sympathy and enthusiasm to liberate them from their age-long trance, and to evoke from their pale, tenuous pages their living spirit, their permanent, immutable beauty over which time has no power. And if the following pages are able to induce in the reader a more receptive and responsive attitude towards the great masterpieces of the past, and to stimulate his imaginative reaction to them, their main purpose will have been achieved.

CHAPTER I

GREGORIAN CHANT

MUSICOLOGICAL research has not as yet provided us with sufficient material to enable us to give a reliable description of the music of primitive races or of non-European civilizations such as India or China, and our complete ignorance concerning the systems of notation employed in ancient times —if, indeed, any were employed at all—effectively prevents us from knowing anything whatsoever of the early history of music. No really authentic examples of Greek music even have come down to us with the exception of one or two fragments so unintelligible as to justify the suspicion that our interpretation of the Greek system of notation is, if not wholly wrong, at least very inadequate. Apart from them, all of it that has been discovered and transcribed up to the present time consists of a few hymns and miscellaneous oddments supposed to date from about the time of Hadrian, together with a small quantity of purely theoretical writings. It will be readily understood, therefore, that an attempt to arrive at an idea of what Greek music was like from such slight and not altogether trustworthy evidence as this is like trying to deduce and reconstruct Greek drama from fragments of the *Hercules Furens* of Seneca, Greek sculpture from a few second-rate busts of Roman emperors, or Greek painting from the descriptions of it which are to be found in the pages of Pausanias or Achilles Tatius. Yet many writers have attempted this well-nigh impossible feat. Gevaert has written two volumes, containing about a thousand pages, on the music of classical antiquity ; Riemann and Ambros have both dedicated whole volumes to it in their respective histories of music, and many others too numerous to mention have similarly devoted a vast amount of time, energy and enthusiasm to its study without, however, any of them succeeding in giving us more than the vaguest idea of what it was actually like. Even on the most elementary and fundamental issues there is still considerable divergence of opinion among the best authorities.

For all practical purposes, therefore, the history of music as we know it to-day is only the history of Western European music from the beginning of the Christian era. This is all we can speak of with any degree of certainty, and even within these comparatively modest and restricted limits we shall still find quite enough scope for indulging in speculations and conjectures without going out of our way into regions where nothing else is even possible.

Our almost complete ignorance of the music of antiquity, both classic and barbaric, and of the music of alien cultures and primitive races at the present time, while it is to be regretted from the standpoint of pure knowledge, has not been altogether a misfortune but in some ways even a distinct advantage. For if the history of music can show a more logical, consistent, and homogeneous idiomatic development and a more unified and unbroken spiritual tradition than any of the other arts, the reason is probably to be found in the fact that Western European music has been able to develop peacefully and autonomously along its own lines, uninfluenced by the tyrannic prestige of ancient precedents and undisturbed by the seductive glamour of exotic cultural traditions. For example, there is no denying the fact that, however admirable the actual artistic achievement of the Greeks may have been, its influence upon modern art has frequently been pernicious in the extreme. Indeed, the two arts which have been most subject to its influence, namely sculpture and architecture seem, in modern times, to have been largely stultified by it ; and the two arts which have attained the highest development with us, apart from literature,—namely, music and painting, are those which have been least affected by it. In fact, it may very well be true that, as Spengler remarks in his " Decline of the West " : " It is to the fortunate circumstance that the whole of the fresco-art of Hellas has been lost that we owe the inward freedom of our oil-painting ", and it is equally probable that the " inward freedom " of our music is directly due to the fact that, apart from a decade or two at the beginning of the seventeenth century—the importance of which has always been greatly exaggerated by historians—the influence of Greek ideals counts for nothing in the history of music.

There is good reason to suppose, moreover, that even if we were so fortunate from one point of view, and unfortunate from another, as to possess authentic examples of Greek music of the best period, we should in all probability be greatly disappointed with them. It is difficult to subscribe to the opinion of Mr. W. J. Turner, for example, when he says in his " Music and Life " that " It is frankly unbelievable that the Greeks, who were capable of a poetic, dramatic and plastic art which has never been surpassed, had not a music of correspondingly high development. . . . It is even possible that the music of the Greeks was richer and finer than any music we have to-day". The fact of the matter is that the transcendent greatness of the Hellenic achievement in other directions is apt to lead us to expect too much of their music, and to imagine that it is a glorious Atlantis sunk beneath the waves of time, whereas actually its loss need not be the cause of anything more than a passing sentimental regret. If we do not know any Greek music worth speaking of, we do at least know enough about it from literary sources to be fairly sure of this. In the first place, it is obvious that the particular ideas and conceptions which are most characteristic of the Greek spirit, in art, in life, and in thought, are precisely the opposite to those which are best suited to musical expression. A race whose outlook is primarily intellectual and logical, and whose peculiar strength lies in the direction of clarity and definition, must inevitably find its most complete and congenial artistic expression in the formative arts, and more particularly in sculpture. For the remote, mysterious, and subjective, which constitute the sphere in which music, the most Dionysian of the arts, moves most freely, all typical representatives of the Hellenic spirit evinced a fear and a repulsion amounting almost to horror.

That the Greeks wholly failed to recognize and appreciate or, more accurately perhaps, chose deliberately to ignore and neglect, the peculiar aptitudes possessed by music as a medium of artistic expression, can be seen in the fact that they regarded it almost exclusively as a mere branch of literature. It was considered to be a part of the poet's training to be able to set his own verses to music. The designation ποιητής meant one who was both a poet and a composer; the term μουσικός was reserved for an executant or a theoretician only. It is

B

related that Hesiod was excluded from taking part in the Pythic contests because he had not learnt to accompany himself on the cithara, and Euripides was severely censured for having entrusted the composition of the musical side of his dramas to another poet.   It was only in later times that music came to be considered by the Greeks as an art which might conceivably have a separate existence apart from literature, and this development, it is significant to learn, was regarded as a symptom of decadence, as it no doubt was from the Greek point of view. But this is not all. With us to-day a song is primarily regarded as a musical composition in which the words are a secondary consideration, and the composer is at liberty to give to each syllable any quantity or duration he may choose. It was quite otherwise with the Greeks, in whose music the time-value of each note was rigorously prescribed by the general metre of the poem and the rhythm of the particular word. The whole musical structure, indeed, was entirely conditioned by the poetry, not only in substance but in detail, and the composer was allowed no latitude or independence whatsoever. In short, music, in the eyes of the Greeks was, to use their own expression, merely a $\dot{\eta}\delta\upsilon\sigma\mu\alpha$ or " seasoning " of poetry.

But with the supersession of the pagan gods by the new cult of Christianity, and the destruction of the ancient social order by the barbaric invaders of the Roman Empire, a complete change takes place. The arts which had been the character-istic means of expression for the old ideals lapsed into decadence or suffered temporary eclipse, while the despised and rejected of the pagan arts came at last into its own. Music, the Prometheus of the arts, bound to the rock of literature throughout the whole period of Greek and Roman cultural ascendancy, was liberated by Christianity and raised by it to the first place among them all—a striking fulfilment in the field of art of the promise made by its Founder that in His Kingdom the first should be last and the last should be first.

It is not difficult to see why this should be so. The whole tradition on which the plastic and formative arts had been built up during the many centuries of Greek and Roman cultural domination was indissolubly bound up with the expression and embodiment of such diametrically opposite values to those of Christianity that it was quite impossible for them to adapt themselves immediately to the new demands which were made upon them, or to achieve at once a perfect expression of the new ideals. The old forms, idioms, and conventions remained wholly intractable, and had to be gradually twisted and bent, and new ones created, before it was possible for the sculptor or architect even to attempt to cope with the task of expressing the ideals of the new order. How could the plastic arts of antiquity hope to depict subjects that were the outcome of inward revelations and ecstatic visions, or realize the infinite in terms of the finite ? Could you house this strange new stable-born God in a stately Greek or sumptuous Roman temple ? Could His image be carved in Parian marble or wrought in gold and ivory like the chrys-elephantine image of Zeus ? Could you sing fitting hymns of praise and glory to His Name in the metres of Sappho or Alcaeus, of Catullus or Propertius ? Music alone of all the pagan arts laboured under none of these disadvantages. While the others were groping about, seeking vainly to adapt themselves to the requirements of the new religion, music alone found itself at once. Euterpe had always been an unwilling and neglected partner in the symposium of the arts of the ancient world, the Cinderella of the Muses, the humble handmaid of literature, ill-treated and despised by her more favoured sisters. Christianity was the fairy prince who rescued her from abasement and servitude, and raised her to the highest place of honour amongst them all. Inarticulate in the expression of the pagan values, music found in those of Christianity its greatest source of strength.

And so the new order came to the plastic arts and, to a great extent to literature also, as a burden and a bondage, to music alone as a triumphant liberation. While the art of painting is sent to school in the catacombs to learn the artistic alphabet of the new religion, while architecture is compelled to lay aside all her worldly splendour and magnificence and to devote herself to the erection of humble and lowly edifices more like barns than temples, while sculpture is practically banished for centuries, music alone was immediately capable of voicing the innermost truths of Christianity in wholly fitting language. The positions are reversed, the rôles exchanged. Formerly a mere adjunct to literature, music becomes not merely an integral part of the liturgy, but its very core ; it is the other arts which in their turn become mere adjuncts or " seasonings ".

No temple is strictly necessary for the performance of the sacred rite, no carven image or pictured representation of the God is needed or even desired, but wherever or whenever His cult is celebrated music is imperatively required. The other arts can speak only of the pomp and splendour of transient things, of mortal desires and earthly passions ; music, free from the tyranny of the concrete and the material, can alone hymn the glories of the Kingdom of Heaven, depict the immortal disembodied soul ascending to its Creator, represent the mysteries of Transsubstantiation, Divine Incarnation, or Immaculate Conception. In the other arts at the commencement of the Christian era we find either the stutterings and dribblings of a dotard on his deathbed, or of a new-born infant in its cradle :—either the fag-end of the old, or the first faint stirrings of life in the new. Alike they have no meaning for us to-day, but a fine example of Gregorian chant, or plain-song, is as perfect and moving a thing now as the day when it was composed. It seems to have sprung fully grown and completely developed from the heart of the Christian religion, like Pallas Athene from the head of her father Zeus.

It is extremely important that this intrinsicality and independence of Gregorian chant should be insisted on and emphasized from the very outset, because the majority of musical historians, afflicted by a morbid mania for seeking origins and derivations, and detecting resemblances and influences where none exist, have professed to find in the music of the early Christian Church a mere continuation of the music of antiquity, or at least an adaptation of it to the purposes of the new religion. It is in reality nothing of the kind, as can easily be shown. In the first place Greco-Roman music is always strongly rhythmic, or rather metric in its structure, so far as we are able to judge it, and its rhythms and metres were strictly conditioned by those of the poem ; plain-song, on the contrary, has only the subtle inflections and irregular rhythms of prose. While the chief rhythmical principle in the former was quantity, or the varying duration of the notes in accordance with the poetic metre, accent was the determining factor in the latter, and all the syllables were of more or less equal duration. Again, the musicians of antiquity seem to have rigorously observed a rule that the accented syllable should coincide with the highest notes of the melodic phrase ; the mediæval musician, on the contrary, did not permit such considerations to determine the melodic movement, but often makes his phrase rise before and after the accented syllable. If our interpretation of its notation is correct, a typical feature of Greco-Roman music consists in comparatively wide melodic leaps and in a marked fondness for the interval of the tritone or augmented fourth, while Gregorian chant moves mainly by conjunct motion and comparatively small leaps, always systematically avoiding the tritone which was regarded throughout the Middle Ages as *diabolus in musica*, probably not so much for æsthetic reasons as because of its frequent occurrence in Greek music and its consequently inevitable evocation of pagan associations. Another important difference between the two consists in the fact that Greek music invariably possessed an instrumental accompaniment, whereas the Christian music is purely vocal and unaccompanied. Finally the dominating mode or scale in the former would seem to have been that which the Greeks called the Dorian (E to E on the white keys of the piano), while in plain-song it is of comparatively rare occurrence.

These are only a few of the more important differences between the two, but the list could be indefinitely extended for technically they possess nothing whatever in common. But the decisive factor in the question lies in their entirely different *stimmung*, or feeling. In Greek music, as Gevaert rightly observes, we find a " beauté froide et sèche, subordination de l'élément féminin, de romantisme, prédominance de l'élément objectif ". Gregorian chant, on the other hand, is the very opposite of cold and dry, and if not feminine exactly, is certainly romantic—in so far as the word has any meaning—and above all subjective.

Other theorists, conscious of these irreconcilable differences, yet equally afflicted by the genealogical malady and unable to contemplate with equanimity the possible existence of a form of art which does not owe all its characteristic features to some other form of art, have suggested, to quote the words of the distinguished French musicologist, M. Gastoué, that " Judaic melody, beyond all possibility of doubt, is at the bottom of the Christian plain-song. It is enough to compare the procedures of Hebrew art, and even its formulæ, with the products of mediæval art, to recognize common traits, witnesses of common origin ".

This sounds very authoritative—quite final in fact—but when we go into the matter more deeply we discover that when the Bible was translated from Hebrew into Greek during the third century no one could be found who was able to decipher the notations of the old Judaic temple music which were in it. The tradition even then was entirely lost, and it follows that we know even less about the ancient ritual music of the Jews than we do about the music of the Greeks, and there is certainly nothing in the modern synagogue music to support the suggestion that it shares a common origin with Gregorian chant. As another equally eminent French musicologist, M. Pierre Aubry, bluntly puts it, " L'art musical des Hébreux nous est absolument fermé, et il faut une étrange assurance pour oser encore aujourd'hui en parler ". We can only hope to form an idea of its general character from the vivid descriptions of it in the Old Testament, and these, one would have thought, would be sufficient in themselves to disprove the theory of the Semitic origin of plain-song. What possible resemblance can one find between the spirit of gentleness, humility, and resignation which is the dominating characteristic of the Gregorian chant, and the brilliant, sensual, and triumphant art which is there so graphically described that we can almost imagine we have actually heard it—the chanting of innumerable voices, accompanied by a vast orchestra of trumpets, pipes, harps, psalteries, and cymbals ?

It is no doubt true that there are certain distinct resemblances to be found in the way in which the psalms are intoned in both Jewish and Christian churches, but similarity of method does not necessarily denote a common origin. When prose speech is heightened into song, or recitative, it inevitably takes the form of ascent to a point (intonation), rest (mediation), and descent (cadence). It does not follow that, simply because this procedure is found in both Hebraic and early Christian melody, the latter must therefore be derived from the former, or *vice versa*, any more than the fact that the Cinderella legend is to be found in the South Seas and in Europe signifies that it was brought from the one to the other. It is simply the most natural and primitive melodic formula in music and particularly in ritual music ; it is not by any means confined to that of

Jerusalem and Rome, but is to be found throughout the entire world. For example it is related—by the Abbé Huc, I believe—that when the first Catholic missionaries came to Tibet they were so astonished at finding a form of chant practically identical with Roman plain-song that they at first believed that someone must have got there before them. It is a pity that such an interesting fact should hitherto have escaped the attention of musical historians suffering from the genealogical mania, for it suggests the most fascinating speculations. Was the music that the missionaries heard in the mountain-girt monasteries of Tibet the Jewish synagogue chant which had travelled to Lhasa via Persia, Afghanistan, and India, or was it the Greek musical tradition which had taken the more circuitous way through Russia and Central Asia and become somewhat dilapidated *en route* ?

But, incidentally, does not the mere fact that it can be seriously and solemnly debated whether Gregorian chant is Greek or Hebrew in origin, conclusively show that it cannot demonstrably be either ? The resemblances between the Odyssey and the Book of Job are not so strikingly noticeable that one might legitimately hesitate before deciding which was Greek and which Semitic, and not even an American tourist from the Middle West would be likely to mistake the Parthenon for a Jewish synagogue or the Praxitelian Hermes for the portrait of a Jewish prophet.

A third theory of the origin of Gregorian chant which claims numerous adherents is that it is a combination of Greek and Hebrew elements ; that, in the words of Gevaert, "on pourrait comparer la melopée liturgique à la langue du Nouveau Testament : le vocabulaire est grec, la forme de la pensée est sémitique ". But is the New Testament merely Jewish thought embodied in Greek language ? Does not the essential significance of the Christian religion lie precisely in its difference from the traditions of both Athens and Jerusalem, in its unlikeness to anything and everything that had gone before ? And similarly, even if it were true that certain procedures were deliberately borrowed from the old synagogue music and grafted in some weird and inexplicable fashion on to the old Greek modal system, or *vice versa*, it does not and cannot alter the obvious fact, which is alone of the slightest importance, that the resultant art bears no more resemblance to the music of either Greece or of Israel than the teaching embodied in the New Testament bears to the cult of the Olympian gods or to that of the Talmud.

Other and even more fantastic theories have been evolved in the attempt to ascribe a definite ancestral origin to plain-song, some going so far as to suggest that it is descended from the music of the ancient Phœnicians, others that it is the continuation of the Egyptian musical tradition, still others who profess to find in it evident traces of Gnostic ritual chants, and so forth, but they are all equally absurd and equally lacking in confirmatory evidence. The plain fact of the matter is that the essential character of Gregorian chant lies in its absolute novelty, its quality of sheer creation, its utter difference, so far as we are in a position to judge, from everything that had preceded it. Anything that it shares in common with other musical traditions consists in small and superficial resemblances, largely accidental, and wholly unimportant and unessential.

Once that fact is grasped we may, if we like, regard the mere outward idiom of plain-song as an amalgam, like Corinthian brass, not only of Greek and Hebraic but probably of many other elements also, fused together in the conflagration of the old civilization, but becoming in the process something entirely new. And the crucible in which this alchemy took place, the melting-pot of the ancient world, was Byzantium, the gateway between Europe and Asia, the point of contact between East and West, possessing a culture neither oriental nor occidental, but both—and yet neither. It was at Nicæa, Ephesus, and Chalcedonia that œcumenical councils fixed and established the dogmas of the Church : it was at Alexandria and at Antioch that the great heresies first arose : it was in Egypt and Syria that monachism first developed. Similarly, it was Constantinople and the provinces of the Eastern Empire that offered the most suitable ground for a meeting-place between the artists of Greece, Rome, Egypt and Syria, who were there able to denationalize their artistic procedures and, so to speak, pool their resources and weld them into a new, universal, cosmopolitan, specifically Christian style. It was there that the first Christian architecture had its origin, the first characteristically Christian painting, mosaic, sculpture and decorative arts ; it was there, almost certainly, that we must similarly look for the origins of the liturgical chant of the Church.

It is only natural that the creative impulse of the new order in all fields of activity should be centred in the Eastern rather than in the Western Empire. In Rome the temples, circuses, theatres, baths, were all so many irresistible reminders of the old religion; at every step some ancient monument, with long-established traditions and associations, rose up to bring forcibly to the memory of the inhabitants the old empire and the cult of the ancient gods. In Constantinople, on the other hand, there were no such traditions and associations; it was essentially a new city, to a great extent the creation of Christianity. In Italy itself, during the whole time that the liturgy of the Roman Church was in the process of formation—roughly 425-700—the capital was no longer Rome itself but Ravenna, and Ravenna was essentially an eastern city under the domination of the oriental emperors.

The legitimate and entirely logical assumption that plain-song was in the main, if not entirely, a Byzantine creation, is further strengthened by the fact that it was on his return from Constantinople that Pope Gregory the Great, who gave his name to it, set about the formation and organization of his *Schola Cantorum*, and so gave a definite shape and form to the church ritual; and there is also a great deal of minor evidence pointing in the same direction which it is unnecessary to give here.

We shall almost certainly be right, then, if we agree to regard the liturgical chant of the Catholic Church as neither Greek nor Hebrew, nor even a combination of both, but an entirely new form of musical art corresponding to the church of Hagia Sophia at Constantinople or the mosaics of Ravenna. It unmistakably reveals not only the same spiritual characteristics but even the same technical features as all the other forms of Byzantine art. The melodic principle to which reference has already been made, of the ascent to and descent from a central point—a simple formula which, nevertheless, underlies practically the entire *corpus* of Gregorian chant—is essentially the musical equivalent of the curved arch and flowing semi-circular lines which constitute the dominant structural motive of Hagia Sophia and practically all Byzantine architecture; and the inner spirit that informs the liturgical chant is recognizably one with that which finds expression in Byzantine mosaics. And the most striking feature of all Byzantine art, the characteristic by which we can infallibly identify it in whatsoever form we encounter it, whether it be in architecture or mosaic, in mural painting or ivory carving, consists in its curiously ethereal, static, arrested, timeless quality—the artistic expression of the πνεῦμα of contemporary Alexandrian theology. As Procopius observed in the fifth century already, " the dome (of Hagia Sophia) does not appear to rest upon a solid foundation, but seems suspended from Heaven by the fabled golden chain", and Mr. O. M. Dalton in his monumental work on Byzantine art and archæology develops the point at length in a suggestive passage which is too long to quote in its entirety. " The Byzantine architect ", he writes, " perceived the majesty of great curves ; he freed construction from the visible tyranny of mass. . . . The eye follows the aerial lines with consummate satisfaction ; they entrance by suggestion of infinity ; they go forth and return upon their appointed course, until in the contemplation of their infallible perfection all sense of superincumbent mass is overcome. There is no dome which floats like that of Santa Sophia; it is poised rather than supported ". With only the alteration here and there of some specifically architectural expression the above might be a description of the effect produced by Gregorian chant on the sensitive and receptive listener.

The plain-song of the Western Church with which alone we are here concerned, was not always uniform as it is to-day, but originally consisted of four separate schools, or traditions, namely : Roman or Gregorian, Milanese or Ambrosian, Gallican or French, Mozarabic or Visigothic. The first of these, by virtue of the prestige of the Papacy and the spiritual power and authority of Rome, gradually superseded the others until finally in the eleventh century a uniform system of chant together with a fixed and systematized ritual prevailed throughout Europe. The church of Milan alone was permitted to retain the old Ambrosian tradition unaltered, and it is still to be heard there to the present day. Some experts profess to be able to discern a considerable difference between the Ambrosian and Gregorian traditions, though one conjectures that if they were to hear a chant of each kind without being told beforehand which was which, they might have considerable difficulty in distinguishing between them. It is sufficient to say that, in the words of an authority, the simple chants of the

Ambrosian ritual are simpler, and the ornate chants more ornate, than the corresponding versions of the Gregorian, which latter are, on the whole, more artistic.

The Gallican tradition gave way to that of Rome at the end of the eighth century at the instance of the Emperor Charlemagne, and the Mozarabic rite was similarly superseded in the eleventh century—save in a few specially favoured churches at Toledo and Valladolid, where it can still be heard —by the Gregorian version which, being the most important, we shall now proceed to consider in greater detail.

The music of the Gregorian collection falls under two main headings : the music of the Mass, called the Missal, and the chants of the Hours or Office, called the Breviary. The artistic interest of the Breviary is very much less than that of the Missal, largely because it is chanted by the clergy whereas the performance of the latter devolves upon a trained choir. We can therefore confine our attention to the chants of the Missal.

The ritual of the Mass is subdivided into two main groups, namely, the Proprium and the Ordinarium ; the former, comprising the Introit, Gradual (or Alleluia), in Lent a Tract, Offertory, and Communion, vary throughout the year in accordance with the day upon which the rite is celebrated, while the latter, consisting of the Kyrie Eleison, Gloria in Excelsis, Sanctus, Credo, and Agnus Dei, are invariable and are repeated throughout the ecclesiastical year. The sections comprising the Ordinarium were originally sung by the entire congregation to simple unvarying melodies which eventually gave place to the elaborate polyphonic settings of the later Middle Ages and modern times. The plain-song repertoire of the Missal then, as it stands to-day, is confined to the Proprium, and consists roughly of about 300 Introits and Communions, 100 Graduals, 100 Alleluias, 20 Tracts, and 100 Offertories. These, allowing for a certain amount of repetition, do duty for the whole round of the church calendar.

The chants are performed in two different ways. The Introits, Offertories, and Communions belong to the category of Antiphonals, in which the choir is divided into two parts which sing alternately. The Graduals and Alleluias are called responsorial chants, in which the choir replies to a solo voice, with a recurring refrain. Of these two methods the latter would seem to be the older ; the former was not introduced into the Western Church until about 400, by St. Ambrose. The responsorial chants, more particularly the solo parts, are, as one might expect, more elaborate and ornate than the antiphonals.

It only remains to mention two species of Gregorian chant which stand somewhat apart from the rest : firstly, a number of hymns possessing a totally different character from that of the ordinary plain-song—so different, in fact, as to warrant the supposition that they, and they alone, are of definitely Greco-Roman origin. It is even probable that they were actual pagan melodies to which sacred words had been adapted in the same way that Luther, and in our time the Salvation Army, adapted secular melodies to the purposes of religion. These hymns are definitely metrical and syllabic, in contrast to the ordinary Gregorian chant, and sometimes possess a distinctly pagan *allure*.

The second of these groups consists of what are called sequences, and the story of their origin is briefly as follows. In the ninth century, so far as can be ascertained, a practice grew up, initiated by a monk called Notker Balbulus, of setting words to the lengthy *jubilati*, or vocalises which are a special feature of the Alleluia chants. Gradually these interpolations were extended ; new music as well as new words were added, and finally, after the limited supply of Alleluias had given out, the new organism detached itself from the chant which gave it birth and assumed a separate existence in the liturgy. Many of these sequences possess great poetic and musical merits, but their illicit existence offended the purists and they were summarily ejected from the liturgy at the Council of Trent. Five of them only were retained, of which the best-known is the magnificent *Dies Irae* of Thomas de Celano, sung in the Mass for the Dead, in which all the sombre and terrible poetry of the Middle Ages finds its most perfect musical expression. It is curious to reflect, incidentally, that Celano was an intimate friend and a follower of St. Francis, for anything less Franciscan in spirit it would be impossible to imagine.

Like the hymns, but in a different way, these sequences differ strikingly from the bulk of the Gregorian repertory. If the former seem to belong to the pagan past and to breathe the air of ancient Rome, the latter, on the contrary, reveal a distinct approach to modern music, not only in the feeling for tonality, but also in the appearance of symmetrical repetitions of phrases, wide melodic leaps, and a more definitely rhythmical structure than is to be found elsewhere.

Apart from their intrinsic musical merits, which are sometimes of a very high order, the sequences played a more important rôle in the history of mediæval literature than is generally recognized. In Gregorian chant the abandonment of a poetic and the adoption of a prose text involved the substitution of accentual for quantitative rhythms. Now, the first sequences were strictly syllabic, i.e., the poet set one syllable to one note of the original Alleluia chant ; consequently the resultant poems, moulded on the musical sentence, as it were, helped to bring into poetic art the new accentual principle and to undermine and finally to destroy the old classical verse metres. The first sequences were irregular prose-poems, with subtle rhythms corresponding to those of the musical moulds on which they were shaped, and not unlike those of Whitman and other writers of *vers libre ;* at a later stage they were organized into the regular forms of modern verse. One of the earliest examples of the regular sequence is the well-known

> Ave maris stella,
> Dei mater alma
> Atque semper virgo,
> Felix coeli porta,

and the sequence beginning :

> Sanctorum meritis inclyta gaudia
> Pangamus socii gestaque fortia

is the first known example of the French alexandrine metre.

The origin, then, of the revolutionary change over from quantitative to accentual verse which constitutes the primary and fundamental distinction between ancient and modern poetry, can be largely traced back to Gregorian chant—to the wordless vocalises of the Alleluia chants of the Mass.

The musical origin and derivation of the accentual principle in verse is, however, less significant than its demonstrably musical character. In ancient poetry the length of the feet was measured and exactly defined, precisely and logically—one might almost say mechanically and mathematically—calculated. In modern poetry on the other hand, the element of the incalculable and the undefinable reigns supreme ; reason and logic are no longer the arbiters of rhythmical values, but the ear alone.   The difference between quantity and accent is the difference between metre and rhythm ; the one is fixed, stable and precise, the other fluid, undefined and variable—in a word, musical.

And so we find that while in classical times it was the poem that dictated the musical structure, in the Middle Ages it was the opposite : the music determined the poetic form, and the poet-musician of antiquity gives place to the musician-poet of Christianity.   And whereas, to quote the words of Professor Tovey in his article on " Rhythm " in the " Encyclopædia Britannica", " ancient Greek musical rhythms were exact translations of verse rhythms, with the quantities interpreted arithmetically ", in mediæval and modern poetry the poetic rhythms are exact translations of musical rhythms, with the quantities interpreted euphonically and intuitively.

A further development of the sequence, called the trope, is also of great cultural as well as musical interest and significance. The main difference between it and the sequence lies in the fact that it did not detach itself from the original organism which gave it birth, but remained imbedded in the liturgy, to the integrity of which it consequently proved an even more serious menace, for, starting from the Alleluia, it rapidly spread like a disease, a kind of elephantiasis, to every part of the Proprium of the Mass.   One of these tropes, sung at Easter, called the *Quem Quaeritis*, is based upon the interview between the three Maries and the angel at the tomb of Christ, as narrated in the Gospel of St. Matthew (xxviii. 1-7) and runs as follows :

> Quem quaeritis in sepulcro, o Christicolae ?
> Iesum Nazarenum crucifixum, o caelicolae.
> Non est hic, surrexit sicut prædixerat.
> Ite, nuntiate quia surrexit de sepulcro.

From this simple beginning the trope gradually blossoms out into a full-fledged musical drama.   The sequence *Victimæ Paschali* is incorporated with it, a scene is added in which Peter and John pay a visit to the sepulchre, then another in which Christ appears, then still another in which the Maries on their way to the tomb buy spices from an *unguentarius* whose remarks impart an element of comic relief—so it grew, like a snowball, gathering fresh tropes, sequences, and scenes around it as it rolled down the centuries. For a long time it remained an integral part of the liturgy ; the rôles were played by priests, nuns, and choristers, and the stage was set in the church. Eventually, however, the music-drama—for such it had now become—was transferred to the churchyard, and then to the market-place ; the parts were entrusted to citizens and finally to professional actors. Such is the origin of the liturgical drama, the mystery play, and the ancestor of the modern theatre. Many subsequent liturgical dramas, or oratorios as one might call them, still exist, and the music is frequently of great beauty and expressiveness.

And so we see that the origins, not only of modern poetry but of modern drama also, can be traced back to the wordless vocalise at the end of the Alleluia chant in the Mass. They have both sprung from the very heart of the music of the Catholic Church. The fact may not in itself be of intrinsic importance, but it certainly is symbolically significant in that it demonstrates more clearly than anything else could the truth of what was enunciated earlier in the chapter : namely, that music is the art in which the early Christian values are best expressed and embodied, and the one which is the model and archetype for all the others.   And if to the enormous importance of the part which Gregorian chant played in the history, not only of music but of all the arts, we add that which it played in mediæval life generally, and consider how, for example, the chant which was used on a particular day would be cited in statutes and chronicles as a means of dating an event ; how official ceremonies and public observances of all kinds were celebrated to its solemn and majestic strains ; how it accompanied the lives of all, noble and peasant, great and humble, rich and poor, cleric and layman, from the cradle to the grave —then indeed we begin to realize the overwhelming cultural significance of this great Roman fountain of song, as sweet and pure and inexhaustible as the Aqua Virgo of the Eternal City itself, and playing endlessly, day and night, throughout the centuries, as do the fountains in the Place of St. Peter before the sanctuary which is the heart and core of Christendom.

At the same time, quite apart from the important place which it occupies in the History of Civilization, it possesses a purely æsthetic appeal as great as that of any other form of art that has ever existed—an appeal which, however, triumphantly defies all attempts at analysis or definition. Wherein lies the secret of its irresistible glamour and fascination, of its immemorial power to move us ? It seems, on the face of it, to be entirely devoid of every attribute of musical beauty which is commonly deemed essential. It has no determinate rhythm, no harmony or accompaniment of any kind, and its melodic scope is severely limited and circumscribed. Nevertheless, when heard in the appropriate surroundings and under fitting conditions, these simple unisonal chants take on a remote, magical, and disembodied quality—a grave ecstasy, radiant yet austere, impassioned yet serene—and glow as with a secret, inward fire. The voices themselves seem to undergo a curious transmutation and become impersonal, sexless, superhuman almost, giving expression to the inarticulate yearnings and aspirations, not only of the living, but also of the countless generations of the dead and the unborn. If we accept the definition of a miracle as a phenomenon contrary to or deviating from the laws of nature, then we may justly call Gregorian chant a musical miracle, for its beauty and appeal are not to be accounted for by any known laws or principles governing musical art, but exist in spite of them, in defiance of them. Are we not almost forced to conclude that, in the words of Huysmans in his " En Route ", " Le véritable créateur de la musique plane, l'auteur inconnu qui a jeté dans le cerveau de l'homme la semence du plain-chant, c'est le Saint-Esprit " ? It is at least a simpler, more plausible, and in every way more satisfying and convincing explanation of its existence than the theory that would assign its origin to a Greek or to a Jewish music about which we know next to nothing, and care rather less.

CHAPTER II

Harmony and Polyphony of the Early Middle Ages

In no art, science, or other department of human activity, has the doctrine of evolution been so enthusiastically welcomed, so eagerly adopted, and so wholeheartedly endorsed, as in music. Indeed, the whole history of the art has almost invariably been conceived and represented as a single, orderly, and undeviating line of progress from the simplest and most primitive beginnings up to the complexities of modern practice; and the account of this gradual process of development which is generally to be met with in musical histories reads exactly like the account given in scientific text-books of the origin and evolution of life from the amœba. In the beginning, we are told, there was rhythm, nothing but rhythm. After a long time melody gradually evolved, and finally, in comparatively recent times, harmony. And in precisely the same way that we are shown how *homo sapiens* is descended from the ape through the intermediate stages of Heidelberg Man and Neanderthal Man, so modern harmony is supposed to have developed from plain-song by way of organum, discant, and other mediæval procedures.

This conception of musical history had the advantage of being logical, inherently plausible, and easily grasped; moreover, it fitted in reasonably well until quite recently with the little evidence at our disposal concerning early developments. But the gradual accumulation of fresh data, together with the new light thrown by a more scientific and unprejudiced scrutiny on that already existing, has clearly shown that many points which had hitherto appeared perfectly simple and comprehensible have now become exceedingly obscure and problematical. In fact from the standpoint of the evolutionary theory, the more we learn of the early history of harmony the less we understand of it. It has been found that a great deal of the new evidence could not possibly be reconciled with the conception of gradual progress and orderly development which had hitherto been entertained, and the most complete and detailed accounts of the evolution of modern harmony, such as those of Riemann and Wooldridge, besides being often completely at variance with each other, are also the most bewildering and unintelligible. For example the latter, in the first volume of the " Oxford History of Music," frankly confesses that " although we may safely conclude, with respect to the original sources of the New Organum, that it was derived from the free species of the Fourth . . . the complete process by which the actual transition was effected is not only unknown to us but is also at first sight somewhat difficult to imagine. . . . Considered as a whole, no method could well be more different from another than the method of the new system from that of the older one. . . . Our inability to trace the actual process of transition . . . is not due to the absence of musical treatises during the transitional period, but rather to a complete silence with respect to this branch of the subject. . . . The writers on music all agree in the omission of any account of the methods of Organum, as if indeed, it formed no true part of music at all ". As for the introduction of discant or mensurable music, we are told that its origin is obscure, " that no absolutely clear or complete account can be given " of the method employed, and so on.

I have quoted at length from this eminent and accepted authority in order to show the confusion and uncertainty with which the whole subject of the early history of harmony was surrounded twenty-five years ago. Since then, so far from diminishing, it has steadily increased until to-day we are no longer merely in doubt as to the actual processes of transition from one stage to another, but have even become increasingly sceptical as to the adequacy and even the validity of the theory which seeks to ascribe the origins of harmony to the practices of the mediæval church musicians.

This state of chaos and confusion, it is interesting and instructive to note, is not by any means confined to music, but is the most characteristic feature in the history of all the other arts during the Dark Ages. Mr. Porter, for example, writing on the architecture of this period, finds precisely the same state of affairs. " For once in architectural history all laws of local relationships in style seem to have been broken. Occasionally three or four buildings in neighbouring localities show a strong family resemblance. But again two churches erected almost side by side and of about the same age will present scarcely any point of contact, while the strongest analogies will crop out between buildings as widely separated as possible in point of time and geographical location. Furthermore, what progress was made was not made consistently. Although many of the improvements usually credited to the later styles were in reality first invented in this epoch, such advances were, as a rule, not followed up, but remained isolated examples until they were adopted by a later age. So the first impression in glancing over the period is one of complexity and confusion, and this confusion, so far from disappearing with closer study, must be emphasized as the leading characteristic of the era " (" History of Mediæval Architecture ").

The position with regard to the music of the period could not be better summed up, for precisely the same phenomena are to be observed there as in the architecture ; but with this difference, that the confusion in music has been worse confounded on account of the refusal of musical historians to discard their evolutionary prepossessions, and their insistence on attempting to explain the phenomena in the light of a preconceived theory concerning the origin of harmony. It will be very much better if, so far from trying to minimize and explain away the confusion on the plea that it is only the result of an insufficiency of data to go upon, as most historians do, we were rather to follow the example of Mr. Porter and, while emphasizing this confusion as the leading characteristic of the era, which an increase of knowledge only serves to intensify, were to examine the facts, such as they are, with an open mind, and see to what conclusions—or, *faute de mieux*, conjectures— they give rise.

In the first place, is it quite so certain as all but a few writers on the subject would have us believe, that the practice of harmony, the simultaneous sounding of two or more different notes of the scale, was totally unknown before the ninth or tenth century of our era ? Such a sweeping assertion and such remarkable unanimity in making it would, one imagines, be supported by a mass of well-nigh irrefutable evidence. Actually, strange to say, there is no such definite and positive, but only negative and circumstantial, evidence For example, it is true that in Greco-Roman music—the only music prior to the Christian era of which we have the slightest knowledge—there is no notation of harmony, but that in itself is of no importance. The exact and comprehensive committal to writing of every element in a musical composition is a comparatively recent invention; even as late as the seventeenth century we know that the bass part alone served to indicate a frequently quite complicated harmonic texture which was improvised by the executants in accordance with a more or less definite tradition, and notation in earlier times was even more rudimentary, and indeed only served as a mnemonic or aid to memory, not as an exact record of the work. The history of music, indeed, consists largely in the progressive and gradual reduction to writing of elements in the musical *ensemble* which had previously been improvised, and it is only in modern times that notation has come to represent for us the whole of a musical work. To take for granted, then, that the notation of the ancients was as comprehensive and precise as our own, and to suppose that because only a bare voice part was committed to writing they must therefore necessarily have been entirely ignorant of harmony, is a quite indefensible position to take up. The *reductio ad absurdum* of such an argument would be to maintain that the Egyptians could not have had any music whatsoever, because, so far as we know, they do not seem to have employed any system of notation at all.

Again, it might perhaps be said that it would indeed be very strange if the Greeks should have omitted to tell us anything about their harmonic practice if they had one, and that this silence on their part should be regarded as a proof positive that they had not. But this does not necessarily follow. It must be remembered that we possess an infinitely smaller quantity of Greek theoretical writings on music than we do of mediæval ones, and, as we have already seen from the passage from Wooldridge quoted above, all writers of a certain period of the Middle Ages omitted all mention of a long-established practice as if it had never formed a part of music at all. Treatises on unaccompanied Gregorian chant continued to be written throughout the Middle Ages, without referring to harmonic practices which had been in existence for many centuries, and if these alone had survived to the present day we should most certainly find musical historians denying the possibility that mediæval musicians could have known anything whatever of harmony. It is just as likely, therefore, that the few Greek theoretical writings which have survived present only a very one-sided and incomplete picture of Greek music, and are consequently more misleading than informative.

The statement, then, found in all histories of music, that neither the Greeks nor any other race prior to about the year 900 A.D. had any notion of harmony, is a purely gratuitous assumption with no positive evidence to support it. It is, of course, equally true that there is no positive evidence on the other side, but it is significant that among the few authorities who are inclined to believe that the Greeks probably did employ some kind of harmonic accompaniment in their songs are Westphal and Gevaert, who, although they are somewhat discredited to-day, are perhaps the two writers that have given the most time and thought to the question. There is an interesting passage in Plato's Laws which would seem to lend support to their contention, in which reference is made to " diversity of notes, when the strings give one sound and the poet or composer another ; also when they make concords and harmonies in which lesser and greater intervals, slow and quick, or high and low notes, are combined ". This passage has never been convincingly explained away by those who would deny any knowledge of harmony to the Greeks. But the principal reasons which lead us to doubt the conclusion arrived at by the majority of writers on the subject are simply common-sense ones. Is it not on the face of it unlikely that a procedure which seems to us elementary and commonplace should have been entirely unknown and neglected up till a few brief centuries ago ? Is it not improbable, to say the least, that, throughout the thousands and possibly hundreds of thousands of years that have elapsed since man began to inhabit the earth, no two notes of the scale were ever sounded together intentionally until the idea of doing so suddenly occurred to some obscure mediæval monk or other ? Is it not asking too much to expect us to believe that harmony of even the simplest description was totally unknown to one of the most daringly speculative and enquiring races that the world has ever seen, and yet owed its origin to the least enlightened period in modern history ? In order to induce one to credit such suppositions it would be necessary to bring forward a mass of well-nigh incontrovertible evidence in support of them, and even then one would probably be more inclined to doubt the evidence than accept such a theory ; but when it is put forward without any evidence at all, one need have no hesitation in rejecting it *in toto*.

But why, it may be asked, if there is nothing to support this belief, was it ever formulated, and how has it come about that it is still unhesitatingly subscribed to by the vast majority of musical historians ? The answer is to be found in the sacrosanct evolutionary theory which has vitiated musical criticism to such an extent that it has ceased to be what it was originally, namely, a credible and eminently workable hypothesis to be retained only so long as the facts and probabilities justified it, and rejected when they did not ; and has become instead an irrefragable dogma, an article of faith which one is not permitted to question or doubt, and to which facts and probabilities must be made subservient or else ignored. As Mr. Belloc so trenchantly puts it in his devastating criticism of Mr. Wells's " Outline of History," " You have to imagine facts without evidence, you have also to distort facts, you have also to suppress them, if you are to present to your readers a childishly simple scheme of regular and, above all, ' slow ' progress. You must make Early Man " —in our case Early Music—" last as long as possible and be as base as possible ".

Now it is obvious that if it were admitted that the Greeks or any other early people might conceivably have possessed harmony, whereas we know for certain that Gregorian chant, which came later in point of time, was purely melodic, the evolutionary doctrine becomes untenable ; consequently the mere suggestion of such a possibility must be summarily dismissed. I do not, of course, wish to imply that there is a kind of secret conspiracy on the part of musical historians to bolster up a theory which its advocates know to be unsound, but simply that the evolutionary habit of mind and way of thinking has become so deeply ingrained that it does not even occur to them to question its infallibility for one moment. Their mode of reasoning is probably as follows : (1) Music has evolved slowly from a primitive condition—this is an axiom ; (2) Gregorian chant is not harmonic, *ergo ;* (3) Greek music which preceded it cannot possibly have been harmonic. To question this reasoning is to destroy the whole basis on which their conception of musical history, both in outline and in detail, rests.

The truth of the whole matter, of course, is simply that we do not possess enough evidence to justify us in saying for certain whether any harmonic practice existed in music prior to our era or not, and it is as well to keep an absolutely open mind on the question. On one point, however, we can be fairly, if not absolutely certain, and that is that even if the Greeks did employ some form of harmony it was at the opposite pole from polyphony, the art of combining different melodies. Even if the device had been theoretically familiar to them, everything that we know of their conception of music and of art generally serves to convince one that they would in practice have rejected it unhesitatingly as a barbarous and inartistic invention ; their whole attitude of mind was clearly homophonic, and it is largely because we believe that harmony can only originate in polyphony that we decline to entertain the idea that the Greeks might conceivably have possessed any harmony at all.

One thing, however, is absolutely certain, namely, that even if the Greeks did not employ harmony in our sense of the word they clearly recognized the existence of definite harmonic principles which rigorously prescribed and controlled the melodic movement. In other words, even if the melody was entirely unaccompanied, it was nevertheless constructed in accordance with a definite, preconceived, harmonic scheme ; and if they did not possess our conception of harmony in space, i.e., as the simultaneous sounding of different notes, they certainly possessed a conception of it in time, i.e., as a successive sounding of different notes bearing a definite harmonic relation to each other. In fact the idea of harmony in one sense or another entirely dominates the Greek conception of music, and might almost be regarded as the tonal equivalent of the idea of σωφροσύνη or ἀταραξία, which is the guiding principle of the Greek conception of life. To assert that harmony played a more preponderant rôle in Greek music than it does in that of to-day even is therefore no mere idle paradox but a literal fact, an incontrovertible truth. In short, Greek music was primarily and essentially harmonic in conception, even if it was entirely unaccompanied harmonically, which we are at perfect liberty to doubt.

Gregorian chant, on the contrary, is primarily and essentially melodic, and remains so even when it is provided with an accompaniment as it often is in churches to-day—a procedure, by the way, that cannot be too emphatically condemned, for harmony of any kind is completely foreign to its nature. This fact explains to a great extent the aërial, floating, disembodied quality which we have already observed to be the distinguishing feature of this music. And if it should be asked why, supposing the Greeks to have employed harmony, the anonymous creators of plain-song should have deliberately rejected such a fruitful technical resource, the reply simply is that they did not want it and had no use for it. That is the all-important point which the evolutionary, materialistic conception of musical history entirely fails to grasp, and the source of this failure can be traced back to the mistaken notion that Gregorian chant is only the continuation and adaptation of the old pagan art, whereas actually, as has been shown in the preceding chapter, they stand at the opposite poles to each other ; and the fact that the early church musicians neglected harmony, so far from invalidating the belief that the Greeks cultivated it, tends rather to support and confirm it, for the mere fact that harmony was the guiding principle of Greek music would in itself be sufficient to entail its exclusion from the new Christian art on account of its profane and secular associations. In his emphatic rejection of every semblance of harmony or instrumental accompaniment the mediæval musician aptly symbolized the early Christian denial of the flesh and all earthly and material things. In Gregorian chant the disembodied melodic soul, freed from the harmonic shackles and encumbrances which had clogged and impeded its movements in ancient times, released from the tyranny of harmonic flesh, soars ecstatically upwards to Heaven like the Holy Dove of the Scriptures.

It is necessary to emphasize this purely melodic nature of plain-song, and its intolerance of and aversion to harmony, for it will be seen to provide a key to many problems which would otherwise be totally inexplicable. In the first place, the procedure called organum, which originally consisted in the addition of parallel fourths and fifths to the plain song, is not harmonic or polyphonic at all, but is only an adaptation and extension of the device called by the Greeks " magadizing ", i.e., a doubling of the melody in octaves. Even if the plain-song had been doubled at every interval of the scale in parallel motion, it would still make no difference in principle. For example, in the Buddhist temples of China, we are told, it was and perhaps still is, customary for each of the singers to intone the melody in the key best suited to the compass of his voice ; but however weird and complicated the result might sound in performance, it could not possibly be called harmonic or contrapuntal, since it merely consists in the reduplication of the melody at different intervals. Similarly, as Professor Tovey rightly points out in his article on Harmony in the " Encyclopædia Britannica ", " when mediæval musicians doubled a melody in fifths and octaves they believed themselves to be doing no more than extending and diversifying the means by which a melody might be sung in unison by different voices ". Neither can any element of harmonic prevision be said to enter into the later development of organum, in which one voice stood still while the other moved, for, as Professor Wooldridge points out, this innovation was due, not to artistic reasons, but simply to a rule " which obliges the organal voice from time to time to hold a certain sound instead of passing below it ; and it is to the continuance of the melody under those circumstances by the principal voice which actually creates the discordant intervals ". Similarly the subsequent introduction of contrary movement between the parts was undoubtedly prompted, not by any fertile, creative, harmonic intention, but simply by a desire to preserve the illusion of unisons, and to avoid those discords accidentally arrived at, which, if they had been deliberately introduced might admittedly have indicated the presence of harmonic thought. Finally, it must be remembered that in all species of organum there is no determinate rhythm or measure, and it is a fact—though more easily apprehended intuitively, perhaps, than proved by argument—that true harmonic writing is impossible without definite, periodic, rhythmic stresses.

But even after the introduction of discant, or measured music, it is still impossible to find evidence of any harmonic thought on the part of the church composers. When they were not content merely with rabbeting two or more independently conceived tunes together at random—generally a fragment of plain song and a folk-song or other popular melody—they added parts to the subject in accordance with a rule which strictly prescribed the employment of the perfect consonances of the fourth, fifth, and octave on the strong beats, and paid no attention whatsoever to what happened in between them. Since these consonances, as we have already observed, were felt and regarded as unisons rather than as harmonies—as, in a sense, they are—the whole method of composition employed resolves itself into a series of unisons, or pseudo-unisons, interspersed with purely fortuitous and accidental combinations of passing-notes which might be consonances or dissonances for all the composers knew or cared.

And yet, in the very midst of this period of utter chaos and confusion which came to an end in the fourteenth century largely as a result of the papal edict of John XXII strictly forbidding the introduction of such methods of composition into the church service, we find ourselves suddenly confronted with a perfect specimen of polyphonic music, namely, the celebrated Reading Rota or Rondel " Sumer is icumen in " which is not merely centuries in advance of its time (*c.* 1240) according to the doctrines of the evolutionary school of musical criticism, but has demonstrably nothing in common with the methods of discant.

It is certainly not going too far to say that this one piece of music is in itself sufficient to demolish the theory that polyphony came into existence by way of organum or discant, for it must either have been the outcome of a common practice dating back to a very much earlier period, or else it is an isolated exception which fell out of the skies like an aerolith, referable to no precedent and susceptible of no explanation. Both theories— and obviously there can be no third—are fundamentally irreconcilable with the evolutionary theory of the origin of harmony and polyphony.

This must not be taken to mean that there is quite definitely no such thing as development or evolution in music, but merely that if there is, it is certainly not of the crude and elementary variety hitherto postulated by musical historians. Most modern exponents of Darwinism no longer hold the original view that Heidelberg and Neanderthal Man are direct ancestors of modern man, but that they are only offshoots from the main line of development, tentative experiments which were ultimately abandoned in favour of an entirely new and different type, and predecessors only in point of time ; and if musical historians could be induced to adopt a similarly modified attitude towards organum and discant there might still be something, but not much, to be said for the theory of evolution in music. But to say, as Sir Henry Hadow does (" Music" ; Home University Library) that from organum " sprang the whole scheme of interwoven voices which culminates in the B minor Mass and the Choral Symphony " is as demonstrably untrue as to say that Cro-Magnon Man is directly descended from Heidelberg Man. Such an assertion can only be maintained by a citation of carefully selected facts and a deliberate suppression or rejection of all evidence that conflicts with it.

Some writers, acutely conscious of the difficulty of reconciling the Reading Rota with contemporary church practice, have suggested that it is to be regarded as an example of folk-music. At first sight this seems probable, for it is supported by the remarkable and often-quoted statement of Giraldus Cambrensis, a writer of the twelfth century, to the effect that in his time the common people in Yorkshire and Northumberland were able to sing in two parts " by natural gift and without training " and that the Welsh were wont to sing together in as many parts as there were voices. The precise significance of the second part of the statement has often been debated by historians, and its veracity impugned ; the first part, however, may be unreservedly accepted, for it is borne out by a piece of definite evidence, though admittedly belonging to a slightly later period. This is a recently discovered manuscript of the thirteenth century belonging to a monastery in the Orkney Islands, in which we find an example in notation of the familiar device of singing in thirds in two parts which is in all probability what Giraldus heard in the north of England. It is very unlikely, however, that folk-singers ever went very much further than this ; that untrained musicians could possibly have invented and perfected such a highly organized and, in the best sense of the word, artificial, form as the rondel, and could have produced such a highly polished and flawlessly constructed example of it as the Reading Rota, which would tax the ingenuity of any composer to-day, is frankly unthinkable.

On the other hand we have the definite assurance of the poet Walter Map—a contemporary and friend of Giraldus, by the way—that the round, rota, or rondel, as it was variously called, was a form well-known to and frequently employed by his contemporaries—i.e., at a date considerably anterior to that tentatively assigned to "Sumer is icumen in". We are therefore almost forced to the conclusion that the latter is to be regarded, not as a solitary exception—a kind of musical "sport", to use the language of biology—but as a representative example, unfortunately unique for reasons which we shall consider later, of a method of composition extensively practised in the Middle Ages, not by church musicians, nor even by folk-singers, but by highly trained secular composers ; and that it bears emphatic witness to the existence of a secular musical tradition subsisting side by side with that of the church and independently of it, probably even pre-dating it, and quite certainly as superior artistically to it as the music of Wagner is superior to that of Hymns Ancient and Modern. And if it should be asked why, if such a secular tradition really existed, the church musicians should be content, with what might seem to us at first sight to be an almost maniacal perversity, to ignore it and to confine themselves to the relative puerilities and incoherences of organum and discant, the answer simply is that the secular style of composition was wholly unsuitable to the purposes of the divine service, and completely inadaptable to the nature of Gregorian chant. It would be as ridiculous to expect the church musicians of the Middle Ages to employ the full technical resources of their secular colleagues as it would be to expect our contemporary writers of hymns and anthems to employ the full orchestra of Strauss' *Salome*, or to write in the harmonic idiom of Schönberg's *Pierrot Lunaire*. It must be constantly borne in mind, moreover, when considering the church music of the Middle Ages, that from the very beginning it had to contend with the implacable hostility of the clergy towards the introduction of any innovations into the ritual of the church. And, as music was, of all the arts, the one most intimately bound up with the ritual, it was only natural that these fiercely conservative tendencies should be particularly intensified with regard to it. The attitude of the church authorities in this question has always been remarkably logical and consistent from the earliest times, and has remained so to the present day. The *Motu Proprio* of Pius X only a few years ago maintained essentially the same position as the bull of John XXII already referred to, or the decrees of the Council of Trent ; namely, that "the more closely a composition approaches in its movement, inspiration, and savour to the Gregorian form, the more sacred and liturgical it becomes ; and the more out of harmony it is with that supreme model the less worthy it is of the temple ". The intrusion of secular elements has always been sternly discountenanced. Time and time again, whenever such a development took place the ever-watchful clergy ruthlessly suppressed it and drove it forth from the sanctuary. The sequences and tropes are the earliest examples of these infiltrations. After they had been expelled, the secular influence furtively attempted to creep back again in the form of discant, arm in arm, so to speak, with the sacred chant, as if hoping to be tolerated on account of the unimpeachable respectability of its companion ; and throughout the entire Middle Ages we constantly come across a quite obvious secular song vainly attempting to masquerade in clerical garb—a musical Till Eulenspiegel with merry twinkling eyes peeping from under the monk's cowl. But the offender was almost invariably detected by the vigilant and inexorable authorities, and in the end summarily ejected from the liturgy.

Similarly the respect for the Gregorian chant which was enjoined by clerical decrees automatically precluded the employment of almost every technical resource that was at the disposal of the lay musician. Not only, however, were secular methods of composition wholly unfitted to the church service from a strictly ethical standpoint, but also from a purely musical one. Such a technical device as canon, for example, in which a definitely rhythmic theme has to be carefully constructed according to its eventual harmonic requirements is obviously inapplicable to a rhythmless chant already in existence.

The hostility of the church authorities, then, combined with the obstinate resistance that plain-song opposed to harmonic treatment, are in themselves sufficient to explain the manifest inferiority of early sacred polyphonic music compared with a work such as the Reading Rota and, indeed, the complete failure on the part of the church composers to found any satisfactory harmonic art on the basis of plain-song. And so far from there being any steady development or constant improvement in their efforts in this direction, as evolutionists would have us believe, the least unsatisfactory of their experiments proved to be the very first strict parallel organum which, as we have already seen, was not, properly speaking, harmonic at all—with its derivate or, as Riemann suggests, possibly its original form, *faux bourdon*, or singing in thirds and sixths ; and the most unsatisfactory was the last, namely the elaborate combination of the chant with one or more rhythmically co-ordinated secular songs which was suppressed by the edict of John XXII. In fact, as Professor Wooldridge quite rightly observes, the traditional and correct method of rendering the chant "is compatible only with perfect parallelism in the accompanying parts."

And so we find that the much-abused procedure called organum which has served as a butt for the ridicule of generations of music-students, remains, notwithstanding, the most artistic and appropriate method of treating plain-song—short of leaving it alone, which is best of all—that has yet been devised ; and it is an interesting and highly significant fact that the revival of interest in Gregorian chant, and its deep influence upon many modern composers, have been accompanied by a reversion, largely unconscious no doubt, to this primitive method of treatment. The strict parallelism of parts in the music of such composers as Debussy and Vaughan Williams, together with their predilection for bare consecutive fourths and fifths, must undoubtedly be ascribed in large part to the essentially modal character of their melodic writing, and constitutes a remarkable tribute to the fine sense of artistic fitness and the sure musical instinct possessed by its mediæval originators. Similarly it might be pointed out that the methods of the early discanters, though they are admittedly unsuited to the reverent treatment of the sacred chant, are not by any means so entirely devoid of artistic interest as they are generally represented to be in musical histories. The frequently ingenious manner in which widely dissimilar melodies are combined in their work reminds one strongly of the similar contrapuntal writing of Berlioz, Strauss, and other modern composers, and what seemed to former ages the intolerable cacophony of their harmonic combinations are almost innocuous and sweet-sounding compared with many similar progressions encountered in modern music. The fact of the matter is that our eighteenth and nineteenth century predecessors invariably approached this old music from the point of view of their own age and with their ears prejudiced against it by the music with which they were familiar. To-day, fortunately, things are different, and it is quite possible that we might even derive considerable pleasure from hearing some of these astonishing motets sung in which two or three secular melodies are combined together on the basis of a Gregorian chant.

However that may be, such things have nothing to do with harmony or with the elaborate polyphony exemplified in the Reading Rota. The church chant was inherently incapable of giving birth to any such development, and it is no mere coincidence, but only in accordance with what we are logically driven to expect, that the first example of genuine polyphonic writing and harmonic propriety that has come down to us should be a piece of secular music belonging to an entirely different tradition of musicianship from that of the church.

Too much importance, in fact, has been attributed to the activities of the ecclesiastical musicians and too little to those of their secular colleagues, simply because we happen to possess a large quantity of the music of the former and next to nothing of that of the latter. The reason for this is, of course, to be found in the fact that notation was originally the invention of the church composers and remained their monopoly for a considerable period. The monasteries were practically the sole repositories of learning for many centuries, and one would hardly expect to find that the monks had devoted their energies and the benefit of their invention to the task of conserving a profane art which must have inspired them with pious horror rather than with approval, with jealousy rather than with sympathy or admiration. The survival of the Reading Rota itself is undoubtedly due solely to the fortunate circumstance that it had been thoughtfully provided with alternative sacred words written probably by its supposed transcriber, a monk named John of Fornsete.   And if the early history of polyphony seems chaotic and unintelligible to us, it is largely, though not entirely, because our knowledge of music in the Dark Ages is almost wholly confined to a comparatively unimportant branch of it. An attempt to write the history of mediæval music with only the theory and practice of the ecclesiastical composers to go upon is like trying to write a survey of modern music based upon the textbooks of Prout and Stainer and the music of the Rev. John Bacchus Dykes and Sir Joseph Barnby. The real history of the art throughout the Middle Ages is almost unknown to us, and can only be filled in by means of speculation and conjecture which, incidentally, are often more reliable guides than logical deductions from insufficient evidence.   For while the fair amount we know about mediæval church music leads us nowhere at all in the matter of harmony and polyphony, in the strict sense of the words, the little we know about the secular music, on the other hand, tells us a great deal ; and if it would seem that too much stress is laid here on a single piece of music like the Reading Rota it is because in æsthetic value and interest it outweighs by itself all the rest combined of the polyphonic music of the period that has survived.

It may of course be objected that it is an exceptional piece of music and consequently should not be made the basis of a generalization on the secular music of the period, considered as a whole.   The mere fact, however, that none of the rest of the early secular music that has come down to us can be compared to it, signifies nothing, for there is so little of it.   Bad music is written in every age and always in much greater quantities than good music ; and when we consider how little of the secular polyphonic art of the Middle Ages has survived, the presence of only one supremely beautiful work amongst it is proportionately as much as, if not more than, we are reasonably entitled to expect.   To suggest that it was " in advance of its time " to such an extent as to be a mere freak which can consequently be dismissed as irrelevant, is only the excuse musical historians make in order to escape having to try and explain its existence which, as they well know, cannot be reconciled with their theories concerning the origin of harmony and polyphony.   It was an exception and in advance of its time in exactly the same way that a work of genius always is, but that is all ; it does not stand out more conspicuously from the rest of the music of the period than any other consummate masterpiece in any other period, and it is more than probable that if we possessed as much of the secular music of the time as we do of the sacred, we should find many works equal to it, if not in sheer musical beauty, at least in technical mastery.

CHAPTER III

The Music of the Minstrels and Troubadours

In the preceding chapter we saw that the first known example of true polyphony, as opposed to the pseudo-polyphony of the church musicians, came from these islands, and all the indirect contemporary evidence at our disposal, such as it is, seems to suggest that this is no mere accident or coincidence, but that the origins of contrapuntal practice are to be sought in the northern rather than in the southern or central parts of Europe. This conclusion, which is unanimously endorsed by the most eminent modern authorities, is further substantiated by the fact that, throughout the whole course of musical history, northern composers in general have always displayed a more marked predilection for polyphony and a greater mastery of contrapuntal resources than those of the south, who, with few exceptions, incline rather in the direction of harmonic and homophonic forms.

It will not surprise us, therefore, if we are unable to find any traces of the existence of an art corresponding to the Reading Rota in Latin countries at the time with which we have so far been dealing ; neither is there any indirect literary evidence like that of Walter Map and Giraldus Cambrensis to warrant the supposition that such a form of art was even theoretically known to musicians in France, Italy, or elsewhere until some time later. We find instead, as we should expect to do, a form of solo song with instrumental accompaniment which attained a high stage of development with the Troubadours and Trouvères in France and the Minnesänger in Southern Germany.

While the great intrinsic value and historical importance of the poetry of the Troubadours and their *confrères* has always been recognized and appreciated by literary critics, the musical side of their art has passed almost unnoticed and its significance has been greatly under-estimated. Until quite recently, indeed, owing to the somewhat haphazard and perfunctory system of notation employed by both composers and transcribers, the music of these songs has remained for the most part undeciphered. Now, fortunately, thanks to the labours of scholars such as Beck and Aubry, it is now possible for us to arrive at a fairly accurate estimate of its intrinsic qualities and to appreciate both its great æsthetic significance and its historical importance, despite a certain amount of doubt and difference of opinion which still remains with regard to minor rhythmical problems.

The art of the Troubadours, the earliest and most important of the three, and the one from which the two others were mainly derived, flourished from about the beginning of the twelfth century till the close of the thirteenth, the first important name being that of Guillaume, Comte de Poitiers, born in 1071, and the last that of Guiraut Riquier who died in 1294. The late Professor Ker, in one of his admirable studies in mediæval literature, calls the former " the first modern poet, using the kind of verse which everyone uses now ", and says of the Troubadours in general that " everything that we can think of in modern poetry is related to the French and Provençal literature of the year 1100 as it is not related to anything in the Dark Age. There is nothing abrupt, no shock of sudden transition in turning from the verse of Goethe, Hugo, or Tennyson, to the rhymes of Provence ". It is a remarkable fact that exactly the same can be said of the music to which the poems were set. In striking contrast to the archaic and forbidding aspect of mediæval church music, the melodic *allure* of these secular songs is so akin to that of modern music that it is difficult to believe that they were written eight hundred years ago. Like the Reading Rota they speak to us in our own language, and express identically the same order of ideas and emotions as the songs of to-day.

This familiarity and accessibility is largely the result of the predominating rôle which our modern major and minor scales play in them, and one might say that the change from the modality of Gregorian music and its derivates to the tonality of the troubadour songs is in many ways a musical parallel to the substitution of the *lingua volgare*, or vernacular—whether French, Provençal, or Tuscan—for mediæval Latin in poetry. Certainly it cannot be a mere coincidence that the two phenomena are first observed in intimate association with each other at precisely the same moment of time and in the same place, namely, about 1100 in Provence.

There can be little doubt, however, that the modern major scale had already been in use in secular music for a considerable time before that, to say the least. For although the four original modes employed in Gregorian chant are those of D, E, G, and F (on the white keys of the piano), and it was only comparatively late in the Middle Ages that those of C and A made their appearance in the music of the church, the latter were deliberately avoided by the ecclesiastical composers, we are told, on account of their secular associations and their markedly irreligious character. Glareanus, for example, in his *Dodecachordon*, written in the first half of the sixteenth century, says that these two modes " are particularly adapted to dances, and are to be found throughout Europe ", adding that, in spite of the strenuous opposition of the church, they had been so extensively employed " for four hundred years " that ecclesiastical musicians, attracted by the sweetness of the modern major scale, were in the habit of altering the church melodies in the F mode by the addition of a B flat so as to correspond with it. He also tells us that melodies written in the C mode were apt to induce a frivolous state of mind, and that a writer, adducing illustrations of the depravity of his age, declared that " the marriagable young woman delights in learning Ionian dances " (i.e., dances in our major scale).

It would be a mistake, therefore, to imagine that the systematic employment of the major scale suddenly began with the Troubadours. Indeed, the deliberate avoidance of it by the original creators of Gregorian chant is in itself enough to show that it was regularly employed in secular music in the early Middle Ages, and that in all probability it even pre-dated the composition of the sacred chants of the Western Church. A good early example of a melody written in the major scale is to be found in the hauntingly beautiful pilgrim's song " O Roma nobilis ", originally a Latin love-song with scabrous words, which dates back to a time long before the appearance of the Provençal Troubadours. There can be little doubt that it is only one out of many which happens to have survived, like the Reading Rota, solely on account of the religious words to which it was adapted ; and if the Troubadour music constitutes the first large collection of secular songs that has come down to us, it is only because their composers or transcribers had been initiated into the mysteries of the ecclesiastical notation and were consequently not dependent on the tender mercies of the monks for the preservation of their music. Before the twelfth century the tradition must have been handed down orally and improvised by the minstrels, and it is extremely improbable that the Troubadours did anything more than adapt it to their own purposes.

This assumption is borne out by the fact that one of the earliest, perhaps even the very earliest, of all the specimens of their art which have come down to us, was not invented by a Troubadour. The story about it, recounted by a contemporary writer, was as follows : " At this time (i.e., about 1200) there came to the court of the marquis (Boniface II of Montferrat) two *jongleurs* who knew well how to play the viol. And one day they played an *estampida* (a kind of dance) which greatly pleased the marquis, the knights, and the noble ladies, and Sir Rambaut (a celebrated Troubadour named Rambaut de Vaqueiras) showed so little joy that the marquis noticed it. ‘ What then, Sir Rambaut ’, quoth he, ‘ why do you not sing to us, why are you not more joyful when here is a beautiful viol melody and there at your side sits such a beautiful woman as my sister, whose favours you enjoy, and who is certainly the noblest woman in the whole world ? ’ Upon which Sir Rambaut declared that he would do nothing. The marquis then said to his sister, ‘ Madame Beatrice, for love of me and the assembled company, be so good as to entreat Sir Rambaut that in the name of your love and favour he will recover his former gaiety and sing to us ’. And Madame Beatrice was of such courtesy and generosity as to entreat Sir Rambaut to take comfort and for love of her to show a less careworn countenance, and to make a new song. It was then that Sir Rambaut, for the reasons that you have heard, made an *estampida* on the air which the minstrels had played on their viols ". This was the famous poem beginning with the words " Kalendas Mayas ", and it is possible that many and perhaps most of the poems of the Troubadours were similarly written to melodies played by the *jongleurs* or minstrels, and that they, consequently, not their noble masters, were the real composers of the music which has come down to us under the names of the latter.

Indeed it would be difficult to exaggerate the magnitude of the part played by the minstrels in the history of mediæval music.   As Professor E. K. Chambers says in " The Mediæval Stage " : " nine-tenths of the secular music and literature, something even of the religious literature ", and, he might have added, something even of the religious music, " of the Middle Ages had its origin in minstrelsy ".   In fact, the more one considers the matter, the more evident it becomes that what we know of mediæval music is only an infinitesimal part compared with what has been lost.   The history of mediæval music, indeed, is like an iceberg, of which only a small part appears above the surface ; the rest lies irretrievably submerged and lost for ever beneath the waves of time.

The part, too, that the music of minstrels played in mediæval life was of an importance comparable only to that of the Gregorian chant.   They wandered from village to village, equally at home in the castle and in the humble cottage, as welcome in the guild-hall as in the tavern, and they were sometimes even smuggled clandestinely into the monasteries by the monks in order to beguile the tedium of the cloistral life.   Their presence was imperatively required at all festivals and rejoicings, weddings and tournaments, baptisms and betrothals ; they accompanied the candidate for knighthood at the *veillée des armes*—the long vigil passed in the chapel the night before the ceremonial investiture—attended pilgrims on their journeyings to holy shrines, and even appeared on the field of battle, like Taillefer who, at Senlac, according to the Roman de Rou,

> Sor un cheval ki tost alout
> Devant le duc alout chantant
> De Karlemaigne et de Rolant
> Et d'Oliver et des vassals
> Qui morurent en Rencevals.

Their assistance was even in urgent request in matters of state and church policy.   For instance, the chancellor of Richard I, William de Longchamp, brought minstrels over from France in order that they might sing his praises to the common people and in this way counteract his great unpopularity ; and St. Francis conceived the idea of creating a band of friars who like minstrels *joculatores Domini* were to go forth into the world singing the praises of Christ and His Heavenly Father, and persuading sinners to contrition and repentance through the power of their art of song.

What are the origins of this great minstrel tradition and whence did it come ? In view of its great antiquity, equal to if not more than that of Gregorian chant itself, and in view of its manifest difference from the latter, it is very tempting to suggest that it might conceivably represent the remnant or survival of the old Greco-Roman art which had been driven underground in the early days of the Christian ascendancy but had never entirely died out ; and to see in the *jongleur* and minstrel who played such an important rôle in the musical and social life of the Middle Ages the lineal descendants of the *joculator* and *mimus* of the Roman Empire, and the inheritors of their tradition. But the more one considers it, the more unlikely it becomes. In the first place, we know that when Clovis, the Merovingian king of the Franks, desired, in the sixth century, to revive the music of the Roman Empire, he was unable to find anyone except at Rome who was able to play the cithara, so completely had the old art disappeared and died out in the course of the two hundred years and more that had elapsed since the downfall of the Imperial City. The similar attempt on the part of Charlemagne to reintroduce the arts and culture of the old Roman Empire was equally artificial and also ended in complete failure. In fact it is difficult to resist the conclusion that the old art had become almost, if not entirely, extinct.

In the second place, the Dorian mode (scale of E) which, as we have already seen, played the most important part in antique music, is in character the most dissimilar of all the modes to the major scale which so largely prevails in the secular music of the Middle Ages ; among all the examples of Greco-Roman music that we possess there is not one to be found that is in modern tonality or that bears the slightest resemblance to the songs of the Troubadours and their anonymous predecessors. Indeed the latter are as markedly different from what we know of antique music as they are from Gregorian music ; all three traditions are quite distinct and separate.

If, then, the music of the minstrels is neither the continuation of the late Greco-Roman tradition, nor an offshoot from the early Christian church music, it can only be one thing, namely the continuation and proliferation of the musical art of the northern, and particularly the Celtic and Anglo-Saxon, peoples, disseminated throughout the continent through the agency of the *scóp* and *gleómon* of whom we get such an interesting and graphic account in the conclusion of the well-known early English poem belonging to the fourth century, called Widsith. As Professor Chambers says in the work already quoted, " they wander through realm upon realm, voice their needs, and have but to give thanks. In every land they find a lord to whom songs are dear, and whose bounty is open to the exalters of his name ". They, rather than the *mimus* and *joculator* of classical antiquity, are recognizably the direct ancestors of the minstrel and the Troubadour. The entertainer of pagan times, it must be remembered, was *infamis*, a social outcast, and remained so in the days of the early church ; only the northern peoples regarded him as a man of repute and even the social equal of the highest in the land. " For a Nero to perform among the *scenici* was to descend ; for a Hrothgar to touch the harp was a customary and an honourable act ". (Chambers, *op. cit.*)

It is not merely by the process of elimination that one is led to the conclusion that the art of the minstrels must be the continuation and adaptation of a northern art-tradition, but because it is a conclusion to which all cultural and historical considerations unerringly point. The feudal system on which mediæval society was built was originally a northern institution ; the feeling for nature which is such a marked characteristic of the poetry and literature of the Middle Ages and so alien to both the Greco-Roman and the early Christian spirits, was a distinguishing feature of Celtic and other northern poetry as early as the sixth and seventh centuries ; and whether the Britons who fled before the Teutonic and Scandinavian invasions of the sixth and eighth centuries brought the Arthurian legends to Brittany, according to one theory, or whether, according to another, the tales were preserved in the land of their origin and only communicated later to the Norman conquerors, the fact remains that the Celtic Arthurian cyclo with its mystical idealism, its cult of gyneolatry and knight-errantry, was the main source of inspiration from which all secular mediæval thought and poetry flowed.

Furthermore, it is an exceedingly significant fact that the monastic community of the Abbey of St. Gall, perhaps the most important centre of artistic activities during the Dark Ages, was largely permeated by Celtic and Anglo-Saxon elements, and that the great mediæval art of miniature painting is generally attributed to them—is in any case of Celtic origin. The monks at this abbey, moreover, were continually occupied in training the sons of the nobility in all subjects, but especially in literature and music, and Uhland is probably not far wrong when, in his study of mediæval poetry, he suggests that we may perhaps find here the germ which came to fruition in the poetry of chivalry.

In the same way then, that all the evidence points to the Byzantine origin of the Gregorian chant, so all the laws of artistic analogy lead us to attributing a northern and predominantly Celtic and Anglo-Saxon origin to the musical tradition which we are considering—a theory which gains additional support from the fact that the musicians at the royal and ducal courts where the secular art was most cultivated were largely English and Irish. Finally, and perhaps most important of all, the definite resemblance in melodic idiom and general feeling between the Reading Rota and the most characteristic examples of the art of the minstrels and Troubadours needs no labouring ; they demonstrably belong to the same root tradition.

One important point in connection with the music of the Troubadours remains to be discussed. We know for a certainty that their melodies were habitually sung to accompaniments provided either by the singer himself, or, more commonly, by one or two *jongleurs*, but as these accompaniments were not committed to notation but were only improvised, we are unable to say for certain what they were like. Of course, in accordance with the *a priori* doctrine of the evolution of harmony from the polyphonic experiments of the church composers, most musical historians refuse to countenance the suggestion that these accompaniments might conceivably have been harmonic ; we are asked to believe that the instrumentalists played throughout in unison with the voice part. There is, however, absolutely no evidence whatsoever to warrant such a dogmatic assertion. Rather the opposite, there is every reason—short of positive evidence which does not exist on either side—for believing that these accompaniments were definitely harmonic. In the first place, the mediæval *vielle* on which they were played—which also seems, by the way, to have been of definitely Celtic origin—possessed a flat bridge, in consequence of which it must have often been, if not actually impossible, at least extremely difficult for the player not to sound two or more notes simultaneously, whether he wanted to or not ; and there is no conceivable reason why he should not, unless out of a touching regard for the prejudices and preconceived notions of musical historians who were to come after him. In the second place, the striking similarities which exist between the music of the Troubadours and modern music in all other respects are in themselves good grounds for supposing that they were not so very different in this respect also, except in degree. If two sides of a triangle coincide the third will also be found to coincide ; and in view of the fact that the songs are rhythmically and melodically so startlingly akin to those of to-day, it would indeed be strange if they were entirely different in the matter of the instrumental accompaniment. But there is more in it than that. The important point is that the growth of the harmonic sense, in the modern meaning of the word, the tendency to conceive the texture of music perpendicularly rather than horizontally, as chords rather than as separate parts woven together, coincides in all periods with a definite inclination in the direction of modern tonality and the scale system. The more definitely the music is in our major key, the more definitely harmonic it becomes. This is a matter of common observation. As the author of the article on " Harmony " on Grove's " Dictionary of Music and Musicians " puts it, " the period of the rise of harmony is the period of the decay of the old tonality ". (He is, of course, speaking of the developments which took place at the end of the sixteenth and the beginning of the seventeenth centuries, seemingly oblivious of the fact that the so-called modern tonality is to be found in the secular music of the twelfth and thirteenth centuries, and possibly even earlier. The idea that it suddenly came into evidence about the year 1600, though one of the most dearly cherished legends of musical history, is absolutely untrue. As we have shown, it seems always to have been characteristic of western secular music, so far as we are able to judge.) The fundamental implications of his statement are nevertheless substantially correct, and corollarily it is also true that the tendency in recent times to abandon modern tonality and to revert to a certain extent to modality has brought about, as we have already had occasion to note, a corresponding tendency to abandon the strictly harmonic standpoint, and to revert to the essentially melodic reduplications of organum and *faux-bourdon*. The old modes in fact, it cannot be too often repeated, are wholly melodic in feeling and hostile to harmony ; the modern major scale, on the other hand, is harmonic in feeling, and indissolubly bound up with the harmonic system, and with the very Harmonic Series itself, as a moment's thought will show ; and the fact that we already find it completely developed in a great part of the music of the Troubadours, together with the other considerations already mentioned, almost constitutes *prima facie* evidence of a circumstantial kind in favour of the probable employment by them of a system or method of harmonic accompaniment similar to, though no doubt much cruder and simpler than, that obtaining to-day.

To this it might perhaps be objected that, supposing such a procedure to have existed in the Middle Ages, one would naturally expect to find it reflected to some extent at least in contemporary ecclesiastical practice ; that because no such influence is discernible it could not have existed. But a moment's thought will suffice to show that this is not in itself a valid objection, and is, indeed, an argument we have already dealt with, in a slightly different connection, in the preceding chapter. For it is surely obvious that a system of instrumental accompaniment suitable to solo songs of a definitely rhythmical character is, from a purely technical point of view, completely inadaptable to unaccompanied choral writing, besides, what is even more important, being fundamentally irreconcilable with the whole nature of the Gregorian chant. In short, the methods of the Troubadours and minstrels, whatever they were, must inevitably have been as unsuited to the purposes of the church music as were the methods of the northern secular choral composers as exemplified in the Reading Rota, with which they probably had much in common. There are, therefore, no reasonable grounds for denying the possibility, and even the probability, that the minstrels and Troubadours made use of harmony in their instrumental accompaniments, except the evolutionary prejudice which we have already weighed in the balance and found wanting ; on the other hand there are many reasonable grounds for supposing that they did.

The whole repertory of Troubadour songs can be roughly divided into two main groups or categories, *chansons à personnages* and *poésie courtoise*. The first consists of several different types of poem, of which the most important are as follows :

        (1) *chansons d'histoire,*
        (2) *chansons dramatiques,*
        (3) *chansons de danse,*
        (4) *reverdies,*
        (5) *pastourelles,*
        (6) *chansons d'aube,*

and the second and smaller group comprises three main divisions, namely,

        (1) *chansons courtoises,*
        (2) *jeux-partis,*
        (3) *chansons religieuses.*

The *chansons à personnages* are on the whole essentially objective in character, and deal with certain definite themes and set conventions of a purely imaginary order. The first of this group, the *chansons d'histoire* (or *chansons de toile* as they were alternatively designated, probably because they were generally sung by women at their work), are as a rule based upon the theme of the unhappy heroine of romance—Bele Yolanz, Bele Erembors, Aiglantine, Yzabel, or Amelot—deserted by a lover or opposed in the choice of her heart by obdurate parents. The *chansons dramatiques* deal with the situation of the *mal mariée*, and pour ridicule and contempt upon husbands and the institution of marriage in general : and sometimes with that of the nun dissatisfied with her lot and yearning for freedom. The *chansons de danse*, as the name suggests, were for the most part instrumental dance tunes to which words were afterwards set, and include also miniature ballets which seem to have been acted as well as sung. The *reverdie* was a spring-song, the *pastourelle* as a rule consisted of variations on the familiar subject of the young shepherdess and the gallant knight riding past who stops and makes love to her, sometimes successfully and sometimes not ; and the *chanson d'aube*, which constituted the most elaborate *genre* in this first group, was in the form of a dialogue between one of the lovers who are together and the watcher who warns them of the approach of day. The well-known scene in Romeo and Juliet (Act III, Scene 7,), beginning "Wilt thou be gone ? it is not yet near day", will be recognized as a variation on this old mediæval theme, and admired as an example of the ability of great genius to impart fresh beauty and significance to a worn-out and threadbare convention.

The musical settings of this first group of poetic forms are almost invariably characterized by a remarkable freshness and spontaneity of melodic invention. The music of the second group, on the other hand, and particularly of the *chansons courtoises* which are, in contrast to the foregoing, intensely subjective, personal addresses made by the Troubadour to his mistress, is on the whole rather more elaborate, subtle, and artificial. In fact, so far as the music is concerned, the two groups may be said to correspond roughly with the two sharply opposed styles of poetic composition practised by the Troubadours, namely the *trobar clar*—the lucid, simple, straight-forward style—and the *trobar clus*—the obscure, complex, and sophisticated style. The former, as one would naturally expect to find, seems to represent the earlier and more primitive tradition, and approximates closely to the manner of folk-song. Gaston Paris, one of the leading authorities on the literature and art of the Middle Ages in France, finds in the dance-song sung at the popular May festival—the *Kalendas Mayas*—the seed from which all Provençal poetry sprang, and it is quite possible that the music has a similar origin. It would be as well, however, not to lay too great stress upon this popular element, or to lose sight of the fact that the art of the Troubadours, both poetry and music, was in essence the reverse of popular. It was above all an aristocratic form of art, intended for the delectation of the nobility and the courts, and not at all for that of the people ; practised by kings, princes and nobles, and only very seldom indeed by commoners.

But whether Gaston Paris is right or not in his theory of the origins of Provençal lyric, the distinguishing feature of the poetry certainly consists in its preoccupation—one might almost say its obsession—with the imagery of spring ; and the whole feeling of the music is similarly that of a *reverdie*, a re-awakening of nature and of the delight in earthly things in the springtime of the world, after the long autumn decline of the late Roman

Empire and the iron-bound winter sleep of the early Middle Ages. Like the Reading Rota, "Sumer is icumen in", the songs of the Troubadours are full of the soft, mellow pipings of birds and the shrill, blithe songs of insects "in a somer seson when softe was the sonne"; and they are full of the scent of the moist fecund soil, the warm fragrant air of spring, and the mounting sap in the trees. Like all the art and literature of the period they tell of the awakening of the heart of man out of the nightmare of the impending Millennium and the Day of Judgment, the convalescence of the world after the agony of the Black Death, and the re-discovery of the beauty of women and all natural things after the asceticism of the early Church. And in the midst of it all, a living symbol of this spiritual re-birth, stands the gentle friar of Assisi, the *jongleur* of God as he called himself, the Troubadour of Our Lady, the Minstrel of Christ, around whose head wheeled flocks of cooing doves, and to whom the very wolves of the forest came to lick his hands and to lie at his feet.

CHAPTER IV

The Flemish Polyphonic Schools

ALTHOUGH, strictly speaking, the tradition of the Troubadours, Trouvères, and Minnesänger came to an end about the year 1300, its influence still continued to make itself felt during the whole of the following century. Indeed, one of the most prominent figures of the immediately succeeding period— perhaps the first really important single name in the history of modern music—namely, Guillaume de Machault, might almost be regarded as a Trouvère. Like them he was both a poet and a musician, and though he wrote music in many different *genres* his most important work, certainly his most interesting and artistically successful, consists in his solo songs with instrumental accompaniment. The chief difference between him and his predecessors is to be found in the fact that, being definitely a trained professional musician and a man of letters whereas they were for the most part little more than aristocratic amateurs, he himself composed the instrumental accompaniments to his songs instead of leaving them to be improvised by minstrels and *jongleurs*. It must be confessed, however, that his greater musical knowledge and erudition were not altogether an advantage, for even his simpler songs lack entirely the freshness, spontaneity and directness which constitute the most prominent and attractive feature of the art of his courtly forerunners. His melodies seem, in comparison, somewhat crabbed, stilted, and artificial, his rhythms needlessly tortured and complex ; and, as a result of his attempt to apply the current procedures of church composition to secular music, and to polyphonize the texture of his accompaniments in accordance with the scholastic methods of discant then in vogue, his harmony is often inappropriately harsh, arid, and illogical, though frequently very interesting from the modern standpoint.

In view of the fact, too, that the poetic art of the Troubadours was introduced into Italy and gave rise first to a school in

Sicily at the court of the Emperor Frederick II, and later to another in the north of Italy, it is only reasonable to suppose that the music of the school of accompanied song which flourished contemporaneously with the latter, particularly in Florence and Bologna, and attained to a remarkably high level of accomplishment at the hands of Francesco Landini, Giovanni de Cascia, and others too numerous to mention, was also in large measure a continuation, adaptation and development of the musical art of the Troubadours. Like the poetry written in the *dolce stil nuovo*, this music, similarly called the *Ars Nova* to distinguish it from the old art of organum and discant with which it has demonstrably nothing in common, is extremely subtle and sophisticated, deriving from the *trobar clus* rather than from the *trobar clar* of Provençal art. The importance of this school is still further enhanced by the fact that, in addition to this form of instrumentally accompanied song, they also cultivated a polyphonic style of composition in which the device of canon played a prominent part. It seems likely, however, that this form was a foreign importation rather than an indigenous growth; it certainly failed to maintain itself and soon died out.

A third and later development of the art of the Troubadours is probably to be found in the *chansons* with instrumental accompaniment of the first school of Flemish composers, of whom Guillaume Dufay and Gilles Binchois were the leaders. The melodic idioms of these songs, with their marked predilection for the major and minor scales rather than for the church modes, are strikingly similar to those encountered in some of the Troubadour songs; and another striking resemblance is to be found in the texts, which are still largely in the tradition of the *Kalendas Mayas*, and exhibit the same preoccupation with the imagery of spring. The fact, moreover, that there is hardly a single example—if, indeed, there is one at all—among the songs of the composers of this school, of the same poem being set to music by two of them, would seem to point to the conclusion that, like the Troubadours, they also were in the habit of writing their own words; and it may be observed in passing that the loose construction of these poems would seem to suggest that the music was written first and the words added afterwards. We are probably justified, therefore, in regarding the melodies of these songs as the transplantation and continuation of the Troubadour tradition—in contra-distinction to the Florentine school, of the *trobar clar* rather than of the *trobar clus*—and the instrumental accompaniments as essentially the notation and elaboration of what had hitherto been generally improvised by the *jongleurs*, minstrels, and other secular musicians of the Middle Ages. However that may be, it is at least certain that these songs belong to an entirely different artistic tradition from the contemporary church music. And the fact that canonic imitations appear frequently in the accompaniments suggests the possibility, or rather the extreme probability, that imitation was a procedure known to and practised by mediæval secular musicians in their accompaniments, and that, in the words of a German musicologist, W. Fischer, " secular music which was the guiding model (führendes Vorbild) of church music from at least the time of Hucbald and Scotus, practised free imitation in *chansons*, long before the Netherlanders took the lead in music ".

Now, whether the Florentine school referred to derived their knowledge of canon and imitation directly or indirectly from the English, as Professor Wooldridge might seem to suggest. (see vol. II of the Polyphonic Period in the " Oxford History of Music ", pp. 49-50), whether the early Netherlanders derived theirs from the Florentines, as Hugo Riemann thinks, or whether it came direct from the minstrel tradition of the Middle Ages as Fischer would have it, the fact remains that it is no mere coincidence that the first satisfactory examples of polyphony known to us should all make use of canon or imitation, for this familiar device constitutes the innermost core and guiding principle of all true contrapuntal writing, wherever it may be found. In Greek the word κανών signifies a straight bar or staff, a rod used in weaving, a level used by masons in building, and finally anything that serves to regulate or determine other things. And in polyphonic music canon performs all these functions. It is the staff on which the early composers leant in their first tentative, uncertain footsteps ; it is the warp or shuttle on which they wove their most intricate and sumptuous tapestries of tone ; it serves to determine the proportions and dimensions of each separate section of the structure, and dictates the movement and conduct of each constituent voice in the *ensemble*. In canon we find the utmost freedom reconcilable with law and order, the utmost discipline consistent with individuality and independence, for in it euphony of the whole is arrived at through consideration of the movement of the individual parts, while the melody itself is compelled to develop and unroll itself with due regard to the harmonic progressions it will ultimately engender. In it are combined the ideal of the liberty, equality, and fraternity of all the parts with that of their strict subservience to the needs and demands of the organism considered as a whole, for each voice is of as great interest and importance as any other voice, yet at the same time an integral and necessary component part of the structure with a definite function to perform. In a word, canon is the musical equivalent of the ideal socialist state, a kind of tonal communism.

So closely and intimately related to life is art, even such an ostensibly abstract and detached manifestation of it as music, that it is probably no mere accident that the triumph of the canonic principle should coincide with the decay of the feudal system, the emancipation of the common people from the tyranny of the barons, the growth of the communes and free cities, and the rise and development of the guild system ; neither is it a coincidence that the stronghold of this popular, communistic, guild music should be in Flanders, where all the foregoing social and political tendencies were more in evidence and more highly developed than anywhere else in Europe at the time which we are about to consider. It was at the battle of Courtrai in 1302 that the French patricians were defeated by the Flemish handicraftsmen, the *leliaerts* by the *clauwaerts*, and it was similarly in that part of Flanders of which Courtrai is the centre that the old aristocratic art of the Provençal Troubadours was finally overthrown by the canonic choral art of the great Flemish composers of the fifteenth century. To the composers of this time and place is almost exclusively due the credit for the application of the device of canon to the music of the church, and for the creation of the ideal polyphonic choral style. And in the same way that the Flemish weaving industry was based on the wool imported from England, so the Flemish musicians wove their elaborate tonal textures by means of the canonic method of composition which, since it is first perfectly exemplified in the Reading Rota, may with justice be called English.

E

The triumphant solution of the problem which had hitherto baffled ecclesiastical composers, namely, how to adapt the devices and resources of secular art to the very different purposes of the church, and to reconcile musical beauty and interest with religious propriety and the integrity of the liturgy was, strangely enough, to a great extent the direct consequence of the edict of John XXII to which allusion has already been made, forbidding the alteration and deformation of the plain-song by means of the methods of discant in vogue during the thirteenth and fourteenth centuries.   For it is surely obvious, as we have already said, that the employment of canonic devices in particular was quite impracticable so long as the Gregorian melodies belonging to the Proprium section of the Mass served as the thematic basis of the polyphonic structure.   In the first place, it would be impossible to present the plain-song canonically without an amount of modification and alteration greater even than that demanded by discant—melodic as well as rhythmic distortion ; secondly, the clear enunciation of the text which was deemed essential to the integrity of the service would have been gravely impaired by its repetition in several parts simultaneously at different distances from each other. But with the enforced abandonment of the method of discanting upon the plain-song of the Proprium, musicians turned their attention to the Ordinarium section of the Mass, and began to compose polyphonic music based upon themes of their own choice in place of the original unvarying Gregorian chants to which it had previously been sung (see p. 19).   Once the composer was free to make use of any thematic material he liked, the employment of the device of canon became a practical possibility, and followed as a natural consequence.   Furthermore the reproach of obscurity, incongruity, and irreverence which would have been well-founded if the text of the Proprium had been subjected to canonic treatment, does not apply to the text of the Ordinarium, or at least in a much lesser degree, since for the most part the texts of the sections which comprise that category of the Mass consist merely of a very few words, and, being in any case invariable, are thoroughly familiar to all. For example, the entire text of the first number is simply Kyrie eleison, Christe eleison, Kyrie eleison.   So far from it seeming irreverent or incongruous here, the infinite repetition of the words produces rather a profoundly devotional effect, suggesting the heartfelt orisons of the whole of mankind, of all races and climes, of all sorts and conditions of men, ascending like incense to the throne of the Almighty.

One might almost say that the relation between the Proprium and the Ordinarium of the Mass is very much the same as the relation between recitative and aria in conventional operas. In the former section the " plot " of the ritual, so to speak, is developed, the words being all-important and the musical interest secondary ; the sections of the latter, on the other hand, constitute the lyric and emotional points of repose, lending themselves to, and indeed almost demanding, a high degree of purely musical elaboration. That this development was permitted, and, it would seem, even encouraged, speaks highly for the instinct and understanding of the clerical authorities who, incidentally, were invariably in the right in their age-long conflict with the musicians. The latter when left to their own devices almost invariably went wrong, and it was only the strict prohibitions enforced by John XXII that turned their attention, and brought them almost in spite of themselves, to the solution of the problem which had baffled them for so long.

Freed from the tyranny imposed by the necessity of employing the Gregorian chant of the Proprium unaltered as the thematic basis of their compositions, Dufay and his successors at first inevitably turned to secular song for the source of their inspiration—inevitably, because a secular melody would naturally lend itself much more readily to musical treatment and development in general than the austere and intractable chant of the church, and to the device of canon in particular which, besides being secular in origin, demands the easily recognizable melodic contours and definitely rhythmical accents that the latter does not ordinarily possess. The masses were then customarily called after the secular songs around which they were constructed ; hence the lovely and suggestive titles which they often bear, such as *Se la face ay pale*, *Rosa bella*, *Puisque j'ay perdu*, *Fortuna desperata*, *L'homme armé*, *Douce mémoire*, and so forth. The Flemish composers have often been unthinkingly reproached on this account with impiety and irreverence, but it is difficult to see why such an innocent procedure should merit any more censure than the practice of painting pictures of the Madonna after living models rather than in accordance with the idealized, lifeless, and hieratic conceptions of the

Byzantine tradition, and calling them *Madonna del Cardellino,
del Gran Duca, della Perla,* and so on.

It might perhaps be asked why it was necessary for the
Netherlanders to use ready-made themes as the subjects of
their musical discourse instead of simply inventing themes of
their own. The answer is not, as is generally imagined, that
they were in any way lacking in creative power. It would
indeed be absurd to suppose that they were incapable of
writing melodies at least as interesting and significant as the
frequently trivial and commonplace little wisps of tune which
they chose. The reason is rather to be found in their whole
conception of musical art. In the Middle Ages a distinction
was always made between the *phonascus* who invented his
subject-matter and the *symphonetes* who worked on existing
material ; generally speaking the secular musicians belonged
to the former—indeed, the very terms Troubadour and
Trouvère imply one who discovers, invents, or creates—and the
church musicians to the latter. To-day of course, we rate the
phonascus very much higher than the *symphonetes,* but in the
fifteenth and sixteenth centuries it was exactly the opposite.
This may perhaps at first sight seem to us to be a very strange
standard of values, but if we divest our minds of modern
prejudices and preconceptions we shall find that it is in reality
very much less irrational and absurd than might be supposed,
and that there is even a good deal to be said in favour of it.
Reduced to its essence, the whole question resolves itself into
the eternal opposition between the artist who creates and
cultivates a manner of his own and possesses an intensely
personal outlook, and the artist who reverences tradition and
inherits his entire technical equipment and spiritual outlook
from his predecessors, or shares them with his contemporaries.
We to-day lay great stress, perhaps too great stress, on
originality, at the expense of all other qualities ; we willingly
tolerate and even condone weak craftsmanship and poverty of
technical resource in a composer who makes amends for these
defects by possessing a highly personal attitude of mind or
great imaginative power and expressiveness. The musicians
of the Middle Ages, on the contrary, would seem to have
regarded originality of outlook as a somewhat reprehensible
eccentricity, a thing to be avoided and suppressed so far as
possible, not encouraged or cultivated ; and that a composer

should have to provide his own thematic material would have seemed to them as absurd as to expect that an architect should make his own bricks and mortar. In their eyes the thematic content of the work was of little consequence ; the treatment of it alone mattered. To write a fine work on a theme of one's own invention was probably regarded as a comparatively easy matter, like a conjuring trick performed with one's own specially constructed apparatus ; but the composer who could take any insignificant theme that lay to his hand and reveal in it an inexhaustible wealth and variety of unsuspected possibilities was analogous to the conjuror who borrows a hat from a member of the audience and produces from out of it an endless number and diversity of objects. This, in their eyes, was the only real magic, the only true test of a composer's talents ; and to a certain extent, of course, this is absolutely true even to-day. Everyone will admit that it often demands a higher degree of invention, resource, and creative imagination, to write variations on an unpromising given theme than to compose an entirely new and original work.

The composers of the first Flemish school, of which Dufay and Binchois were the chief, belong to the period of transition from the individualistic and inventive ideals of the Troubadours and their successors, to the collectivist, democratic, guild conceptions of the later schools. They were in fact alternately *phonasci* and *symphonetes*—the former in their secular music, the latter in their work for the church. From the point of view of intrinsic artistic interest their secular solo songs with instrumental accompaniment are undoubtedly superior to their religious music, although they have always received less attention from musical historians than they deserve. They represent the last fruits—for the time being—of the old minstrel tradition which stretches back into the Dark Ages and perhaps even further, and many of them possess a rhythmic spontaneity and a melodic freshness and charm which are still capable of arresting our attention. Their sacred music, on the contrary, is more important historically than æsthetically, as revealing the first deliberate and conscious effort to adapt canonic devices to the purposes of the church music. The employment of them there, however, is extremely tentative, fitful, and haphazard, compared with the assured handling they receive in the secular music.

The main characteristic of the music of the first Flemish school consists in the deliberate pursuit of euphony for its own sake, resulting in a sweetness almost amounting to effeminacy, a listless beauty, and a wayward charm, which are apt to become monotonous and slightly enervating. It lacks entirely energy and virility; it has no bones or muscle, and moves with the artless and engaging gawkiness of a newly-born colt on its spindly little legs. The effect of the church music in particular is curiously vague, dreamy, and hypnotic; one voice after another emerges inconsequently from a pale and misty twilight of sound, drifts and hovers uncertainly above the others for a brief moment, and then recedes into the gently undulating background whence it came.

With the second Flemish school, of which Johannes Okeghem was the acknowledged leader, the whole art of polyphony undergoes a complete change. In fact it would be difficult to imagine a more striking contrast than that between the music of Dufay and his school and that of Okeghem and his. The balance of interest shifts over definitely from secular to church music; the indolent, feminine grace and charm give way to a strenuous masculinity and intellectual force, austerity takes the place of sensuousness, and the aimless and amorphous arabesques of sound of the earlier school are submitted to a rigid discipline and an unbending logic. With Okeghem, in fact, the art of polyphony goes to school and is set to perform tasks, frequently dull and thankless in themselves, but constituting the discipline and exercise which are a necessary preliminary to any fruitful development.

In contra-distinction to Dufay, Okeghem is a pure cerebralist, almost exclusively preoccupied with intellectual problems, and the most typical example in music of the kind of artist who, in the hackneyed phrase for which there is no adequate substitute, goes out of his way to create difficulties for the pleasure of overcoming them. Expression was for him a secondary consideration, if indeed it existed for him at all. He seems to have had something of the mentality of Arnold Schönberg to-day, the same ruthless disregard of merely sensuous beauty, the same unwearying and relentless pursuit of new technical means for their own sake. He is the schoolmaster, the drill-sergeant of music.

In a mass of Dufay the melodic material of the work is

provided by the tenor; this part, however, is not actually the most important part æsthetically, but only the warp upon which the other voices are woven. Out of the material provided by the tenor an upper part is constructed and the remaining voices are added afterwards, probably one by one, and are little more than what are called to-day " filling-in parts ", which sometimes move very awkwardly in order to arrive at the notes desired for the purposes of harmonic euphony. Long held notes are common, leaps of a seventh take place occasionally, and the parts frequently cross each other in a somewhat helpless and haphazard fashion. Dufay's whole method, in fact, consists in the sacrifice of the texture as a whole to the benefit of a single part, the pampered princess at the top, deriving her substance from the plutocratic, capitalistic tenor who grinds the faces of the poor lower parts—a symbolic representation in music of society as seen through communist spectacles. Only here and there do we find a tentative canonic combination of the lower parts, as if in a rebellious attempt to unite and to subvert the autocracy of the upper parts.

To this musical capitalist system Okeghem, the Karl Marx of music, sought to put an end, and to substitute for it an ideal organization in which each part shares in the thematic wealth of the work, and all voices are equal. Individual interest of any one part at the expense of the other parts is sternly discouraged, and the system of filling-in parts is abolished ; no parasites are tolerated, and no humble hewers of wood and drawers of water for the benefit of others are permitted. This communist revolution, however, was not immediately or completely carried through by Okeghem. Here and there in his work the tenor still continues to make its structural importance felt, and the uppermost voice its melodic predominance, to much the same extent that imitation occurs spasmodically and unsystematically in the work of his predecessors. It was left to his successors, and in particular to the great Josquin des Prés, the Lenin of music, to perfect and consolidate the method which he, more than any other single composer, had been instrumental in forming.

Comparatively little of Okeghem's music has survived, though whether this is to be attributed to a small output or to the accidents of time it is difficult to say. It is enough for us to know that he was regarded by both his contemporaries and successors as the undisputed leader of the school to which he belonged.   Other prominent members of it whose work has come down to us in greater quantity were Jacob Obrecht, Heinrich Isaac and Alexander Agricola.   (Incidentally, it must be remembered that in speaking of schools there must always inevitably be a certain amount of overlapping in dates, so that it is impossible to ascribe some composers definitely to either one school or another.   Isaac, for example, can just as well be regarded as a member of the third as of the second.)   Obrecht is less exclusively an intellectualist than Okeghem, and shows a greater consideration for the harmonic effect of the *ensemble*. In certain works too, he reveals an expressiveness which to a great extent foreshadows Josquin des Prés.   Agricola is more definitely in the Okeghem tradition, and combines great contrapuntal virtuosity with an emotional dryness and an insensitiveness to the claims of sonority ; indeed, he constantly tends to sacrifice harmonic felicity to the greater vitality of his part-writing.   Isaac, the greatest of the three, and also the most prolific, adds to the profound intellectuality of their common master a quality of stern grandeur and solemnity, and a melodic force and vigour which the latter does not ordinarily possess.   Leaps of a sixth, seventh, or octave in the parts are a common feature of his style, and even a leap of a tenth can occasionally be found.   Such cases, however, are not referable, as with Dufay, to harmonic exigencies, but to strictly melodic purposes not always unconnected with an attempt at word-painting.   A further peculiarity which may be noted in his melodic style is a tendency to begin with long notes which gradually dissolve into notes of shorter value as the phrase progresses, like a tree-trunk breaking into branches, or a Gothic pillar into streams of lines where it meets the vaulting.   He chiefly lives to-day, however, by virtue of an exquisite little secular choral work, " Innsbruck, ich muss dich lassen ", the melody of which was eventually, at the time of the Reformation, adapted to sacred words, " O Welt, ich muss dich lassen ".

But the beauty of all these lesser stars pale into insignificance beside the incomparable splendour and magnitude of Josquin des Prés, the leader of the third, and strictly speaking, the last of the great Flemish schools.   In the words of a very fine musician and musical critic named Martin Luther, " other composers do what they can with the notes ; Josquin alone does what he wishes ".   In the works of his predecessors one always feels the tremendous strain and effort ; in the music of Josquin there is a sense of ease and a virtuosity in the accomplishment of even the most difficult and exacting tasks which he sets himself.

In his work we find united all the finest qualities that are to be found separately in the work of his predecessors : the intellectual power of Okeghem, the sonority and expressiveness of Obrecht, the austerity of Agricola, the mystical grandeur of Isaac, together with an added mastery which raises his work to a height of perfection never before and only seldom since attained.   In fact, he occupies much the same eminent position in Flemish music that the Van Eycks occupy in Flemish painting.

It is in his masses on secular themes, such as the famous *L'homme armé*, and the *Faysant regrets*, that his most remarkable feats of virtuosity are to be found ; in those built on fragments of liturgical themes, such as the *Ave Maris Stella*, *Mater patris*, and *De beate virgine*, a simpler and more devotional style is encountered.   Still, it is in the motets on the whole, rather than in the masses, that the more expressive and religious side of Josquin's genius is revealed.   In fact one might almost say that the motet bears much the same relation to the mass that the altar-piece does to the fresco in painting, and there are even distinct formal analogies to be perceived between the two cases.   The motet, particularly in the hands of Josquin, frequently tends to assume the form of the triptych, while the six or more movements of the mass (for the great Flemish composers sometimes included several settings of the Agnus Dei in the same work), all of which were built on the same theme, bear a distinct analogy to the series of detached scenes or episodes in the lives of saints and so forth, which are to be met with in the fresco-painting of the Middle Ages and the Renaissance.   And in the same way that the painters were wont to display their technical prowess in frescos and to reserve their more devotional impulses for their altar-pieces, so the great Flemish composers tend to make the mass the main field of activity for their feats of contrapuntal virtuosity, while in their motets a more restrained and sober method of composition, and a more pronouncedly expressive purpose, are generally to be encountered.   And so with Josquin, not even in the work of his greatest successors, Palestrina, Lassus, or

Victoria, do we find anything more profoundly moving than the *Absalon Fili mi*, the *Planxit autem David*, the *Stabat Mater*, or the elegy on the death of his master Okeghem—and these are only four of many magnificent examples mentioned at random.

Another interesting aspect of Josquin's many-sided genius is to be found in the strain of impish and satirical humour which continually peeps out in the most unexpected places, even in the most solemn moments of the divine service. It is a mistake, however, to reproach him on this account, as is generally done, with irreverence or impiety. Such things are conceived in much the same spirit as the gargoyles of Gothic architecture or the curious pictorial fantasies of Breughel, and remind one of the beautiful and touching legend of the Jongleur de Notre Dame, who turned somersaults and stood on his head before the image of Our Lady, for Her delectation and entertainment; for which act he was most graciously thanked and suitably rewarded by Her. They are, in fact, characteristic of an age of faith, and can only seem repellent to the taste of unbelievers and those sour Puritanical souls who willingly grant to their deities the possession of every conceivable human attribute, including many exceedingly unpleasant ones, save only a capacity for gaiety and a sense of humour.

Finally, Josquin was more intensely preoccupied with problems of pure sonority than any of his immediate predecessors. His was no mere paper music, and he would frequently alter his work after having it tried over by the choir. Despite his very large output he was intensely scrupulous and conscientious, and never produced a work until he had kept it by him, sometimes for many years, during which it was subjected to constant and drastic revision.

The third school can count many more eminent figures than either of its forerunners, each of whom possesses a distinct individuality of his own and all of whom attain to such a high and uniform level of excellence that it is difficult to discriminate between those who are deserving of special mention and those who are not, or to assign to them any definite order of precedence. After Josquin the most important name is perhaps that of Pierre de la Rue, who combines his master's contrapuntal virtuosity with at least an equal depth and spirituality. He is, however, a somewhat austere and inaccessible composer, lacking the geniality and robustness, the breadth and universality of outlook of the great Josquin. The work of Antoine Brumel, on the other hand, reveals a marked predilection for harmonic brilliance and at times an almost modern turn of melody and rhythmic accentuation. In strong contrast to him stands Aloyse Compère, disdaining transcendant technical feats to a greater extent than any of his colleagues, and aiming rather at a softness and sweetness of texture strongly impregnated with a vein of wistful melancholy. Ambros indeed calls him a romanticist, but in a few examples of his secular music which have survived, however, he shows himself to possess a comic verve and exuberance excelling even that of Josquin. The music of Jean Mouton, again, has great freshness, vigour and spontaneity, and, like that of Brumel, a pronouncedly secular accent not entirely suited to the church. This is perhaps to be accounted for by his Gallic rather than Flemish origin, for already by this time one is able to discern the rise of a definitely French school of composition which, though it derived technically from the Netherlanders, developed nevertheless certain strongly marked characteristics which distinguish it sharply from the Flemish schools we have so far been considering. While the members of the latter, with few exceptions, confined themselves almost exclusively to the composition of church music, the achievement of the French school in this sphere was relatively small in quantity, and very much less interesting than their achievement in the field of secular composition. Considerable technical differences also distinguish the two schools. The melodic invention of the more representative French masters is shorter-winded than that of the Flemings, and more continually punctuated by full closes. One notes also a fondness for syllabic declamation, rhythmic precision, and dapper, clean-cut, well-knit musical sentences, together with a deliberate avoidance of contrapuntal ingenuities and a predominantly harmonic rather than polyphonic bias. Even when the music is contrapuntal in texture it generally gives one the impression of having been conceived harmonically and only afterwards broken up into independent parts. Together with this tendency, as we should naturally expect, may be perceived a distinct preference for the modern major and minor scales as opposed to the modal preferences of the Netherlanders.

The leader of the school was Clément Jannequin. Whether he was a Frenchman or a Fleming by birth is still disputed, but there can be no question about his music, which exhibits all the qualities which are most characteristic of French art throughout the ages—lightness, swiftness, gaiety, grace, verve, wit, *finesse* and so forth ; it is, in fact, the first authentic expression in music of the *esprit gaulois*. His best and most original works, of which the most celebrated examples are the *Chants des oiseaux, La Guerre, La Chasse, Caquets des femmes*—titles which sufficiently indicate their nature and the programmatic predilections of their composer—apart from their intrinsic musical qualities, conjure up for us a vivid and arresting picture of old France, the France of Montaigne and Rabelais, of Ronsard and Marot ; of old Paris with her narrow, winding, crowded ways, filled with the chatter and gossip of women and the cries of street-merchants ; of the bird-haunted woodlands of the Ile de France, echoing to the clamour of the deer-chase in full cry ; of sieges and capitulations, victories and defeats, and deeds done on the field of battle. In smaller and less ambitious canvases such as the exquisite and justly famous *chanson* " Ce mois de Mai ", we find, both in the words and in the music, the old Troubadour tradition of the *reverdie* and the *Kalendas Mayas* still persisting intact, with a melody written in our major scale, and harmonized throughout in plain blocks of simple chords, as its predecessors no doubt also were some three centuries or more earlier.

Guillaume de Costeley is perhaps the most important composer of the French school after Jannequin. He is essentially a miniaturist, however, and never attempts the large manner and vivid style of the latter. Gascogne and Claude de Sermisy are other masters, practising on the whole a somewhat more contrapuntal and more sophisticated form of art. Their work, slightly lacking in vitality perhaps, is delicately wrought and finished, and full of an undeniable charm and fragrance.

Finally, for the sake of completeness it may be mentioned that there was also a French school of Protestant or Huguenot composers, chief among whom were Claude Goudimel— formerly but erroneously supposed to have been the master of Palestrina—and Claude Le Jeune, who also achieved great distinction in the field of secular music. Like the above-mentioned composers they wrote in a more homophonic and harmonic style than their Catholic and Flemish contemporaries, without, however, achieving anything like the same high standard of musical excellence.[1]

Another group of composers remains to be mentioned which cannot properly be said to belong either to the Flemish school of Josquin, or to the French school of Jannequin, but to a great extent combines the qualities of both. In the work of its members the constant tendency of the Flemish style to degenerate into arid scholasticism and pedantry is held in check by the clarity and simplicity of the French style, and in return the intellectual strength and consummate technical mastery of the former acts as a corrective to the frequent triviality and insipidity of the latter. The defects of the one, in fact, are modified by the virtues of the other. So definitely does this school differ from both, however, although it is derived from both, that it almost deserves a distinguishing name to itself, and might be called the Franco-Flemish, or Gallo-Belgian school. Nicholas Gombert, perhaps the most versatile and richly gifted artist of the post-Josquin age, may be called its leader. He handles with equal ease the brilliant and elaborate contrapuntal style of the great Flemish masters and the simple, harmonic manner of the French. He is equally at home in secular and in sacred music, at one moment emulating the naturalism of Jannequin in his *Chant des Oiseux*, and at another rivalling even Josquin himself in the nobility and deep feeling of such motets as the *Salve Regina* or the *Miserere nostri*. A parallel also to the alleged irreligiousness of his great predecessor is to be found in the *chanson* " Alleluia me fault chanter ", in which the Gradual Alleluia of the Easter Mass is grotesquely parodied and distorted.

Other members of this brilliant group are Jacques Clément, generally called, quite unnecessarily, Clemens non Papa, in order to distinguish him from the reigning Pope Clement VII, and Thomas Crecquillon. It is enough to say that both display the same facility of invention, the same nonchalant ease of execution, the same astonishing fecundity, the same unvarying grace, purity, and clarity of style. Clément excels as a church composer, whereas Crecquillon, although he wrote a great deal

---

[1] Goudimel's early work, written previous to his conversion, is, on the other hand, in the pure Flemish tradition.

of sacred music, is perhaps better known on account of his secular *chansons*, many of which are to be found in the same collections as those of Jannequin and his school, published by Attaignant in Paris.

It is depressing to reflect that among all these great masters —and we have only considered a few of the more eminent— there is hardly one that is anything more than a mere name even to professedly cultivated musicians, and not even that to the ordinary listener or concert-goer.   Indeed, as we have already observed in the Introduction, about nine-tenths of the world's greatest music is absolutely unknown to all but a very few, and these few even are generally scholars and antiquarians without a spark of aesthetic sensibility or discernment.   In the same way that in the eighteenth century all painting anterior to Raphael was considered unworthy of notice, a mere museum curiosity, incapable of arousing any other emotions than wonder and contempt, so even to-day the idea still persists that music begins with Palestrina, and that everything and everybody before him only " led up " to him, as the saying is, and is contained in him.   Nothing could be further from the truth.   The music of such masters as Josquin, Isaac, Jannequin or Gombert is every bit as aesthetically satisfying as the painting of Giotto, Duccio, Masaccio, or any other of the great masters of painting formerly despised and now admired, and there is just as much for composers to learn from our so-called primitives in music as painters have learnt from their primitives.

But even if it were true that the music of these early composers is not intrinsically significant, one would at least have expected that their immense historical interest would have been better recognized.   Even if they are, compared to Palestrina, like the early race of gods in Greek myth who were superseded by the new order of Zeus, Apollo, and the rest, they might well say, in the superb words of Oceanus in Keats's *Hyperion :*

> On our heels a fresh perfection treads
> A power more strong in beauty, born of us
> And fated to excel us, as we pass
> In beauty that old darkness ; nor are we
> Thereby more conquered than by us the rule
> Of shapeless Chaos. Say, doth the dull soil
> Quarrel with the proud forest it hath fed,
> And feedeth still, more comely than itself ?

Can it deny the chiefdom of green groves ?
Or shall the tree be envious of the dove
Because it cooeth, and hath snowy wings
To wander wherewithal and find its joys ?
We are such forest trees, and our fair boughs
Have bred forth, not pale solitary doves,
But eagles golden-feathered, who do tower
Above us in their beauty, and must reign
In right thereof ; for 'tis the eternal law
That first in beauty should be first in might.
Yea, by that law, another race may drive
Our conquerors to mourn as we do now.

But there is even more in it than that.   Even if we were to
admit that Apollo is fairer than Hyperion and the music of
Palestrina more perfect than that of Josquin, it would still be a
mistake to imagine that it is all pure gain.   On the contrary,
there is a stern grandeur, a rugged strength and sublimity in
the music of these old Flemish masters which are certainly not
transmitted to their Italian successors, but disappear from
music entirely until the time of Bach.   They are no more
contained and summed up in Palestrina than Giotto and
Duccio are in Raphael.

It has for a long time been the fashion among people who
know nothing whatever about this music to condemn it
wholesale on account of its alleged intellectuality.   Now it is
certainly true that the appeal of a great part of it is predominantly intellectual, and that some of it even has not much
more aesthetic significance than ingenious crossword puzzles
have, but this represents only a comparatively small part of
their output, the importance of which has always been greatly
exaggerated.   There is no reason to suppose that the composers
themselves attached any more value to such things than we
do, or that they regarded them as anything more than a
useful and diverting form of mental exercise—a kind of mental
gymnastics designed solely for the purpose of keeping
their technique supple and adaptable.   Furthermore it should
always be remembered that nothing is more deceptive than the
appearance on paper of *a cappella* music, and that nothing
could be more unlike its sound in performance than a rendering
of it on the piano.   Indeed, it is probably no exaggeration to
say that it is easier for the average intelligent musician of
to-day to form a fairly accurate idea of the sound of a modern

orchestral work from a study of the score, than to imagine the sound of elaborately contrapuntal vocal combinations such as those of the Netherlanders. The values of instrumental *timbres*, though capable of infinitely subtle gradations and complex combinations, seem nevertheless to be comparatively constant and readily calculable; those of unaccompanied voices, though very much simpler in theory, seem in practice to vary in different contexts, in different works, and with different composers. Speaking from personal experience, I may say that I have often been unable to recognize at once in performance an old mass or motet that I had not only studied carefully but had even scored from the parts. Unaccompanied voices constitute what is perhaps the most exquisitely sensuous medium in all music, in all art one might even say, and what may often seem to be on paper the dryest and most pedantic exhibition of contrapuntal ingenuity, becomes in performance a thing of purely sensuous beauty, and the most insignificant and commonplace progressions take on a radiant glow that we could never have foretold or expected. There is little doubt that if we had more opportunities of familiarizing ourselves with the medium and of hearing performances of this music which we stigmatize as intellectual after playing it on the piano or reading it in score, we might begin to reconsider our opinions of it—or, more accurately, the opinions handed down unquestioningly from generation to generation of writers on music who have in many cases never even played it on the piano or read it in score, much less taken the trouble to have it performed. Intellectual this music certainly is, but the possession of intellect does not necessarily exclude the possession of other qualities. The music of Bach, it is as well to remember, was scornfully dismissed as mere " mathematics " by critics of former times in precisely the same way as we to-day dismiss that of the great Flemish composers.

But even if we were to admit for the sake of argument that the appeal of this music is entirely and exclusively to the intellect and that it possesses no sensuous or expressive beauty whatsoever—which is certainly not true—why is this necessarily a fault ? Why this *parti pris* against intellect as such ? It seems to be the one point on which all schools unite—classic and romantic, ancient and modern—a shrill, petulant, querulous denunciation of intellect. The idea at the back of it would seem to be that art and intellect are irreconcilable, antagonistic even, that music in particular exclusively appeals to or expresses the emotions—one of the most pernicious and pestilential heresies that have ever devastated aesthetics.   Music is an art which is capable of expressing any aspect of life and of appealing to any and every faculty without exception, and it is this fanatical proscription of intellect that is largely if not entirely responsible for the predicament that music is in at the present time.   There are signs, however, that a change of attitude in this matter is immanent ; it is certainly long overdue.   But when it comes, we may be sure that these grand old Titans, this Saturnian dynasty of composers, will eventually receive the appreciation to which they are entitled, and will be installed in their rightful places of honour in the Pantheon of musical history, along with the great ones of all time.

F

CHAPTER V

The art of vocal polyphony, as we have already had occasion to remark, was of definitely northern provenance and character. Indeed, one might say that just as Gregorian chant corresponds with Byzantine architecture, so does the art of the Flemish composers and their successors constitute the musical equivalent of Gothic architecture. The stylistic analogies are striking and have often been pointed out before. The leading characteristic of Gothic style, in the words of an eminent authority (Moore, " History of Mediæval Architecture "), consists in " a system of balanced thrusts " and a " logical adjustment of parts whose opposing forces neutralise each other and produce a perfect equilibrium ", and the same words might be used, without any alteration, to define the essential structural principle underlying the art of the great Flemish composers of the fifteenth and early sixteenth centuries. Another instructive and perhaps even closer analogy is to be found in the art or craft of tapestry, in which, as in contrapuntal music, separate threads of material are woven on a frame in such a way as to produce a complex tissue of lines and colours. Indeed, one could not hope to find a better definition of polyphonic music than that it is a tonal tapestry, or a weaving together of several voices into a definite formal design.

The analogy is not only stylistic, but historical and even geographical as well. It is a curious and interesting fact which cannot be a mere coincidence that both contrapuntal music and the art of tapestry weaving should have flourished side by side, both in time and in place. Both reached their highest pitch of development at about the same period, and both simultaneously declined : and it is in Flanders, and more especially in north-western Flanders, that the central point of both artistic activities is to be found.

Such parallels are not only interesting in themselves but are also highly instructive, as showing the close cultural relation which exists between different modes of artistic thought and expression at the same period of time or in the same locality, and the way in which they can be made to throw light on each other. For just as there is no trace or vestige of the existence in Italy of any indigenous schools of Gothic architecture or tapestry until a long time after they had attained to a high level of perfection in northern Europe, so we do not find any Italian adaptation of the Flemish art of vocal polyphony until about the beginning of the sixteenth century. They were all three foreign importations, exotic growths, and wholly alien to the spirit of Latin culture and civilization. The Florentine school of canonic composition, which flourished for a time in the fourteenth century, died out completely for this reason, and the new transfusion of Italian music by foreign elements would also undoubtedly have come to nothing if it had not been found possible to adapt, modify, and naturalize them in such a way as to change the character of the original Flemish style entirely. Speaking of the Italian as opposed to the Flemish school of tapestry, Denuelle says in his " Rapport au nom de la commission de la manufacture des Gobelins ", that " le style s'élargit et s'épure, les compositions deviennent plus libres, plus gaies, plus abondantes, elles perdent leur forme rigide— les nuances tendent à se substituer aux couleurs si nourries, si franches, si éclatantes de la période gothique " ; and again, the very same words admirably serve to describe the transformation that the art of counterpoint underwent in the hands of the Italian composers of the sixteenth century. And the difference between the Flemish polyphony and that of the Roman school in particular might also be instructively compared to the difference between a northern Gothic cathedral with its dim, religious light filtering through stained-glass windows, its atmosphere of brooding mystery and solemn grandeur, and an Italian Gothic cathedral such as that of Orvieto, with its exquisite symmetry and proportion, its richly sculptured polychromatic marbles and brilliant painted frescoes, its soft voluptuous light and warm harmonious colouring.

But there is one important difference to be observed between the two cases. Whereas northern, indigenous Gothic is on the whole more devotional in character than its southern derivate the contrary is true in music. The constant preoccupation of the Flemings with intellectual conceptions and problems of purely musical texture and design, coupled with their frequent employment of secular thematic material as a basis for their masses, inevitably imparted a pronouncedly worldly aspect to the greater part of their music, and especially that of it directly associated with the celebration of the mass. With Josquin and his contemporaries the ritual of the mass was seldom anything more than a pretext for an elaborate vocal concert in which the composer proceeded to develop a magnificent musical discourse, during which the performance of the rite must inevitably have been either completely suspended or at least momentarily disorganised. The main feature of the contrapuntal music of the Roman School, on the contrary, consists in its absolute fitness to the purposes of the ritual. No purely musical development was permitted by its masters to interfere or conflict with the reverent unfolding of the symbolic drama enacted at the altar, and no musical reference to the profane world, nor suggestion of the joys and sorrows of every-day existence, were allowed to intrude upon the sanctity of the Divine Presence. In the music of the Roman school, then, we find for the first time a completely satisfactory solution of the problem which had beset musicians for some six or seven centuries, namely, how to create a polyphonic style of church composition which was at once musically satisfying and yet in no way incompatible with the demands of the ritual.

The first great master of the Roman school of whom we have any knowledge is Costanzo Festa. So little of his work survives, however, and so little even of what survives is accessible, that it is not possible to say anything very definite about him except that in what we know of his music the distinctively Roman tendency to which we have alluded can already be perceived in embryo, lying within the Flemish matrix from which it definitely emerges in the work of his successor Giovanni Animuccia, the immediate predecessor of Palestrina in the post of *maestro di cappella* of the Sistine Chapel. In the preface to a volume of masses (1567) Animuccia writes that it has always been his intention " to sing prayers and the praises of God in such a way that the understanding of the words should be least impaired, but also in such a way that art should not be lacking or the pleasure of the ear neglected ". In order to achieve this compromise some loss of purely artistic interest was unavoidable.   For in the same way that strict attention and deference to dramatic exigencies in opera inevitably entails some voluntary sacrifice of musical resources on the part of the composer, so the masters of the Roman school, in their desire to comply with the demands of the church, were compelled to throw overboard a considerable part of the rich technical equipment that they had inherited from the Flemings. The gain of religion, like the gain of drama, invariably and inevitably spells the loss of music to some extent at least, and it cannot be denied that the intrinsic musical interest of the work of the Roman school is frequently slight and impoverished in comparison with that of the work of Josquin and his compeers.

A definite tendency, then, in the direction of the clarification and refinement of the opulent, exuberant technique of the Flemish composers can be clearly discerned in the work of Palestrina's predecessors ; all that he did in this respect was to complete their task and carry their art to a higher pitch of perfection.   The popular legend which attributes to him the virtual creation of the characteristically Roman style, at the instance of the Council of Trent, is a pure myth.

The super-eminent position that Palestrina occupies by universal consent among all composers of the sixteenth century is due not so much to his innovations—actually, like so many great composers, he invented very little, if anything at all, either technically or stylistically—as simply to his possession of a higher degree of genius than any of his colleagues, but of essentially the same order.   If one is able to distinguish between his work and that of, say, the Nanini or Anerio brothers, it is not so much by virtue of any essential difference in mentality or any marked originality of style—although of course every creative artist has a definite individuality of his own to some extent—but simply on account of its superlative merit and its well-nigh flawless perfection.   This absolute impersonality may or may not be a characteristic of the very greatest art : it is certainly, however, a necessary attribute of the greatest religious art.   In the same way that the priest officiating at the altar ceases temporarily to be an individual and becomes a mere passive vessel or instrument of Godhead, so the fitness of music to the celebration of the divine rite depends largely on the extent to which the composer has been able to submerge his individuality and become an impersonal agent. And it is because Palestrina is more successful in fulfilling this condition and in achieving this state of compositorial humility and self-abnegation that he must be accounted the greatest of all religious musicians, with the possible exception of the anonymous creators of Gregorian chant.

Giuseppe Baini, the biographer of Palestrina, professed to have been able to distinguish no fewer than ten separate styles or periods in the work of the master, but the worthlessness and artificiality of this characteristic example of the pedantic and hairsplitting tradition of Italian art-criticism current in the eighteenth and nineteenth centuries, is shown by the fact that in the first of these ten styles he clearly detects traces of the influence of Goudimel, formerly supposed, and only recently proved not to have been the master of Palestrina. It is exceedingly doubtful, to say the least, whether he would have made this attribution had he known that Goudimel, so far from being the master of Palestrina, had never been in Rome in his life, so far as can be ascertained.

It is certainly true, however, that at least three distinct styles can be discerned in his work, as in that of so many other great artists. In his first book of masses, and in several other compositions published later, but probably written about the same time, he appears rather in the light of a disciple and follower of the Netherland school than as a practitioner of the method and manner introduced by Festa and Animuccia. They are highly complex and artificial, and as full of ingenious contrapuntal contrivances as the most elaborate productions of the Flemish school. His second period is characterized by a constantly increasing tendency in the direction of melodic suavity and harmonic clarity, culminating in the *Missa Papæ Marcelli*—the most famous as it is likewise one of the best of all his masses—in which the utmost sensuous beauty is united to a great wealth and subtlety of technical resource, without, however, detracting from the profoundly devotional character of the music. Finally, in the work of his third period, the formal structure becomes more concentrated and precise, the polyphonic texture still more refined and simplified, and the harmonic and melodic idioms undergo a further process of clarification, resulting in the formation of a style from which every vestige of the old Flemish style has been finally eliminated.

The difference between the old and the new music might be compared to that between a trackless mediæval forest with its gnarled and moss-grown tree-trunks and its thick tangled network of spreading branches through which no light can penetrate, and a cultivated park with neatly trimmed hedgerows, well-kept paths, smooth lawns and terraces, and swans floating serenely and majestically on ornamental lakes. In the later works of Palestrina one finds a deliberate and systematic avoidance of the modal asperities of the older music, and a definite inclination in the direction of modern tonality, resulting in a more vertical, harmonic style of writing, in which parts are continually disposed so as to produce full three note chords at the expense of interesting individual melodic progressions ; and this tendency is further accentuated by a preference for syllabic declamation and conjunct motion of the parts within a restricted compass, which together inhibit the superabundant melodic flow, the energetic bounding leaps, majestic soaring sequences, and rich tonal arabesques that are such prominent features of the style of the great Flemish masters. Precisely the same change, it may be noted, takes place about the same time in French literature, when the rich, exuberant, vivid, and picturesque idiom of Rabelais and Montaigne gives place to the elegant, refined, and somewhat colourless language of Malherbe and Descartes.

It may safely be said without fear of contradiction, for it is one of the few points on which all critics are agreed, that in the works of his last period Palestrina comes as near to absolute perfection as is permitted to mere mortals—certainly nearer than any other composer who has yet lived. Nevertheless all our admiration for his marvellous art should not blind us, as it is naturally apt to do, to the fact that this perfection is the outcome of a narrowing and not a broadening of artistic resource. The man who aspires to artistic perfection, like the man who aspires to moral perfection, must take vows of poverty and divest himself of all his material possessions ; and Palestrina, in throwing away the rich inheritance of the Netherlands and stripping himself of all his artistic resources as it were, is a kind of musical St. Francis, and as such is entitled to our reverence and admiration. But it does not follow that we must all go and do likewise ; indeed, for the majority the ascetic ideal is generally a fatal one to pursue, in art as in life. For one saint we get a horde of lazy, parasitic, worthless friars, and for one Palestrina we get a race of musical weaklings. In short, while one can only unreservedly admire the great personal achievement of Palestrina, it cannot be denied that the effect of his example on other composers led to the emasculation, impoverishment, and rapid decadence of contrapuntal art. Despite its undeniable beauty and sublimity the so-called Palestrina style is a delicate hothouse plant, carefully reared and nurtured in the close, incense-laden atmosphere of the church, and liable to wilt and wither away when taken out of its surroundings and brought into contact with life and reality. Its beauty is essentially cloistral ; its absolute fitness to the purposes of the ritual is to a great extent attained at the expense of musical interest and vitality. For example, to hear the celebrated *Miserere* of Allegri, one of the most distinguished members of the Roman school after Palestrina, in its proper place in the Easter service, is a profoundly moving experience on account of its liturgical felicity ; from a purely musical point of view, however, it is quite uninteresting— there is practically nothing at all there, in fact. And even in the work of the master himself we frequently encounter an extreme tenuity of musical substance which, however apt it may be to the ritualistic purposes, is hardly sufficient to hold our aesthetic, as distinct from our religious, attention.

It will be seen, therefore, that the Palestrina style, so far from being the culminating point of perfection and the unsurpassable model of the contrapuntal style, as it has generally been represented to be by musical historians, is, from a purely abstract point of view, a decadence and an emasculation of it. It may be the most perfect form of devotional art the world has ever known, but it is certainly not the ideal polyphonic style. It contained the seeds of death, and deprived polyphony of the strength and energy necessary to resist the continual assaults of homophony ; it is the wooden horse in whose belly lay concealed the Greek monodists who laid siege to the Trojan citadel of counterpoint at the end of the sixteenth century.

Until comparatively recent times it was customary to regard the Spanish school of church composers in the sixteenth century as a part or at least an offshoot of the Roman school, and any difference that might be perceived between them was generally vaguely ascribed to the greater influence of the Flemish masters upon the former. It is now generally recognized, however, that it represents a separate, autonomous tradition which can be traced back as far as the foundation of the Roman school, that although they intermingle with each other to a great extent, each nevertheless preserves a certain individuality and independence, and that the influence of one upon the other was reciprocal. And in spite of the close political and artistic relations between Spain and the Netherlands in the course of the sixteenth century, and the fact that many of the Flemish masters are known to have visited Spain (Agricola, for example, would seem to have passed the greater part of his active career there, first in the service of Philip, King of Castile and Aragon, and later in that of the Emperor Charles V), there is evidence which would seem to point to the existence of a native school possessing certain clearly defined characteristics which differentiated it sharply from the Flemish school even.

A writer of the sixteenth century, describing the various styles of singing practised by different races, says that " Les Anglais jubilent, les Francais chantent, les Italiens ou bien bêlent comme des chevres ou bien aboient comme des chiens, les Allemands hurlent comme des loups, et les Espagnols pleurent parce qu'ils sont amis du bémol ". We also learn that Spanish singers were greatly sought after for the choir of the Sistine Chapel at Rome, on account of the great expressiveness of their voices and manner of singing. This expressiveness tinged with melancholy, combined with an intensely mystical and devotional turn of mind, are also the most distinctive traits in the music of the Spanish composers. Three figures stand out prominently among them, namely Cristobal Morales, Francisco Guerrero, and, greatest of all, Tomás Luis de Victoria. The art of Morales is perhaps less directly moving than that of most of his compatriots, and has in it something of the ceremonious stiffness and solemn, courtly demeanour of a Spanish grandee ; nevertheless this somewhat forbidding aspect conceals a vein of sombre and passionate intensity which is often exceedingly compelling and impressive. Particularly noteworthy in this respect is an Easter motet in which three parts are sung to the words *Emendemus in melius quæ ignoranter peccavimus*, while the tenor inexorably intones the plain song melody to the words *Memento, homo, quia pulvis es, et in pulverem reverteris.* This is a favourite device of Morales, reminding one of the sombre pictures of Zurburan and other Spanish painters, of monks praying devoutly while surrounded by skulls and other grisly relics and reminders of human mortality. The music of Guerrero, on the other hand, is a feminine counterpart to that of Morales, and more immediately attractive, more sensuous and lyrical, with the same soft veiled melancholy and wistful sweetness that one finds in the pictures of Murillo, but saved from the reproach of effeminacy by the limpid purity and gravity of his style.

These two widely different aspects of the national genius, the first and second subjects of the Spanish symphony, are combined and worked out in the person of Victoria, the greatest and last of the school, and one of the crowning glories of the polyphonic style. He is often spoken of as if he was only an imitator or humble camp-follower of Palestrina, and has even been impolitely called " the ape of Palestrina " by one of the latter's admirers. Nothing could be more unjust or more lacking in critical perspicuity. The qualities which both admittedly have in common are not the unique possession or creation of the Roman master but his inheritance, shared to a greater or lesser extent by every composer of the age ; anything that Victoria owed directly and exclusively to Palestrina is more than counterbalanced by what the latter in his turn owed to Morales, whose art played a very important part in the formation of the Roman style and method. Indeed, the interaction of the Roman and Spanish schools on each other is very similar to that of the French and Flemish schools which we have already noted in the preceding chapter ; the easy, graceful, fluent manner of the former corrects the somewhat stiff and awkward movement of the latter, and acquires in return an emotional depth and expressiveness which the work of the earlier Roman masters, such as Festa and Animuccia, assuredly did not possess. On the whole, though, it would seem that the Roman school actually owed very much more to the Spanish school than the Spanish to the Roman, and it would be very surprising if it were not so when we consider that during the greater part of the sixteenth century Italy lay under the heel of Spain, not only politically and militarily, but culturally also ; the manners, customs, dress, and the particular variety of religious and artistic sentiment which prevailed during the whole of the period called the Counter-Reformation are predominantly Spanish in character and origin. As Miguel de Unamuno says, "Was there not something akin to cultural hegemony in the Counter-Reformation, of which Spain was the champion, and which actually began with the sack of Rome by the Spaniards, a providential chastisement of the city of the pagan Popes and the pagan Renaissance ? " It is also a fact moreover that Rome, throughout her entire history, pagan and Christian, has never succeeded in creating a form of art proper and peculiar to herself. All she has ever done has been to arrange, transform, and adapt to her own purposes the materials which she gathered from extraneous sources.

The resemblances between Palestrina and Victoria, however, such as they are, are merely stylistic and idiomatic ; in spirit they are worlds apart. In order to define the difference between them it is only necessary to say that the one was a typical Italian, the other a typical Spaniard. It is the difference between the soft, undulating, sensuous line of the Alban hills near which the Roman master was born, and the mystic, arid, treeless plains of Castile in the midst of which stands Avila, the birthplace of Victoria and St. Theresa ; it is the difference between Raphael and El Greco, between St. Francis and St. John of the Cross. While Palestrina did not disdain to turn his hand to secular music, and actually wrote four books of madrigals, Victoria's output does not include a single work that is not sacred. His attitude towards his art is expressed in the preface to his book of Hymns (1581). "Many evil and depraved men abuse music as an excitant in order to plunge into earthly delights, instead of raising themselves by means of it to the contemplation of God and of divine things. . . . The art of song should be entirely devoted to the aim and end for which it was originally intended, namely, to the praise and glory of God ". Palestrina was a layman who was able to reconcile the practice of his art with a partnership in a prosperous fur business, a musician who wrote for the church but did not despise natural beauty ; in his work, to quote the words of Animuccia, the pleasure of the ear is never neglected. Victoria, on the other hand, was a priest who happened to write music, and a man for whom the external world did not exist. With St. Bernard he would have said :

Quisquis amat Christum, mundum non diligit istum
Sed quasi fetores spernit illius amores,
Aestimat obscoenum quod mundus credit amoenum
Et sibi vilescit quod in orbe nitescit.

In no other music, in hardly any other art whatsoever, do we find such intense religious exaltation, such unearthly ecstasy, such white-hot incandescence of spirituality, such burning aspiration towards the infinite. In fact his art is sometimes almost too intensely religious to be altogether devotional. He resembles that saint who, when celebrating mass, attained to such a pitch of ecstasy and illumination that he was often suddenly levitated to a considerable height above the ground, to the wonder and admiration of the onlookers, but somewhat to the detriment of the divine rite. And Victoria's frenzied, exultant rhythms and soaring melodic lines frequently generate an emotional intensity which is apt to be slightly disturbing, and is certainly less conducive to the cultivation of a devotional mood than the calm, tranquil, self-possessed movement and suave concord of his Roman rival. For this reason his peculiar genius is perhaps best suited to specially solemn occasions, such as the Tenebrae in Easter Week, and his best work on the whole is to be found in his motets; Palestrina is the more harmoniously balanced artist of the two, and his music is consequently better fitted than that of Victoria to the ordinary church routine, and particularly to the ceremony of the mass.

Another great figure of the age, Orlande de Lassus, more commonly but less correctly known by the Italianized form of his name, Orlando di Lasso, has also suffered like Victoria from the narrow, Procrustean standard of values which would set up the Roman style as the only true polyphonic style, and Palestrina as the measure to which all sixteenth century composers must conform or else be rejected. It is true that in sheer perfection of style Lassus is not to be compared to Palestrina; on the other hand he possesses qualities which his great rival entirely lacks—a breadth and vitality inherited from his Flemish predecessors, and a universality and versatility which he shares with no one else. While Palestrina achieves greatness through exclusion and refinement, Lassus achieves it through inclusion and enrichment of resources. Although strictly speaking he is a Flemish composer by birth and training, and the legitimate successor of Josquin and Gombert, he is very much more besides. Like his great contemporary in politics, the Emperor Charles V, his sway extended over many provinces besides the Netherlands. He was a consummate master of every means of expression, every idiom and every form of composition current at the time : the canonic, imitational style of his countrymen which he generally employs in his masses, the freer and more expressive style of the motet, the harmonic, homophonic style of the French *chanson*, the elaborately pictorial style of the Italian madrigalists whom we shall consider in the next chapter. He is equally at home in both secular and sacred music, and as much at his ease in writing for twelve voices as for two. In this enormous diversity of styles he gives expression to every variety of human experience. In the *Penitential Psalms* he attains to the sublimest heights of religious feeling, and in the *chansons* to the most perfect utterance of worldly sentiments, not even excluding a quite Rabelaisian obscenity, as exemplified in " En un chasteau "—the musical equivalent of an indecent limerick. And at the same time that he sums up in himself all past and contemporary styles and forms, he foreshadows also to a great extent those of the future. He closes an epoch and inaugurates another ; he is at once a conclusion and a commencement, a lake into one end of which a river empties itself while from the other a new stream takes its departure—one the stream of the Middle Ages, the other the stream of modern music. While Palestrina may be considered as the last flowering in music of the mediæval spirit, stylistically modified no doubt by the artistic tendencies of his age but nevertheless fundamentally unaltered, and Victoria the musical representative of the Catholic Revival or the Counter-Reformation, so Lassus is to a great extent the musical embodiment of the spirit of the Renaissance. Like Euphorion, the offspring of the union of Faust and Helen, the ancient and the modern worlds, Lassus is a dual personality in whom two opposite tendencies meet in perpetual conflict. As a man he seems to have oscillated continually between outbursts of extravagant gaiety and moods of extreme melancholy and depression. Two extracts from his correspondence show this antithesis clearly. The first is a fanciful description of Heaven as he imagined it or would have it to be : " Estans la trouverons assez de quoi passer le temps ;

en tous temps estans toujours jaloux, sain, gagliard, point pagliard, jeune, beau, non pas veau, bien en ordre, sans faire désordre, content sans argent, chantant, dansant, oiant musique bien magnifique, en louant Dieu en chascun lieu, o quel plaisir, sans desplaisir, o allégresse plein de liesse, o lieu heureux, bien plantureux, tout plein d'odeur, garni de fleur, o grand douceur, le grand faveur, que le Sauveur donne à tout cueur, qui pour lui meur ".

There is much that is self-revelatory and descriptive of his own art in this quaint and charming medley of epithets. What better adjectives, indeed, could be found to define the more robust and happy side of his genius than " sain, gagliard, plein de liesse, bien plantureux " ?   But the next moment we find him writing as follows : " Quant à l'état ou je me trouve, jamais de ma vie je ne me suis senti plus mélancolique, je suis toujours seul, à moins que je consente a m'énivrer jour et nuit ".   This is the other side to the picture, and this striking contrast is reproduced in his art.   As in the fresco in the Campo Santo at Pisa entitled *The Triumph of Death*, attributed to Orcagna, we are shown a gay cavalcade of fair women and gentle knights riding through the forest, surrounded by all the pomp and pageantry of earthly pleasures, and coming suddenly upon a swollen and bloated corpse lying by the wayside : as in the famous *Melancholia* of Albert Dürer we are shown a brooding figure disconsolately seated among the littered confusion of symbols of human effort and knowledge, science and art ; so in the music of Lassus we come at every turn, amidst all the robust and jovial creations of his genius, upon the anguished prescience of decay and death, the cankering obsession with the nothingness and futility of all mortal things.   The spirit of his religious music, unlike that of Palestrina or Victoria, is one of remorse and contrition rather than of adoration or aspiration, of fear of death rather than of hope of immortality or salvation, of the irremediable defeat of the flesh rather than of the triumph of the spirit. Hence the fullest expression of his strange and contradictory personality is probably to be found in his *Penitential Psalms*. The masses of Palestrina, then, the motets of Victoria, these psalms of Lassus, are the three unapproachable summits of religious music in the sixteenth century, all equally great in their different ways, complementary rather than antagonistic.

He whom Ronsard, prince of poets, had praised, he who had received a knighthood from the Emperor Maximilian, the Order of the Golden Spur from Pope Gregory XIII, the Cross of Malta from the King of France—loaded with all the fame, wealth, and honours that the heart of man could desire, Orlande de Lassus, prince of musicians and friend of princes, died insane, of melancholia.

CHAPTER VI

The Venetian and Other Italian Schools of the Sixteenth Century

Political, commercial, and cultural relations between the Netherlands and Venice had always been close, and just as the pupils of the van Eycks in the fifteenth century brought the art of painting in oils to the city of the lagoons, so Adrian Willaert, a pupil of Mouton, brought there the Flemish polyphonic art and became *maestro di cappella* at St. Mark's in 1527. But there is ample evidence to show that long before this, and perhaps always, Venice had been a pre-eminently musical city. Even as far back as 379 St. Jerome praises the musicians of Aquileia—the city on the mainland whence the first settlers in the lagoons had come—in extravagantly laudatory terms : " Aquilienses clerici quasi chorus beatorum habentur "—and throughout the entire history of the republic one finds a quite remarkable preoccupation with and cultivation of the art of music.   In Venice the cult of the state almost usurped the place occupied elsewhere by religion : " siamo Veneziani e poi Cristiani ", as the inhabitants were wont to say, and festivals and state occasions, such as the election of the Doge or the celebration of victories were always made the pretext for elaborate musical festivals. Musical academies abounded throughout the city, and in the many schools or *Studi*, there were large collections of musical instruments and scores.   It was in Venice, too, that the first musical publishing house was established by Petrucci da Fossombrone in 1498, under the direct and active patronage of the State ; and Marco d'Aquila, a Venetian, " incomparabile nel toccar del liuto ", was the inventor of the tablature system of lute notation.   And when we consider the remarkable frequency with which we encounter pictorial representations of concerts and other musical subjects in Venetian painting, it becomes evident that music played a larger part in Venetian life, both public and private, than in that of any other city or country in Europe.   As familiar instances of this one need only mention the *Trionfo di San Giorgio* of Carpaccio, the *Fête champêtre* of Giorgione, the *Venere che si recrea con la musica* of Titian, the *Fantasia sulla Musica* of Tintoretto, the picture at Hampton Court of the *Sonatrice di clavicembalo* of Licinio, the *Ricco Epulone* of Bonifacio de Pitati, but especially the *Wedding Feast at Cana* of Veronese, in which the painter has represented himself together with Titian, Tintoretto, and Bassano, all playing musical instruments.

In spite, therefore, of the great eminence displayed by the Venetians in the other arts we may safely say that Venice was above all a musical city.   By his statue of Apollo in the Loggetta the famous sculptor and architect Sansovino wished to signify the love of his city for music " which seems there to be in its natural and proper abode " (Temanza, *Vita di Sansovino*), and in the similar tributes on the part of the painters, and particularly in the picture of Veronese already mentioned, we may see the wish to pay honour to the art which, more than any other, seemed best to express the Venetian spirit, and an almost unconscious and involuntary recognition of the essentially musical quality of their own, and indeed of all, Venetian painting and all Venetian art generally.   " Musical, " in fact, is the one adjective which recurs most frequently in any attempt to describe or define the haunting emotional quality, the rich harmonious colouring, the melting indefiniteness of line and contour, that are so characteristic of Venetian art, and even of the very city itself ; as Nietzsche says in his *Ecce Homo*, " if I try to find a new word for music, I can never find any other than Venice ".   It is hardly too fanciful to point out that the very form of the city is musical, for it is constructed like a six-part double choir in which the *sestieri* of Castello, San Marco, and Cannareggio on one side of the Grand Canal respond to Polo, Dorsodura, and Santa Croce on the other ; and the Grand Canal itself is one long, sweet antiphonal in which a group of palaces on one side replies to a group on the other, like choir to choir, until they finally unite in the majestic full close of the Piazza di San Marco.

It is interesting to observe that this characteristic structural feature of the city is reproduced in its music, for the Venetian masters particularly cultivated the method of writing for two or more choirs, generally composed of four parts each, which

G

come together at the end. The introduction of this practice, attributed to Willaert, has often been accounted for by the fact that the church of St. Mark's possessed two choirs, one on each side of the aisle. But this seems to be putting the cart before the horse, because from the earliest days of the church, long before St. Mark's was built, it was a familiar and well-established custom to chant the psalms antiphonally. This custom originated in the Eastern Church, and since Venice, Ravenna, and the surrounding country were the door through which the Byzantine influence penetrated into Italy, and in view of the markedly oriental character of most early Venetian art, it seems probable—if not absolutely certain—that this method of intoning the psalms was earlier and more extensively practised in Venice than anywhere else. The chances are, therefore, that the two choirs of St. Mark's owed their existence, not to a purely architectural conception, but to a desire to regularize and perpetuate this old and familiar musical device, the eventual application of which to polyphonic music was a wholly natural and inevitable development. The supposition that this later Venetian practice was only an adaptation of the traditional method of chanting the psalms and not due merely to a structural feature of a particular building, receives additional support from the fact that it first makes its appearance, if not exclusively at least predominantly, in settings of the psalms.

Willaert was a figure of greater historical than aesthetic importance. He was the founder of a great school, the creator of a new musical style, the first of a long line, and a teacher of great masters, rather than a great master himself. Nevertheless he remains an impressive and striking figure. In the remark which he made in his old age to his pupil Zarlino, the famous theoretician—" Non mi doglio d'esser vicino agli anni della decrepità, ma bensi mi doglio che mi converra morire allora che comincio ad imparare "—we are inevitably reminded of the similar saying of old Haydn, " I have only just learnt in my old age how to use the wind instruments, and now that I understand them I must leave the world ", and the words of Hokusai, the great Japanese painter, uttered on his deathbed, " if Heaven had lent me but five years more I might have learnt to become a good painter ". Only fine artists are capable of such touching modesty and humility.

Willaert's music, though somewhat crabbed and stiff in style, possesses an undoubted grandeur and dignity; he makes amends to a certain extent for his deficiency in melodic invention by his great mastery in handling massed voices. He is perhaps the first of the Flemish composers to give the impression of writing in chords rather than in separate interwoven parts, and this definitely harmonic bias remains and becomes increasingly intensified in the work of his Venetian successors. It is, of course, largely or at least partly the outcome of the double-choir system of writing, which inevitably leads to the counter-balancing and blending of homogeneous masses of sound rather than to the weaving of an elaborate contrapuntal texture.

Willaert was succeeded at St. Mark's by another Fleming, Cyprian van Rore. He was only Flemish by birth, however, and came to Venice at an early age. His music, as far as can be ascertained—for very little of it is accessible—is written in two widely divergent styles ; in the one he follows more or less in the footsteps of his predecessor, while in the other he reveals himself as a daring experimentalist, particularly in the direction of chromatic harmony. He is more important as a secular than as a church composer, however, and the same may also be said of his successor Claudio Merulo, the first leader of the school to be an Italian by birth, who, though he wrote a vast amount of vocal music, is better known on account of his instrumental compositions.

It was left to the two Gabrielis, Andrea and Giovanni, uncle and nephew, to develop, extend, and bring to perfection the style of composition introduced by Willaert, and to raise the Venetian school of polyphonic sacred music to as great artistic heights as any attained by their Roman, Flemish, or Spanish rivals. While their predecessors only made use of a double choir, each of which was made up of the ordinary four-part, soprano, alto, tenor, bass combination, the Gabrielis frequently wrote for three and sometimes even four choirs, consisting of combinations of all kinds of different voices. For example, in one work of Andrea we find two choirs of the ordinary four voices, and a third one of male voices alone, which are pitted against each other and blended in such a way as to produce remarkable effects of subtlety and diversity of colour—a quality of the music of the Gabrielis which is still further intensified by their frequent employment of instruments, the parts of which are no mere accompaniments or doublings of voice parts, but constitute an integral element in the texture and design of the whole.

In the work of Giovanni, even more than in that of his uncle, colour is the principle aim and end to which all other considerations are sacrificed. The canonic art of the Netherlanders has at last vanished almost completely, leaving nothing but an occasional point of imitation which is never continued for more than a few notes. By means of harmonic richness—often chromatic—skilful grouping of voices, and blending of instrumental *timbres*, he attains to a grandeur, brilliance, and fiery energy which music had never before known. It is impossible to resist the obvious and almost necessary comparison between such an art and the painting of the Venetians, and of Tintoretto and Veronese in particular, whose gigantic and grandiose compositions, quite apart from the predominantly colouristic interest which they have in common with the art of the Gabrielis, are often constructed in a strikingly analogous fashion. See, for example, the great *Crucifixion* of Tintoretto of which the French critic Taine, knowing nothing about the multiple choir music of the Venetian composers, or even about music at all, writes in his *Voyage en Italie*, " Il se déploie comme un chœur qui correspond à un autre chœur ".

And so we see that just as Palestrina and his school assimilated the art of the Flemish masters and transformed it into an entirely new and indigenous Roman style, so the Gabrielis also modified it in a similar manner, though in quite the opposite direction, in such a way as to arrive at a characteristically Venetian form of art, and at the musical realization of the contradictory union of spirituality and worldliness, of gravity and brilliance, of nobility and sensuality, of strength and beauty, which imparts such a distinctive character to all the finest art of the proud republic. Needless to say, this music cannot for a moment be compared to that of the Roman school as regards its fitness to the purposes of divine worship ; like the sacred pictures of the Venetian painters, it hymns the beauty of earthly rather than of heavenly things, and glorifies man rather than God ; but nevertheless, considered solely and simply as music, one can no more say that the art of Giovanni Gabrieli is inferior to that of Palestrina than that the art of Titian, Giorgione, or Tintoretto is inferior to that of Perugino or Raphael.   It is simply different, that is all, but just as great in its own way.

In studying the proliferation of the polyphonic tradition in Italy, we have so far confined ourselves almost entirely to church music, mainly for reasons of convenience, seeing that, with only very few exceptions, those composers who excelled in sacred music played no part at all, or only a very small one, in the field of secular music, and *vice versa*.   But it would be a great mistake to suppose that the great Flemish Conquest of music, the defeat of monody by polyphony, the invasion of the South by the North, which set in about the end of the fifteenth century and lasted until the end of the sixteenth, was confined to the music of the church, for it also exercised as important an influence on secular music.   In Italy, however, and more particularly in the north of Italy, secular composers still continued to write in a form which, in view of the fact that the text of the poem is often found underneath the notes of the upper part only, while the remaining parts are harmonically conceived and consist for the most part in simple note-against-note chords with a bass part frequently leaping by fourths and fifths in a recognizably characteristic instrumental manner, we may safely conclude were performed by a solo voice with instrumental accompaniment—probably a lute and bass viol—although they could also have been rendered by voices alone. These little works were variously designated as *frottole*, *villanelle strambotti*, *villotte*, and *rispetti*, distinguished from each other by small and comparatively unimportant structural differences rather than by stylistic ones.   Many of these compositions, though simple and unpretentious, are very pleasing, and both in their melodic and harmonic idioms, as in practically all secular homophonic music, reveal a definite inclination in the direction of modern tonality.   The most important composer of such works is one rejoicing in the sonorous patronymic of Bartolomeo Tromboncino.

About the beginning of the sixteenth century, however, a new form called the madrigal makes its appearance. (The early Florentine school of the fourteenth century also wrote works which were called madrigals, but there is nothing whatever in common between them and those we are about to consider.)   The exact meaning and origin of the term is not known, but musically speaking it may be defined as the outcome of the union of the vigorous, plebeian style of the North and the delicately nurtured patrician art of the South—a cross between the French or Flemish *chanson* and the Italian *frottola*, between the polyphony of the church and the harmonic monody of the court.   Traces of this dual origin persist throughout the history of the form   Sometimes the one element predominates, sometimes the other, but they are seldom to be found in complete equilibrium ; they perpetually tend to separate out, and to resolve into their primary constituents, even in the course of the same work, and generally refuse to blend into a homogeneous style.   This inherent weakness is probably the main cause of the inability of the madrigal to survive as a form, despite the great beauty of much of the music written in it.

As a result of this union of contraries, this cross between different species, two separate schools come into existence ; in the madrigals of the Southern or Roman school the polyphonic element tends to predominate, while those of the Northern or Venetian school are more harmonic in character.   In the early madrigals of Palestrina, for example, sacred words might frequently be substituted for profane ones, without any sense of incongruity between them and the music resulting from it ; and although in his later ones he came to adopt a more distinctively secular style, the atmosphere of the cloister never entirely disappears.   The same applies to most of the madrigals of his Roman colleagues, and this close assimilation to the style of the church music is the reason why, beautiful though they often are from a purely musical point of view, they cannot, generally speaking, be regarded as completely satisfactory examples of secular composition.

At Venice, however, and in the surrounding country— particularly at Ferrara—a style more sharply differentiated from that of the church, and better suited to the expression and satisfaction of earthly delights and passions, was successfully cultivated by Willaert and his successors.   In fact the predominantly wordly bias of the Venetian school which is responsible for the inferiority of their church music compared to that of the Roman school, from the religious standpoint, makes for their incontestable superiority in the domain of secular music.   The most interesting and significant feature of their style consists in the systematic exploitation for the first time—in written music at least—of the resources of chromaticism, to the origin and development of which a few words must now be devoted.

We have already had occasion several times to emphasize the essentially melodic and anti-harmonic nature of the Gregorian Chant, which had effectively prevented early church composers from founding a satisfactory harmonic art on the basis of plain song, and to lay stress upon the corollary that harmony is bound up with the major scale and the modern tonal system.   As the historian Ambros puts it, " only so long as the Gregorian chant was sung in unison could the diatonic modal system be strictly maintained.   In polyphonic music this was not possible without afflicting the ear to an intolerable extent by means of unnatural harmonic combinations ".   On the other hand the secular and even definitely irreligious character of the major harmonic scale effectively excluded it from the church. In order to surmount this difficulty the church musicians evolved a cunning compromise.   They left the old modal system intact so far as notation and theory were concerned, thus satisfying the objections of the ecclesiastical authorities, who in turn consented to close their eyes, or rather their ears, to slight violations and infringements of it which were made in practice for the sake of euphony, consisting in the chromatic alteration of certain notes in order to obtain satisfactory and natural harmonic progressions, and particularly the leading-note cadence.   The result of this custom was to establish a working compromise between the rival claims of the melodic modal system and the harmonic tonal system, and that is, in effect, what the counterpoint of the Middle Ages and the Renaissance is—a working compromise between harmony and melody, an equilibrium between the conflicting claims of scale and mode.

This alteration of notes, called *musica ficta*, was the only kind of chromaticism countenanced, strictly speaking, within the fold of the church music, though no doubt abuses of it were liable to creep in now and then, in secular music, on the contrary, a different kind of chromaticism came into use—may, indeed, always have existed—and is referred to in a vague and somewhat perfunctory manner by various musical theorists of the Middle Ages, such as Tinctoris and Prosdocimus de Beldamandis.   In this case chromatic notes were employed, not in order to mollify the harmonic asperities inseparable from pure and undiluted modality, not merely so as to produce the perfect cadence—which secular music had always possessed from the earliest times, as in the Reading Rota and the pilgrims' song *Roma nobilis*, for example—but simply whenever desired for purely expressive or colouristic purposes.

In short, while the former variety of chromaticism is a modification of the modal system and a half-way house in the direction of the modern scale system, the latter variety may be regarded more in the light of a modification of the modern scale system, and a reaching-out towards the chromatic or twelve-note scale of to-day. The distinctive feature of the former consists in the inflection of a semitone below a note, in order to form a leading note cadence, that of the latter in the inflection of a semitone above. They are, in fact, two entirely different things and should be carefully distinguished from each other; and seeing that two different expressions were used, more or less indiscriminately, to denominate both forms of chromaticism—namely, *musica ficta* and *musica falsa*—it would be a great advantage if the first of these were used to denote the relative, pseudo-chromatic, modal variety, and the other definitely restricted to the designation of the true and absolute form of chromaticism which now begins to play such an important rôle in the madrigals of the Italo-Flemish schools of Venice and Ferrara.

Although Willaert was probably the first important composer to make use of chromaticism to any appreciable extent, his employment of it was wholly tentative, haphazard, and experimental. He would not seem to have perceived clearly its possible value as a means of expression, and rather resembles a man who has by accident hit upon a remarkable discovery without having any very clear perception of the uses to which it could be put. Its exploitation as a means to the musical realization of emotions and states of mind, especially those of a somewhat gloomy and tragic order, was left to his pupil and successor, van Rore, some of whose madrigals, and particularly his setting of a Latin ode—*Calami sonum ferentes*—though undoubtedly somewhat crude, reveal nevertheless a very acute perception of the great expressive possibilities latent in this new resource. Many other composers, above all those of the school of Ferrara, the importance of which city as a centre of experimental activities during the second part of the sixteenth century has not yet been sufficiently appreciated by musical historians, followed him hesitatingly and tentatively in these slippery paths, and even the great Lassus in his youth seems to have dabbled experimentally in chromaticism ; but it cannot be said that the full implications of this new means of expression were thoroughly grasped, or its resources turned to great account, by any composer before Carlo Gesualdo, Prince of Venosa, one of the most remarkable figures of his age.

Although a Neapolitan by birth and musical training, Gesualdo may be legitimately regarded as belonging to the school of Ferrara, since his early work is comparatively conventional in style, and it was not until he went to Ferrara that the characteristic qualities of his art made their appearance. It is only natural, therefore, to suppose that he was influenced in his direction by the composers already referred to ; on the other hand his treatment of chromaticism is so bold and original, his whole method and style so strikingly different from theirs, that he can hardly be considered to be the member of any school whatsoever. He stands apart from all his contemporaries, and seemingly bears no relation either to predecessors or successors. Indeed, he bears a striking resemblance to the Spanish painter El Greco, both in the qualities of his art and in the isolated position which he occupies in musical history.   It is interesting to note, moreover, that their careers coincide exactly in point of time, both of them dying in the same year (1614). Gesualdo, indeed, is as far in advance of his time as El Greco, and has similarly had to wait until the present day for a recognition of his importance, both historical and artistic. It is certainly not going too far to say that not until we come to Wagner and Debussy do we find chromatic progressions that can be compared to those which we encounter at every turn in his madrigals, and even then the comparison, both as regards audacity and sureness of touch, is not by any means to his disadvantage. He is certainly more original than Wagner, whose chromaticism, however daring and novel it may appear at first sight, is in essence only a development and extension of a pre-existing tradition ; and his harmonic conceptions are much less limited and mechanically arrived at, much more directly the outcome of a definite musical thought than those of Debussy which are little more than a development of *faux bourdon*, consisting of chords whose constituent parts move entirely by similar motion, which they never do in the work of Gesualdo.

But it would be a mistake to regard Gesualdo as being merely a daring and ingenious experimentalist in harmony and nothing else, for he is equally remarkable in other directions. No composer of his time, and very few since, have possessed such a talent for inventing small, pregnant, melodic phrases— jewels five notes long—which continue to haunt the memory long after one has heard them. In sheer expressiveness and dramatic intensity, too, he is unrivalled by any composer of his day, and he particularly excels in the musical delineation of the darker and more sombre aspects of things, such as death, pain, grief, and so forth.

The most conspicuous fault of all Gesualdo's work lies in its stylistic inequality. He seldom succeeds in reconciling his chromatic harmonic manner with the traditional polyphonic style, and perpetually oscillates between the two. His predilection for vivid word-painting, too, results frequently in a certain formlessness and lack of cohesion, and for the most part his madrigals consist of a series of short and strongly contrasted sections which are seldom welded into a unified whole. For this reason alone it may perhaps be conceded that he is a less completely successful composer, though unquestionably a much more powerful and arresting personality, than his contemporary Luca Marenzio who is generally, and with reason, regarded as the greatest Italian master of the madrigal. In the latter's best work formal balance and design are never sacrificed, as in that of Gesualdo, to expressiveness ; neither are we conscious, in the superb opening section of his *Solo e pensoso*, for example, of any fundamental irreconcilability between the rival claims of chromatic harmony and traditional polyphony. In his work, to a greater extent than in that of any other composer of madrigals, the radical defect of the form, which consists in its fundamental instability resulting from the duality of its character and origin, and so strikingly exemplified in the work of Gesualdo, is completely overcome. Marenzio, indeed, is one of the great stylists of music, and achieves much the same high level of perfection in the madrigal that Palestrina achieves in the music of the church.

Another outstanding figure among the Italian madrigalists is Orazio Vecchi, best known for his remarkable and interesting experiments in the direction of choral drama or dramatic cantata, written in the form of a series of madrigals, analogous to the sonnet-sequence in poetry.   Of these the *Amfiparnasso*, described by the composer as a *commedia harmonica*, is the most famous.   It is written with an astonishing verve and brilliance, a wit and humour which have rarely been equalled and certainly never surpassed ; the comic chorus of Jews in particular is a masterpiece of musical characterization, reminding one of the dispute between the Jews in Strauss's *Salome*. Apart from works of this kind, of which there exist several, Vecchi also wrote madrigals in the ordinary manner, many of which are equal to the very best of the period.   In the dramatic comedy form he was followed by Adriano Banchieri, with whom, however, wit and vivacity are apt to degenerate into mere riotous buffoonery.

The history of instrumental music before and during the sixteenth century is extremely difficult and perhaps even impossible to write, on account of the fact that there was then no hard and fast line drawn between it and vocal music as there is to-day.   Music, indeed, was frequently written and published with a view to its performance by either voices or instruments and sometimes expressly designated on the title page as being equally adaptable to both *media*.   But it would be a mistake to assume, as Sir Hubert Parry does in his volume on the music of the seventeenth century in the "Oxford History of Music," that instrumental music therefore "evolved" from vocal music ; that composers for the lute, for example, at first "strove in vain to present formulas of polyphonic art", and that only their gradual realization of the inherent technical disability of the instrument to perform such a task, compelled them, almost in spite of themselves, "to look for a style of music which was more apt for it".   This is surely putting the cart before the horse, for in the first place it is inherently improbable that an instrument should come into existence with a distinctive and fully formed technique, and that a search should then be made for a style of writing suitable to it.   Mere common sense tells us that it is much more likely that an instrument should be invented and constructed in a certain definite manner in order to realize certain conceptions and satisfy certain artistic needs which no other medium, instrumental or vocal, was able to do. In the second place, it is an undoubted fact that the lute, and the viol too for that matter, was in common use long before the formulas of choral art to which Sir Hubert Parry refers came into existence.   It is certainly true, of course, that music originally written and conceived in terms of voices was frequently performed by instruments as an alternative or makeshift, but the reverse is probably equally true ; for, as we have already seen in a previous chapter, the first Troubadour song of which we have any record was originally an instrumental piece to which words were subsequently fitted.   Indeed it is more than probable that the Reading Rota itself, and the very device of canon and imitation which constitutes the earliest and most fruitful " formula of polyphonic art ", were also instrumental in origin ; for apart from the fact that canon is obviously a device that would occur more readily to an instrumental than to a vocal composer on account of the somewhat incongruous and unnatural effect produced by the reiteration of the same words in various voices at different distances from each other, all the evidence at our disposal goes to prove that it was in the instrumental accompaniments of songs that the origin of the canonic art of the Flemish composers is to be found.   It is certainly a fact that the deliberate, conscious, and systematic employment of imitation is to be found there long before its appearance in choral music.

So far then from it being true that instrumental music evolved slowly and painfully from vocal music, the contrary is, if any-thing, much nearer to the truth.   The fact of the matter is, however, that we are too apt, from the standpoint of the present day, to make an artificial and arbitrary distinction between the two categories, and to regard them as separate and independent, even antagonistic.   This is not to say that they do not possess certain clearly defined characteristics that differentiate them, or that music does not lose something in transcription from the one to the other, but only that what one medium has in common with the other greatly exceeds, both in quantity and import-ance, that which belongs to it alone.   In fact we may liken the different *media* in music to different languages belonging to the same root stock.   The substance of the thought will remain unchanged in translation ; the peculiar felicity of style, and the more subtle shades of meaning only, will be lost.   In the process of transcription some works will undoubtedly lose more than others, but it is probably safe to say that nine-tenths of the world's greatest music could be transcribed for any medium within reason without losing more than a comparatively unimportant part of its substance and appeal ; and that, generally speaking—for naturally there are many exceptions— the greater a work is the less it will lose.

To suggest, therefore, that because the instrumental music of the sixteenth century has a great deal in common with the choral music, it must consequently have been derived from it, is like saying that French is derived from Italian or Italian from Spanish.   What they have in common is what they both derive from the fundamental roots of musical language and thought. It is impossible to say, for example, that a melody such as the *Kalendas Mayas* is either instrumental or vocal in character ; it can be equally well sung or played, and the same may be said of a great part of all music, whether mediæval or modern. To suppose that musicians only gradually came to realize that it was possible to make use of purely instrumental resources and to write music which could not well be executed except by the instrument for which it was originally written, is an entirely gratuitous assumption. Many of the earliest published examples of instrumental music that have come down to us, such as the lute music of Luis de Milan, reveal as genuine and highly developed a sense of instrumental style as any subsequent music, and are in no sense mere adaptations of the choral art.

The idea, therefore, of the gradual evolution and emergence of instrumental music from the formulas of polyphonic vocal art is only another aspect of the great evolutionary myth which we have already encountered so often.   It is certainly true that most early keyboard music does seem in a sense to derive from the choral technique, but that is simply because, properly speaking, there never has been and is not yet even such a thing as a definite organ or piano style.   To revert to our linguistic simile, if the different *media* of chorus, accompanied solo song, string music, and so forth, might be likened to so many languages belonging to a common stock, like French, Italian, and Spanish, the various forms of keyboard instruments might be regarded as a kind of musical Esperanto or universal language, a synthesis or amalgam of all of them, possessing no special aptitudes or individuality, but capable of everything to a certain extent.   The organ style of Bach, for example, is largely if not entirely based on the methods of contrapuntal choral art ;

the piano writing of Chopin and Liszt is founded on a combination of the *bel canto* of Italian operatic arias and the violin writing of Paganini ; and the piano in the hands of Beethoven becomes a kind of miniature orchestra. All piano and organ music, indeed, is in a sense transcription or arrangement ; it possesses no distinctive characteristics which it does not share with or take from some other medium, save perhaps a certain mechanical aptitude for the presentation of florid figurations and decorative arabesques, which we already find fully developed and realized in the earliest examples of specifically keyboard music that have come down to us, such as the *Intavolature per organo* of Girolamo Cavazzoni (1542) ,and the *Toccate, Ricercari,* and other organ works of the great masters of the Venetian school, such as Merulo and Andrea Gabrieli. It must be confessed, however, that the best organ music of the sixteenth century is that which is based on choral precedents, and the least satisfying that which seeks to exploit the only positive individual resource of the instrument. The *Toccate* in particular are generally mere windy displays of virtuosity, consisting of endless strings of meaningless figurations devoid of either melodic, rhythmic, harmonic, formal or any other conceivable kind of musical interest. Of much greater value and significance is the organ music of Jan Pieterzoon Sweelinck, a Dutch composer deriving from, if not actually belonging to, the Venetian School. He excels all other instrumental composers of his time by reason of his more highly developed structural sense, and more particularly by his resourceful treatment of variation form, both types of which he successfully exploits : namely, that in which the melody remains unaltered throughout with constantly changing harmonies, and that in which the harmonic progressions are retained intact while the melody and rhythm undergo alteration. Both as regards the intrinsic merit and the historical significance of his work, Sweelinck may be considered to be the first really important figure in the field of purely instrumental composition, and the first whose achievement in this direction can be compared without disadvantage to the finest choral art of the century.

CHAPTER VII

The English Polyphonic School

Enough has already been said in preceding chapters to show the utter inadequacy and falsity of the narrow code of æsthetic values which seeks to postulate one single standard of beauty to which all composers must conform, in accordance with which the so-called Palestrina style has been set up as the ideal polyphonic style and all other music adjudged good or bad in so far as it approached to or receded from it—the great Flemish masters hastily brushed aside as mere forerunners sent to prepare the way, Victoria and Lassus patronizingly commended as worthy imitators, the Venetians reproached and ignored for having gone in an entirely different direction. Similarly it is this narrow and bigoted conception that is mainly responsible for the indifference and neglect with which the English polyphonic school has had to contend up till the present century. Fortunately, so far as this country is concerned at least, this prejudice has been largely overcome, and the great masters of the Tudor and Stuart ages are at last beginning to receive the attention and appreciation that they deserve. Unfortunately, however, as in all such cases of neglect followed by rediscovery, there has been a tendency to go to the opposite extreme, and to allow extravagant and excessive praise to take the place of the former under-estimation. This is in every way as great a fault and must be carefully guarded against, for it inevitably tends to engender an attitude of scepticism and suspicion in the minds of those who are not themselves acquainted with the music in question. For example, when Mr. Davey, in his " History of English Music,", remarks airily, *en passant*, that in the middle of the sixteenth century " Palestrina and Lassus were still groping their way through foggy obscurities to the serene light of the clear style already attained in England " ; and when Dr. Eaglefield Hull, in his " Music ; Classical, Romantic and Modern ", observes that " if all the works of Palestrina had been lost and those of Byrd and his compatriots preserved, the world would not have been much the poorer ", they are merely talking nonsense, and doing very real harm to the cause they are championing.

But even when we have made due allowance for the reckless extravagance of such statements we are still bound to recognize the fact that in the sixteenth century and earlier England possessed a school of composers which, if not superior to, was probably at least the equal of, any other school existing contemporaneously on the Continent, taking it all round: and that it quite certainly boasted a larger number of eminent names than any other, not even excepting that of the Netherlands. Dunstable, Fayrfax, Aston, Appleby, Cornyshe, Davy, Farrant, Johnson, Ludforde, Mundy, Redford, Shepherde, Taverner, Tye, White, Phillips, Tallis, Byrd, Dowland, Wilbye, Weelkes, Gibbons—these are quite literally only a few of the more important names chosen more or less at random. To treat even these few adequately, moreover, would require an amount of space that the limits of this book do not permit.

It is a remarkable fact that although the first example, by a long way, of perfect canonic art came from this country, English church composers avoided making use of the device for a very long time, largely, no doubt, on account of its secular associations and its originally somewhat irreligious character. That the old tradition had not entirely died out in secular music is shown by the fact that although John Dunstable—the first great name in English music—does not seem to have made any noticeable use of imitation in his church music, he did employ it in his secular music—in the *chanson* " Puisque m'amour ", for example.

Dunstable actually preceded the first Flemish school of Dufay and Binchois in point of time, and is generally supposed to have influenced it considerably, especially in the direction of euphony and harmonic propriety. This influence has probably been greatly exaggerated, however ; in so far as it exists at all it was purely transitory, for the direction in which the Flemish schools ultimately developed was precisely the opposite to that pursued by Dunstable and his followers. Besides, most of the music in early collections, such as the Trent Codices, inscribed with the words *de Anglia* or *Anglicanus*, referring either to the nationality of the composer or to the style of composition employed, has a specific character of its own which differentiates it from other contemporary schools on the Continent.

So far as we are able to judge the music of Dunstable from the little of it that has so far been made accessible, it would seem to reveal in embryo the characteristic features of most subsequent English music ; a remarkably sure instinct for harmony and euphony, great melodic freshness and spontaneity of invention, though not of a very robust order, combined with a certain distaste for academic discipline and a marked fondness for variation form.

The same preoccupation with sensuous beauty and avoidance of scholastic devices for their own sake persist in the work of Robert Fayrfax (*c.* 1500), the next outstanding figure in English church music, despite the important changes which had in the meanwhile taken place in the general technique and style of composition. The device of imitation certainly occurs, but is never carried through in the rigorous and systematic manner of the Flemish masters. In his *Tecum Principia* mass, for example, its employment is almost entirely confined to passages written for not more than three voices, and he seems to be unable, or unwilling, to apply it to a larger number of parts, preferring rather to build them up into a somewhat loose and ungainly harmonic structure which frequently attains to a high level of sonorous beauty, but is, however, apt to become monotonous on account of the formal invertebracy of the whole. The same criticism applies in the main to the work of his immediate followers, of whom Hugh Aston is perhaps the most gifted ; but whereas Fayrfax would seem to be chiefly preoccupied with the attainment of massive harmonic effects, Aston, at any rate as exemplified in his fine *Videte Manus* mass, aims rather at extreme rhythmic subtlety and melodic elaboration.

It is not until we come to John Taverner that we find ourselves in the presence of a master who can justly be placed on a level with the greatest of his continental contemporaries ; for although he cannot be compared to Josquin in sheer technical virtuosity and absolute command of every resource, he is in no way inferior to the Flemish master in expressive power and grandeur of conception. His part-writing may at times seem to be somewhat clumsy and uncouth yet he never for a moment ceases to hold our attention. He is one of those artists whose very imperfections command our respect and seem almost to be positive qualities ; without them, one feels, he would lose a great deal of his powerful and impressive personality. Although he employs canon and imitation to a much greater extent than his predecessors, they never play such an overwhelmingly important rôle in his music as they do in that of the Flemish masters ; the chief weapon in his technical armoury consists rather in a very personal use of sequential melodic progressions which imparts an organic vitality and a stern purposefulness to his texture which are lacking in that of Fayrfax and his school.

John Shepherde, on the other hand, is an artist of a very different stamp, bearing much the same relation to Taverner that Guerrero bears to Morales in the Spanish school. If the prevailing characteristics of Taverner's music are a forbidding grandeur, a rugged strength and Titanic energy, those of Shepherde's are rather a sweetness and serenity, a calm tranquil beauty, which is lyric rather than epic. The former reaches his greatest heights when handling a large number of parts, as in the magnificent six-part masses *O Michael* and *Corona Spinea* ; Shepherde, on the contrary, would seem to prefer a somewhat more restricted medium, and particularly excels in his superb four-part *French Mass*, and in that written on the beautiful secular melody called the *Westron Wynde* (also employed by Taverner and Tye) for the same number of voices.

The foregoing masters all write in a style which offers many striking points of contrast with that of their contemporaries in other countries ; with Christopher Tye and Robert White, however, we find ourselves in the presence of a form of art more closely assimilated to that of their continental colleagues, and more clearly under the influence of foreign and particularly Flemish methods. Indeed, it is interesting to note that in this respect the English school develops in quite a different way from all the other national schools we have so far been considering. While the Roman and Venetian Schools, for example, arose directly out of the Flemish school and only gradually attained to distinct individuality and independence with Palestrina and Gabrieli, the English school began with a distinct individuality and gradually came more under the Flemish influence. This influence, however, was mainly stylistic ; the specifically English quality of thought remains unimpaired.

The high tide of Flemish domination is to be found in the work of Thomas Tallis, and is particularly exemplified in the degree of attention which he devoted to canon and imitation, which play a very much more important part in his work than in that of any of his predecessors. His counterpoint is frequently somewhat crabbed, austere and intellectual, like that of the great Netherlanders, but displays of technical ingenuity are never for a moment, as they so often are with the latter, allowed to detract from the profoundly devotional quality of mind which all his work reveals.   The finest examples of his art are probably to be found in his motets such as *O bone Iesu* and *Audivi media nocte*, and in the superb *Lamentations*, which constitute one of the outstanding pinnacles of the English school.

All these great masters however, are overshadowed by William Byrd, the one member of the school who can fitly be placed side by side and compared with the very greatest masters of the century in other countries—Palestrina, Lassus, Victoria and Gabrieli—and yet have nothing to fear from the comparison. He may not attain to the absolute formal balance and clarity of style of the Roman master, but neither does he sacrifice musical interest and vitality in pursuit of them.   His mysticism may lack the sombre vehemence and passionate intensity of the Spaniard, but it has a greater serenity and restraint.   His colour may not glow with the same deep fire and gem-like brilliance as that of the Venetian, but it is always free from the slightest taint of worldliness or sensuality.   He may not give to quite the same degree as Lassus the impression of exuberant vitality, inexhaustible fecundity, and easy mastery of every technical resource, but then neither does he ever indulge in displays of sterile and meaningless virtuosity for its own sake, as the latter, like all his countrymen, is apt to do.   In short, while it may be admitted that most, if not all, of his admirable qualities may perhaps be found singly developed to a higher pitch of perfection in the art of other masters, Byrd's possession of all of them to a high degree gives his finest work a breadth and universality which cannot be found elsewhere in the music of the period, and can only be compared to that of Shakespeare in any art.   This must not be taken to mean that Byrd is a personality of quite the same transcendant magnitude as his great countryman and contemporary in the world of letters, but simply that he does possess much the same quality of mind, though in an infinitely less degree—the same mellow wisdom and serenity, the same overpowering sweetness without the slightest trace of sickliness, which are the abiding characteristics of the greatest English art of all periods, and are to be found united to their highest degree in the art of Shakespeare.   And if one were asked to name the work which, more than any other, may be said to represent Byrd's greatest and most characteristic achievement, one would surely choose the great five-part mass : a work which, in its combination of the wide-eyed candour and virginal innocence of a child with the grave dignity and quiet strength of a man, the unearthly ecstasy and illumination of a mystic with the sanity and restraint of a sage, the lover's delight in physical beauty with the austerity and unworldliness of a saint, is without a parallel in the whole field of English church music, and is only equalled by the highest flights of the greatest masters in other lands.

The secret of Byrd's greatness as a composer of sacred music is to a great extent explained in the preface to his first book of *Gradualia*, published in 1605, in which he says that " there is a certain hidden power in the thoughts underlying the words themselves, so that as one meditates upon the sacred words and constantly and seriously considers them, the right notes, in some inexplicable fashion, suggest themselves quite spontaneously ".   And in all his music for the Roman rite one gets this impression of absolute inevitability, resulting from a kind of mystical meditation on divine things, unequalled by any composers except Palestrina and Victoria, and unexcelled even by them.   Admirable though it may be in many ways, the music that he wrote to order for the English church service lacks this quality.   In his attempt to comply with the exigencies of the new regime one feels a certain lack of inspiration and inner conviction, and this applies more or less to all Protestant church of the period in England.   Only in some of the fine work of Orlando Gibbons does the new religious spirit find satisfactory and convincing musical expression, but even it cannot really be considered in any way comparable to the music of the Roman church.

We have so far confined our attention to the church music of the English school, for the sake of convenience.   It is true that Fayrfax, Aston, and many others wrote a certain amount of secular music, but the fact remains that this aspect of their activities is of less importance than that represented by their sacred music.   The first outstanding figure in the history of English secular vocal music is Thomas Whythorne, whose songs for three, four, and five voices appeared in 1571.   No composer has suffered more from slipshod and hasty criticism.   Because some early writer professed to find his work mediocre all subsequent writers have followed him in condemning it, without ever, one can be fairly certain, having taken the trouble to examine it for themselves ; for if they had they would surely have seen that it frequently attains to a high level of beauty and technical accomplishment.   The rehabilitation of this in many ways admirable composer is entirely due to the scholarship and initiative of Mr. Peter Warlock, the first student of his work who has not been content to take his opinions ready-made and second-hand from previous writers.

The secular vocal music of Byrd, like that of Palestrina, beautiful though it undoubtedly is, perhaps suffers to a certain extent from the predominantly religious bias of his temperament, and its range of feeling is in consequence mainly confined to a lofty reflective dignity and a grave serenity which are not always wholly compatible with the texts on which the music is ostensibly based.   That he was not, however, incapable of a lighter style of composition on occasions—indeed, it would be difficult to find anything of which Byrd was incapable—is shown by such numbers as *Though Amaryllis Dance* or *Who likes to love* (in the " Psalms, Sonnets and Songs " of 1588), but the fact remains that it is not a vein in which he frequently indulges.

Thomas Morley, on the other hand, admirably typifies the lighter side of the Elizabethan genius.   He is the musical incarnation of the spirit of Merrie England, and the absolute antithesis of the Italian madrigalists who, almost without exception, incline in the direction of preciosity, effeminacy, and over-refinement.   Not even Marenzio or Gesualdo are exempt from this fault, and perhaps only Vecchi is entirely free from it.   In every work Morley wrote there is a wholesome breezy quality, a freshness and spontaneity, a wayward grace and fragrance, that are entirely lacking in the music of his southern contemporaries.   Thomas Weelkes, on the contrary, though he sometimes rivals Morley in his lighter vein, is, in his most interesting and characteristic work, perhaps in spirit the closest of all the English madrigalists to the Italians, and particularly to Gesualdo. His *O Care thou wilt despatch me*, for example, reveals the same fondness for sharp antithesis and juxtapositions of strongly contrasted moods, and the second part of it opens with bold chromatic progressions strikingly similar to those which are such a characteristic feature of the art of the Italian master. He possesses, however, a greater unity of style than the latter, and is better able to weld his contrasted sections into a satisfactory formal organism.

But it is probably John Wilbye, on the whole, to whom pride of place amongst all the English madrigalists must be assigned. In his incomparable art we find united the sweet gravity of Byrd, the sunny gaiety of Morley, the expressiveness of Weelkes—if hardly the same passionate intensity—together with a dazzling brilliance and sheer perfection of workmanship that are entirely his own. Indeed, he occupies very much the same position in the English school that Marenzio occupied in the Italian school, and possesses many qualities in common with him : the same impeccable purity of line and grace of style, and the same ability to reconcile harmonic interest with the traditional polyphonic methods of construction. On the other hand, although his output was not nearly so large as that of his great Italian rival, he probably possesses a wider range of expression, and the general level of his work is so high that it is virtually impossible to single out any particular example as being greatly superior to any of the others. Each number is carefully polished and exquisitely finished, revealing in every bar the evidence of long and careful deliberation which does not, however, exclude a remarkable spontaneity of invention or give the slightest impression of laboriousness.

Among the later masters of the school who deserve to be singled out for special commendation is Thomas Tomkins, a daring and powerful harmonist, a contrapuntist exceptionally able in the management of a large number of parts, and a brilliantly imaginative tone-painter. See for example his *Weep no more*, in which the phrase " laughs, and weeps, and sighs, and sings ", is delineated in the music with a graphic antithetic intensity unequalled save in the work of Gesualdo. Giles Farnaby, who similarly excels in the rendering of emotions and sensations, possesses a highly personal style, not so much experimental as unconventional, full of curious harmonic progressions and melodic leaps of unusual intervals such as the augmented second and the diminished fourth ; and finally may be mentioned Orlando Gibbons, whose *Silver Swan* in particular is justly famed for the stately grandeur and elevation of its style.

The number of Italian madrigalists is very large and the general level of achievement correspondingly high, but the lesser masters are somewhat lacking in individuality and consequently hardly call for separate mention. The number of English Madrigalists, on the other hand, though probably much smaller than that of the Italians, nevertheless includes a higher proportion who possess definitely personal characteristics, quite apart from the question of relative merit, and therefore demand more detailed consideration. This, as we have already seen, applies equally to the English church music compared with that of the Italian schools, which can each be conveniently summed up in one or two outstanding names : and altogether, speaking generally, this individual liberty and comparative freedom from a uniform discipline would seem to be peculiarly characteristic of the native genius in all arts and in all periods. Indeed, a definite tradition to which all deferentially subscribe has seldom existed for long in English art, and would seem to be foreign to its innermost nature. This is at once a virtue and a defect, for a definite accepted tradition is, in different ways, both a help and a hindrance.

Besides the madrigalists the English school also boasts of a small but brilliant group of composers of solo songs with lute accompaniment, the leader of which, John Dowland, can claim to rank with the greatest song-writers, not only of his own country but of all countries, not only of his own time, but of all time. The richness of melodic invention he displays in his voice parts is truly amazing ; moving within a narrow compass seldom exceeding an octave, they never fail to impress one with their variety and resource. Although he is capable of writing the most exquisite tunes in symmetrical four- and eight-bar phrases, one of the most remarkable features of his finest songs consists in their rhapsodic and impassioned declamation—a kind of prose melody which is, however, at the opposite pole from recitative. His harmonic experiments, though daring and unconventional, are invariably successful ; and the rhythmic subtlety of his flexible periods is unsurpassed even in Elizabethan music. His accompaniments, though always subordinate to the voice part, are nevertheless full of independent interest. (It should perhaps be observed here that some of these *Ayres*, as they were called, of Dowland, were also printed in an alternative version which could be sung by unaccompanied voices alone, but generally speaking one feels that they were primarily conceived as a principal upper part with an instrumental accompaniment.)

To an even greater extent than any of his colleagues Dowland seems to stand apart by himself and reveals a definite personality not merely by virtue of a highly original style, but also of a highly individual quality of mind which he shares with no one else.   It is possible to mistake a work of Byrd for that of one of his contemporaries, never one of Dowland, whose long, subtle, flowing vocal lines have a distinctive and immediately recognizable quality of their own.   Although he frequently writes in a bright and even gay vein, one feels, nevertheless, that his finest and most intensely personal songs are rather those of a somewhat passionate, melancholy, and elegiac temper, such as *I saw my lady weep*, or *In darkness let me dwell*— two of the loveliest songs ever written, and certainly without a parallel in English music.

In spite of his great originality, however, Dowland is, in certain aspects of his work, a profoundly traditional artist, the descendant of a long line stretching far back into the Middle Ages.   He might even be called a Troubadour for all the difference that there is between him and his courtly predecessors of four or five centuries before.   Indeed, certain melodies, or at least phrases, of Dowland so strongly recall those of the Troubadours that one might well be forgiven for being unable to decide at once which were which.   Compare, for example, the beautiful Troubadour melody, *Volez vos que je vos chant* with the *Now O now I needs must part* or other similar melodies of Dowland ; it is not merely that the rhythmic structure of both is strikingly akin, but the whole feeling, the whole style and method.   Resemblances such as these conclusively reveal the utter baselessness and unreality of the conventional division of musical history into cut-and-dried periods and water-tight compartments.   The art of Dowland represents a middle point in an unbroken lyric tradition stretching back to the earliest times of which we have any record, and forward to the song of to-day and no doubt of to-morrow as well.   The different periods and phases that seem to succeed and give place to each other in musical history are as illusory as the apparent succession of the seasons of the year, or the alternation of day and night, which in reality all and both exist simultaneously in different places.   It is only in the eye of the stationary observer that the change takes place from one to the other, and similarly in music, once we are able to free ourselves from this illusion of succession in time we see several immemorial traditions existing side by side throughout the ages ; their coming to fruition and passing away again takes place only in our finite perception. Evolution, so far as it exists at all, is not in one single line or plane, but in several simultaneously, as in a contrapuntal composition in which each voice takes an independent part, first one taking precedence and then another.

If Dowland, then, may be said to be the Elizabethan counterpart of the noble Troubadour or court musician of the Middle Ages, Robert Jones, another member of the Lutenist school, may be regarded as the spiritual descendant of the *jongleur* or minstrel of the lower order.   His art is much less sophisticated and more immediately popular, revealing a vein of charming melody, considerable wit and vivacity, and negligible technical abilities. He excels in songs of the lighter kind and generally fails in his more ambitious flights. In striking contrast to him stands John Danyel, a consummate master of technical resource, who is at his best in works on a large scale of a serious and rather sombre character ; his *Chromatic Tunes* in particular is one of the most daring and at the same time most successful experiments of the age in chromatic harmony. Philip Rosseter, again, is a slighter figure, whose simple and unpretentious, but always, unlike those of Jones, exquisitely finished songs, possess a quiet wistful beauty and a haunting charm that we do not find anywhere else. Lastly may be singled out for special mention Captain Tobias Hume, who, on account of one solitary little song, one perfect lyric, namely, *Fain would I change that note*, assuredly deserves to be remembered long after the ponderous operas, symphonies, oratorios, and concertos of all but a small handful of composers have been entirely forgotten. It should also be mentioned that Thomas Campion, the great poet, belongs to the school, but it cannot be said that his music is on the same high level as his verse. He may be conceded to possess a fertile vein of pleasant, but rather undistinguished melody, and that is about all. As a musician pure and simple he is of the second rank.

Another important aspect of the immense activities of the English school which has hitherto been somewhat unaccountably neglected by historians consists in a large number of songs written for a single voice with an accompaniment of four stringed instruments, many of which are anonymous while others are by Farrant, Parsons, Nicolson, and other eminent members of the school. A selection of these songs, recently reprinted by Mr. Warlock, contains many examples of great beauty. Finally may be mentioned the large collection of pieces for the virginals, an early form of keyboard instrument, by various composers. Except for short dance movements they are practically all in variation form and for this reason they are apt to become somewhat monotonous when considered in bulk ; it is safe to say, however, that with all their limitations they compare more than favourably with the keyboard music of any other school or country at that time. In musical interest they are certainly infinitely superior to the arid *Toccate* and *Ricercari* of the Venetian school. Here, as elsewhere, the most commanding figure is Byrd, whose sextet for strings, incidentally, is also a striking landmark in the history of instrumental music.

And so we see that alike in sacred and secular choral art, in accompanied solo song and in pure instrumental music, the English school is at least the equal and in some aspects even the superior of any continental school ; and when we come to consider its achievements all round—in all fields of activity taken together and not merely in any single one—we are forced to conclude that there is no school that can be compared to it. And in the same way that in many-sidedness the English school excels all others, so within that school, by reason of his protean versatility transcending even that of Lassus—who, so far as is known, wrote no instrumental music—and equalled only by that of Bach, William Byrd must be given the highest place. It is therefore, not going too far to say that Byrd is not merely the greatest of all English composers but also, considered all round, the greatest composer of his time in any country.

So far from it being true, then, that the polyphonic tradition of the Netherlands was taken over and perfected by Palestrina, and that all the other schools should be regarded as so many unsuccessful attempts to achieve the Roman ideal, we find instead several distinct schools with different ideals, each of which excels all the others in its own way. If we value perfection of form and style above all other qualities, then indeed we shall be justified in putting the Roman school at the head of all the others ; if we seek expressiveness and religious emotion primarily we shall prefer the Spanish school ; if intellectual power and vitality of line, the Netherland school ; if richness and brilliance of colour the Venetian school ; if sweetness of sound, radiant serenity of spirit, and versatility, the English school. But if one is wise one will value them all equally, for each of them reveals an aspect of musical beauty that none of the others can reveal, at least to the same extent. And besides recognizing that each school possesses an individuality of its own and virtues and defects peculiar to it, so we shall also do well to recognize that each great composer within each school, besides sharing certain general qualities in common with his colleagues, nevertheless possesses a distinct personality of his own. We are too apt to imagine that all " old music " sounds exactly the same, that it is all the expression of identically the same conceptions and ideals, and that originality is a modern invention, but it is not so in reality. What we call to-day originality is often mere eccentricity only, which can be cultivated or suppressed, whereas true originality cannot. It is implicit in every word or note one writes, in every picture one paints, in every act, however trivial, that one performs. We cannot get rid of it even if we would, any more than we can rid ourselves of our shadows, and this is as true of the sixteenth or any other century as it is of the twentieth. It is only un-familiarity of idiom or superficiality of judgment on the part of the listener that leads him to suppose that all old music is very much alike, in the same way that at first sight one is apt to imagine that all negroes or all Chinamen are very much alike. And if it be true, as it very probably is, that Palestrina is on the whole the greatest composer of his age, the greatest master of the polyphonic style who has ever lived, it is simply on account of his pre-eminent stature and not at all on account of his tendency—rather in spite of it indeed, for, as we have seen, it was, considered abstractly, in many ways a harmful one, and led to the rapid deterioration and downfall of the old poly-phonic art in Italy. It is no part of my intention to detract one iota from the tributes which generations of musicians have rightly paid to the radiant genius of Palestrina, and only those who have completely misunderstood the foregoing pages could possibly suppose it.   I only wish to suggest that there are other great composers of the same age, who, if they do not possess quite the same supreme genius, are nevertheless not so far behind him in their different ways as to justify his triumphant apotheosis and their almost complete neglect and abandonment. To say, as Sir Charles Stanford does, that Palestrina is the only composer of importance up to the close of the sixteenth century " whose works are still alive and still intimately affecting musical ears and thoughts ", is, or should be, quite untrue.   Actually there are many composers of the same time and even of much earlier times, who, though they be of lesser stature possibly, are more congenial to the restless spirit of the present age and more sympathetic to modern ears than the somewhat passionless and tranquil art of the great Roman master.

CHAPTER VIII

The Music of the Italian Renaissance

It can hardly have escaped the reader's attention that, during the whole course of the period known as the Renaissance, very little of the music we have been considering can strictly be said to reflect the characteristic tendencies of the age, as exemplified in all the other arts. It is of course true that we come across composers here and there, such as Lassus or Giovanni Gabrieli, in whose mentality traces of what we call the Renaissance spirit may be clearly detected, but in whose work, nevertheless, it was seldom able to find complete and convincing expression on account of the essentially Gothic nature of the polyphonic style of composition in which they wrote ; even the madrigal was too much of a hybrid, too unmistakably derived, on one side of its family tree at least, from mediæval ancestors, to permit of a wholly characteristic and æsthetically satisfying embodiment of the spirit of the age. In fact it may safely be said without fear of contradiction that, strictly speaking, there is no adequate parallel in music to the great stylistic transformation which takes place in literature, architecture, sculpture, and painting, during the century and a half that elapsed between the fall of Constantinople, from which the beginning of the Renaissance is generally supposed to date, and the commencement of the seventeenth century, which marks its close.

The explanation of this phenomenon is not far to seek. Neither the intellectual curiosity and lust for knowledge which is perhaps the spiritual *leit-motiv* of the period, nor the desire for personal fame and glory which was the dominant impulse behind the munificent patronage and encouragement extended to artists by great nobles and princes of the church,— finding expression in the record of their lives and deeds in poetic eulogies and in dedications, in the preservation of their lineaments for the edification of posterity in sculptured stone and painted canvas, and in the erection of magnificent palaces and tombs to serve respectively as their dwelling-houses in life and their resting-places in death—neither of these two desires could be satisfied to any appreciable extent by the art of music. Similarly the cult of the antique which exercised such a powerful and decisive influence on the styles of all the other arts during the period had little or no repercussion on music, for the simple reason that no examples of Greek or Roman music which could serve as the models for a new style of composition were known to exist—more accurately, perhaps, none had as yet been deciphered. All that musicians had to go upon, in any attempt to revive or reconstruct the musical art of classic antiquity, consisted in a few obscure and fragmentary theoretical writings and in vague literary allusions and descriptions.

But apart from these purely practical considerations there were others even more cogent and deep-lying which effectively precluded the Renaissance impulse from finding a satisfactory outlet in music. Western European music, it must always be remembered, was, to a greater extent than any other art, the direct creation of Christianity and indissolubly bound up with the expression of the Christian values. In order to express those of pagan antiquity, therefore, it would obviously be necessary for composers to cast aside practically the entire traditional legacy that they had inherited from their predecessors, on account of the strength of the associations that music had contracted and the peculiar aptitudes and disabilities it acquired in the course of centuries of service in the interests of the church and its ritual. In fact the course of development followed by the various arts at the time of the Renaissance is the exact opposite of that which we observed at the beginning of the Christian era. Then it was music that found itself at once and took the leading place among the arts, while the plastic arts, and sculpture in particular, were relegated to positions of secondary importance and compelled to discard the highly organized technical equipment they had possessed under paganism in their endeavour to adapt themselves to the expression of the Christian values. Now, however, the positions were reversed. Already as early as the thirteenth century the Renaissance spirit began to manifest itself in sculpture, while for its repercussion in music we have practically to wait until the beginning of the seventeenth century ; and even when it did eventually come, it brought about the same impoverishment and limitation of resources, the same temporary eclipse that signalled the advent of the Christian ideals in the field of the plastic arts. The explanation of this is to be found in the fact that the reaffirmation of the pagan ideals logically and inevitably entailed the degradation of music from the proud position of unqualified and acknowledged supremacy which it had enjoyed in the symposium of the Christian arts, and its relegation, in accordance with Greek æsthetic, to the rank that it had held prior to the advent of Christianity—that of a mere decorative adjunct, or $\eta\delta\upsilon\sigma\mu\alpha$ of poetry.

While the Renaissance, then, was a period of liberation and vast expansion of resources for the plastic arts, it threatened music with ignominious chains of servitude and involved an impoverishment of its resources amounting to its virtual extinction as an independent art. The acceptance of its ideals and principles by musicians would be tantamount to a voluntary renunciation of practically all that had hitherto been achieved, a betrayal of the interests of music in favour of those of literature such as no genuine musician could possibly have contemplated with equanimity, much less have set his hand to.

It need not surprise us, therefore, to find that the men who carried the Renaissance ideals into execution and initiated a form of musical art which they fondly imagined was equivalent to that of ancient Greece, consisted of a group of literary men and aristocratic *dilettanti* such as Jacopo Peri, Emilio Cavalieri, Vincenzo Galileo, Giovanni Battista Doni, Jacopo Corsi and other members of the *camerata* who were wont to foregather in the palace of one Count Bardi at Florence in the last decade of the sixteenth century ; together with a sprinkling of renegade professional musicians like Giulio Caccini who, as even one of his warmest admirers, Pietro della Valle, is compelled to admit (in his discourse *Della Musica dell'età nostra*), had entirely failed to distinguish himself in any works written prior to his conversion to the new ideals. Caccini is, in fact, the earliest representative in musical history of the type of artist, unfortunately only too familiar to us at the present day—the stuff out of which nine-tenths of so-called revolutionary artists are made—namely, the type of ambitious mediocrity who finds in new movements and experiments an opportunity for advertising himself, and seeks to conceal the essentially poverty-stricken nature of his inspiration, and the technical short-comings of his practice, by means of arrogant manifestos and specious theoretical disquisitions. Few, indeed, of his modern exemplars, not even the egregious Signor Marinetti himself, have given vent to quite such bombastic and self-laudatory utterances as did Caccini in his prefaces. Not only does he claim to have invented an entirely new form of art, but he even actually goes so far as to say that " neither in ancient nor in modern times, so far as I know, has music of such transcendant beauty ever existed as that which I hear resounding in my own soul ". That such grandiloquent words should refer to the puny and insignificant little works that he actually wrote is truly amazing—never did so great a mountain give birth to quite so small a mouse—but it is even more amazing that he should have been taken seriously and at his own valuation by a considerable section not merely of his contemporaries but of posterity even, and accorded an honoured place in musical history. The moral of this would seem to be that there are absolutely no limits to what can be achieved through sheer brazen impudence and effrontery. At most it may be conceded that a few numbers of his *Nuove Musiche* possess a certain delicacy of outline and a vague insipid charm which might still be capable of faintly stirring our languid interest, but that is about all ; it is only necessary to confront them with the work of his great contemporary John Dowland to realize their extreme narrowness of range and poverty of both invention and execution. As for such works as the *Euridice* of Peri, and the *Rappresentazione del animo e del corpo* of Cavalieri, their musical interest is so slight as to be virtually non-existent, apart from a very occasional phrase of expressive declamation—they are mere ἡδύσματα of literature, in fact. The latter in particular is one of the dullest and most helplessly incompetent works ever written.

Most musical critics and historians, while disposed to admit the intrinsic aesthetic insignificance of the achievement of Caccini and his colleagues, claim that it was nevertheless of great historical importance, constituting a wholly new departure in music which was eventually to give rise, in the hands of subsequent composers, to important results ; and that in consequence the innovators should at least be given the credit for having made such developments possible. Indeed, such great historical significance has been assigned to the experiment of the Florentines that it has become customary to divide the history of music into two distinct sections at the year 1600— which coincides roughly with the commencement of their activities—and to regard all music lying on one side of this date as " ancient ", and all that lies on the other side as " modern ".

At first sight this division might seem to be largely justified, for the superficial differences between the music of the sixteenth century and that of the seventeenth are so striking as to be readily apparent even to the most casual and uninitiate eye. Nevertheless, when we come to enquire more closely into the matter we discover firstly, that the hard and fast line which has been drawn between the two periods is exceedingly arbitrary, and that in so far as it is justified it is no more due to the Florentines than to any other composers of the time ; secondly, that the innovations and revolutionary changes popularly ascribed to them are more apparent than real, and that inasmuch as they can be said to constitute a new departure they were not followed up by their successors to anything like the extent that has generally been supposed.

For example, in their creation of the form of entertainment known as opera, which is probably the most important aspect of their activities, they were by no means without precedents. As we have already seen in the first chapter, a form of sacred opera or oratorio was extensively cultivated in the Middle Ages, and the *Sacre Rappresentazioni* of the late fifteenth and early sixteenth centuries were nothing but religious music-dramas in embryo. Similarly their invention of the method of declamatory singing called recitative, which constitutes the only important difference between their opera and a work such as the *Orfeo* of Poliziano, in which music, both vocal and orchestral —not merely incidental—played a large part, is little more than an adaptation to secular and dramatic purposes of the methods employed in Gregorian chant and psalmodic intonation. Even in this, however, they were by no means alone, and were anticipated by several of the madrigalists, notably Gesualdo and Vecchi, in whose works dramatically expressive passages in a declamatory style frequently occur ; and in the *Sacrifizio* of Alfonso della Viola, performed in Florence in the year 1554, the whole text was set to music, and a kind of recitative employed.

I

Secondly, we have already seen enough in preceding chapters to know that the modern tonal system or major scale, which is commonly represented to have been first consciously and systematically cultivated by the Florentines in place of the modes, can be traced back to the earliest times of which we have any record ; indeed, many of the melodies of the Troubadours and minstrels, many even of the church sequences, are very much more definitely tonal in feeling than the music of Peri and Caccini.   And even if the instrumental accompaniments of the Troubadours consisted merely in a doubling of the melody in unison, which is extremely improbable, there is abundant literary evidence to show that a form of solo song with harmonic accompaniment existed long before Caccini wrote his *Nuove Musiche*.   For example Castiglione, in his celebrated work, *Il Cortegiano*, written about the beginning of the sixteenth century, expressly indicated his preference for accompanied solo song over choral music, and statements made by very much earlier writers such as Boccaccio, leave no room for doubt that the *cantori a liuto* were a definitely recognized class of musicians, and that solo singing was probably always much more popular and more extensively cultivated, in Italy at least, than choral singing—which is only what one would naturally expect.   In any case, the songs of the Spaniard Luis Milan, with lute accompaniment, date back to 1536 and, as Gevaert rightly says, " l'œuvre de Milan . . . ne peut représenter à nos yeux le début d'un genre d'art, mais son efflorescence.   Elle implique une tradition technique déjà solidement établie, et suppose consequemment une succession d'artistes habiles remontant à plusieurs générations ".   In short, we have made the mistake of taking Caccini at his own valuation when he called his solo songs with instrumental accompaniment the *Nuove Musiche*.   There is nothing new about them whatsoever.

Similarly there is now ample evidence at our disposal to show that the system of notation called the figured bass—by means of which only the upper part, whether for voice or instrument. and the bass part, were written out in full, the rest being filled in by the accompanying player in accordance with certain numerical indications written in under the notes—was not actually invented by the Florentines, as has generally been supposed, but was only a development and extension of a pre-existing practice. As we have already had occasion to observe, it was customary during the sixteenth century and even earlier, to write music indifferently for performance by voices or instruments, or for some kind of arrangement or combination of both. The rôle of the organ or *cembalo* in such cases was, if possible, to double the whole of the parts as written by the composer ; if, however, the number of parts or their intricacy in crossing rendered this impracticable or undesirable—quite apart from the time and labour involved in the preparation of the necessary full score—it was usual for the player either merely to support the voices by playing blocks of chords, or to improvise counterpoints and figurations of his own which were better adapted to the potentialities and limitations of his instrument. For this purpose he was often provided with a bass part upon which he constructed this *contrappunto alla mente*, as it was called. So well-recognized and established a procedure was this that in Venice during the sixteenth century competitors for the post of organist at St. Mark's had to satisfy the examiners with regard to their ability in this improvising a polyphonic texture on a given part. A manuscript copy of a work of Alessandro Striggio is still extant which contains a part for the organ consisting of the bass only, and if other tangible evidence showing the popularity of this procedure is wanting, the explanation is to be found in the fact that such a bass part would only be rapidly written out as a makeshift, and thrown away when it was no longer required. In a treatise on organ-playing, however, written by a Spaniard called Diego Ortiz, in 1553, pieces for viol and *cembalo* are given in which only the bass of the latter instrument is provided, leaving the rest of the accompaniment to be filled in by the executant. The fact that the writer makes no suggestion that this was a novel or in any way unusual proceeding leads one to suppose that it was, on the contrary a familiar and well-established practice. This in itself leads one to question whether the monodic art of the early Florentine school of the fourteenth century, also consisting of a voice-part and an instrumental bass, was not similarly interpreted. As Riemann says *à propos* of a work of Giovanni da Florentia, a member of that school, " es wäre keine verlorene Mühe, den Satz, wie er da ist, als eine Generalbassnotierung zu behandeln, und entsprechend der 300 Jahre späteren Praxis zu ergänzen

—er konnte sich getrost neben den *Nuove Musiche* des 17 Jahrhundert sehen lassen ", and the same idea has occurred to other distinguished critics, amongst them M. Romain Rolland. Conjecture apart, however, there are certain resemblances between the so-called *Nuove Musiche* of Caccini and the *Ars Nova* of the early Florentine school which are too striking to be dismissed as mere coincidences ; indeed, the flowing *melismata* and *fioriture* of the one are frequently almost indistinguishable from those of the other.   The highly significant fact, too, that Florence is the one great artistic centre in Italy where the Flemish choral technique never took root, and where no great contrapuntal school ever came into existence, is in itself strong circumstantial evidence in favour of the assumption that Florence—as we should naturally expect from the stronghold of the Renaissance impulse in all the arts—was always hostile to the foreign, Gothic, choral art ; and that her ancient monodic tradition, dating at least as far back as the fourteenth century, never really died out, but continued to exist in some form or another throughout the centuries of Flemish domination elsewhere.   However that may be, enough has been said to show that the figured bass of the Florentines was only an adaptation of a familiar and wide-spread practice, rendered less improvisatory and more precise by the addition of figures indicating the constituent notes of each chord.

Finally, the whole idea, sedulously fostered by musical historians, that a harmonic or vertical mode of thought only came into existence about the beginning of the seventeenth century, that before then music was exclusively conceived as a combination of separate parts viewed horizontally, is so demonstrably ridiculous and so contrary to all established facts that it is difficult to understand how or why it ever originated.   Leaving all conjecture aside, there are innumerable passages in even the most severely contrapuntal compositions of the Flemish masters that consist of mere successions of blocks of chords which are as harmonic in feeling and in style as anything in modern music.   It is equally false to assume that counterpoint died out in any way or was superseded by harmony as a result of the activities of the Florentines and their immediate successors.   On the contrary, it was precisely in the seventeenth century that the most extravagant contrapuntal excesses took place, far beyond anything conceived or even dreamt of by the Netherlanders in their wildest moments.   As an example of this it is only necessary to mention here—we shall return to the subject later—the twenty-part canons of Pierfrancesco Valentini, and the so-called *Canone nel nodo di Salamone* of the same composer, for no fewer than ninety-six voices.   Performances such as these, so far from being exceptional, were frequent and indeed highly characteristic of the age.

Similarly, it is quite untrue that music suddenly becomes secularized about the year 1600, as we are invariably told in text-books.   A secular tradition, as we have already had occasion to observe, existed side by side with the church tradition from the earliest times, and sacred music continued to engage the active attention of almost every eminent composer of the seventeenth century from Monteverdi to Scarlatti.   This important side of their activities, however, has always been consistently ignored by musical historians in the same way that the secular music of earlier times is consistently ignored by them, in order to justify their preconceived ideas, and to sanction the division of the history of music into two sharply contrasted sections at the year 1600. And if it may be conceded that on the whole sacred music seems to be more important than secular before that date, and that after it the balance seems to incline in the opposite direction, it is probably only because more of the latter was written down, published, and otherwise preserved, instead of being merely improvised or handed down orally.   In fact, the whole gradual process of the secularization of music, as conceived in musical history books, probably consists to a great extent merely in the development and more frequent utilization of notation by secular composers.   To suppose that the Florentines were in any way responsible for this seeming change of balance is to attribute to them an importance that they do not possess.

And so we see that Peri, Caccini, and their colleagues actually initiated very little.   As Sir Hubert Parry rightly observed in his volume on the music of the seventeenth century in the " Oxford History of Music ", " so far from the *Nuove Musiche* being a kind of spontaneous generation, it was little better than a crude attempt to redistribute and readapt existing artistic means and devices to novel ends ", and even the novelty of these ends, as we have seen, has been greatly exaggerated. Their achievement was almost entirely negative, consisting in the neglect of traditional resources rather than in the invention of new ones ; and the factitious appearance of novelty that their work presents is less the consequence of what they created than of what they destroyed.

And so we see that the art of the Florentines is not only almost entirely devoid of aesthetic beauty or significance, but also that its historical significance has been greatly exaggerated. It is important that this should be recognized, for it is generally maintained that the whole art of the seventeenth century, the whole of modern music even, is essentially the continuation and development of the movement initiated by the Florentines. This is a complete misconception ; their influence on their successors was by no means as deep-seated or as lasting as it has generally been represented to be. In the first place there is already not a vestige or trace of the Renaissance spirit in the *Orfeo* of Monteverdi written (or produced) in 1607. Anything less classic it would be difficult to imagine. Monteverdi was above all the child of his age, and his whole art, with its violent and lurid contrasts of light and shade, its frenzied and hysterical emotion, its restless and exaggerated sensationalism, is essentially the musical equivalent of the " naturalist " painting of Caravaggio and his school. It is true, of course, that some of the technical procedures employed by Monteverdi might have been taken over from his Florentine predecessors, but it is just as likely that he evolved his style and method independently of them. For example, in his third book of madrigals published in 1592 many passages are to be found written in a dramatic and declamatory style which clearly point the way to their logical conclusion in the recitative of *Orfeo*—in itself a vastly different thing from the recitative of Peri and Caccini. In his hands the languid, arid, and expressionless style of declamation cultivated by the Florentines becomes the vehicle of a dramatic intensity and an emotional power which had never before found expression in music, save only here and there perhaps in the madrigals of Gesualdo ; and instead of aiming, in the characteristic words of Caccini, at a " nobile sprezzatura di canto "— noble disdain of song—he invested his voice parts with a degree of linear melodic interest which raises them at times right out of the category of recitative altogether. His recitative, indeed, is generally heightened song rather than heightened speech, an intensification of melody rather than a disdain of it. Similarly, while the Florentines sought to eliminate every trace of independent musical interest from their work, and to reduce music to its old Greek rank of the humble handmaid of the written word, Monteverdi tends rather to treat the text as a mere peg on which to hang his own graphic musical delineations of dramatic situations and human emotions ; and while Doni, the theorist of the Florentine secessionists, laid it down as an axiom that " the smaller the number of instruments employed the less defective will be the harmonies (*concenti*) " Monteverdi brought to the service of his conception of music-drama every artistic resource, both vocal and orchestral, at his disposal. In *Orfeo*, to quote the words of M. Henri Prunières, " by the side of *ritornelli* on strictly metrical lines we find *sinfonie* in homophonic or polyphonic style, *toccate*, *ricercari*, *morisques*. By the side of dramatic recitatives we find aria recitatives, strophic airs, *airs mesurés*, choruses in homophonic style or in counterpoint, and ballets played, sung, and danced ". We are here obviously a long way from the dessicated and anæmic art of the Florentines ; indeed, Monteverdi's whole conception of opera is diametrically opposed to their's, and strikingly similar to that recently enunciated by Ferruccio Busoni in his " Entwurf eines Vorwortes zur Partitur des Doktor Faust "—namely, a superform capable of including within itself every conceivable musical form from the simplest song, march or dance, to the most elaborate contrapuntal structure ; affording opportunities for the employment of every means at the musician's disposal, both instrumental and vocal, and for the expression of every state of mind and every mode of thought, both lyrical and dramatic.

Another important difference between Monteverdi and his Florentine predecessors is to be found in the fact that he did not by any means turn his back on the music of the past and confine his attention exclusively to the field of the so-called New Music. Indeed, by far the larger part of his output consists of madrigals, and he also wrote masses in the strictest polyphonic style of the sixteenth century. The fact of the matter is that far too much emphasis has been laid on one side of his activities and far too little on the other, with the result that we have got a wholly wrong conception of him. It is at least indisputable that the intrinsic musical interest of many of his madrigals and of his superb six-part mass *In illo tempore* is equal if not actually superior, to that of his dramatic works and other experiments.

The same remarks apply with even greater cogency to the music of Marco da Gagliano—the most gifted of the immediate followers of the Florentine innovators with the exception of Monteverdi—whose madrigals and other compositions written in the traditional style are immeasurably superior to anything he achieved in the new directions ; and the art of those composers who wholeheartedly espoused the Florentine cause, such as Benedetti, Belli, and Saraceni, is only interesting on account of its harmonic audacity which, however, is quite unmistakably derived, not from Peri, Caccini, and their colleagues—whose harmony is tame and inexpressive to a degree—but from Carlo Gesualdo, prince of Venosa.

For all practical purposes, therefore, we may say that music stepped straight from the Middle Ages into the Counter-Reformation, from Gothic to Baroque. The Renaissance, so far as music was concerned, is only a momentary digression, a mere side-show, having no connection with anything that preceded it or followed it. The *New Music* was an old man's child, posthumous and sickly, for by the time that the Renaissance impulse had spread to music—the artistic citadel of the Christian, Mediæval, Gothic ideals—the movement was already dead, and its forces entirely spent.

CHAPTER IX

Italian Schools of the Seventeenth Century

FROM Florence and Mantua the centre of operatic activity
passed for a time to Rome, where the reaction against the
Florentine tendencies, already adumbrated in the *Orfeo* of
Monteverdi and the *Dafne* of Gagliano, asserts itself with
increasing force and definiteness.   In 1626 Domenico Mazzocchi
produced his *Catena d'Adone*, in which a more polyphonic
style is clearly discernible, particularly in the choral sections,
which are of more frequent occurrence than in the work of
any of his predecessors in the operatic field ; and what he
expressly designates as " il tedio del recitativo " is greatly
alleviated by the introduction of a considerable number of airs.
Mazzocchi, incidentally, also wrote motets, masses, madrigals,
and so forth, in the old polyphonic manner, for which he quite
openly proclaimed his preference, saying that " il più ingegnoso
studio che abbia la musica e quello dei madrigali ".

In this reactionary but essentially wholesome tendency
Mazzocchi was followed by Stefano Landi, whose *Sant' Alessio*
and *La Morte d'Orfeo* both possess a high level of purely
musical interest ; and in the latter work there is a scene in which
Charon takes a glass of water from the Styx and sings a jovial
and quite modern-sounding drinking-song, which is perhaps
the first example of the comic scenes and interludes which
subsequently gave rise to the *opera buffa*, or comic opera.

But the composer of this Roman school who best exemplifies
the reaction against the destructive, anti-musical activities of
the Florentines was Giacomo Carissimi, often called the father
of the oratorio.   Like Mazzocchi and Landi, but to an even
greater degree, he was in secret sympathy with the old polyphonic ideals, to the extent of writing a mass for no fewer than
twelve voices on the old theme so beloved by the Flemish
composers of the fifteenth and sixteenth centuries, called
L'homme armé ".   The choral writing in his oratorios also,
though naturally strongly imbued with the spirit of his time, is

nevertheless always fundamentally traditional in feeling and in style ; and even in those parts of his works in which he employs the Florentine system of figured-bass notation, his basses stand on a very much higher level of interest and reveal a much greater degree of melodic independence than those of any other composer of the early seventeenth century. The distinctive qualities of his music are a pathos and a sweetness which sometimes hover perilously on the verge of sentimentality and effeminacy ; his *Jephtha*, however, perhaps the best of his works —certainly the best-known—possesses considerable vigour and dramatic power.

Another form particularly cultivated by Carissimi was the " cantata a voce sola " with figured-bass accompaniment, consisting of a series of ariosos freely interspersed with passages of declamatory recitative, which rapidly attained a great vogue and popularity about the middle of the century. Luigi Rossi, another composer of the Roman school and a contemporary of Carissimi, also excelled in this *genre* ; his *Gelosia* in particular is one of the most famous early examples of it that have come down to us, and a remarkable instance of the employment of *coloratura* as a means of emotional expression.

In the field of instrumental composition, too, this Roman school is of primary importance. Girolamo Frescobaldi was the greatest organist of his time, and the first of the great line of masters of that instrument which eventually culminated in Bach a century later. Both his subjects and the manner in which they are treated are more pronouncedly instrumental in character than those of any of his predecessors, whose sole resource apart from the traditional choral technique which is the foundation of all organ music, consisted, as we have already had occasion to observe, in the writing of empty, whirling scale-passages and similar ornamental figurations for the most part entirely devoid of musical significance. It should perhaps be mentioned that Frescobaldi, although he was organist of St. Peter's in Rome, and lived, worked, and published his compositions in that city, was a pupil of Luzzasco Luzzaschi, one of the most eminent masters of the school of Ferrara to which reference has been made in a previous chapter, and to this source are no doubt to be ascribed the frequent chromaticisms and other harmonic experiments which are to be found here and there in his works. It must be confessed, however, that in this particular direction Frescobaldi is not conspicuously successful, certainly not at all successful in comparison with Gesualdo or Monteverdi. His genius was essentially diatonic, the natural bent of his mind strongly traditional and averse to innovations which, when they appear in his music, lack spontaneity and inevitability. Their presence would seem to be due to extraneous influence and to the general tendencies of his age rather than to inner conviction or artistic necessity.

In music for the violin also the Roman school was pre-eminent with Arcangelo Corelli, one of the greatest masters of the seventeenth century, and one of the very few amongst them all whose work is still occasionally to be heard at the present time. His style of writing has served as the basis and foundation of all subsequent violin music, and as the unsurpassable standard and model by which it is to be judged. But while his music is conceived in terms of the violin and would undoubtedly lose considerably if transferred to any other medium, its interest is not, as with that of so much writing for the instrument, conditioned by the medium alone, but is a direct consequence of the intrinsic value of his ideas, considered abstractly. Particularly characteristic of his work is a note of majestic dignity and gravity which, however, never degenerates into mere pomposity, as with so many of his contemporaries, and does not exclude a vein of quiet pathos and searching tenderness, as so many of his expressive adagios testify. It should also be mentioned that, apart from his sonatas for solo violin, Corelli is also to be credited, if not with the invention, at least with the first important cultivation of concerto-form.

His more eminent successors in the field of violin music, although some of them belong to a later period and none of them were Romans, can be more conveniently dealt with here than elsewhere, for they certainly belong unmistakably to the tradition established by him. Francesco Maria Veracini's style, in marked contrast to the somewhat stiff and scholastic severity of his forerunner, is distinguished by its debonair grace and elegance, his thought by a greater spontaneity and freedom, and by a vein of impassioned lyricism which is lacking in the tranquil art of Corelli. Francesco Geminiani tends rather in the direction of facile virtuosity, and is apt to overload his melodic lines with ornamentation; an occasional unexpected point of harmonic or modulatory interest, however, redeems his work from the reproach of superficiality. Pietro Locatelli is chiefly interesting for the remarkable degree of elaboration that is sometimes to be encountered in the accompaniments of his concertos ; in his eighth concerto, for example, the six-part, wide-spread, interlacing **arpeggios** constitute a striking anticipation of the complex string figurations in the last scene of Wagner's *Rheingold*. In comparison with the foregoing masters Giuseppe Tartini seems slightly lacking in brilliance and vivacity, and bears a closer spiritual affinity to Corelli than any of the others do. His best and most characteristic work possesses a rugged grandeur and an expressive power that give it a place apart in the literature of the solo violin. His successor, Pietro Nardini, on the other hand, achieves an exceptional purity and suavity of style, a harmonious balance between the conflicting claims of the musical thought and the artistic medium, which is only made possible by the deliberate avoidance of both the heights of virtuosity and the depths of expression.

Finally it should not be overlooked that in church music the old Roman polyphonic tradition still reigned supreme during the first part of the seventeenth century, and produced in the person of Gregorio Allegri one of its greatest masters, second only to Palestrina himself. It is interesting to note that he came of the same family as the painter Antonio Allegri, better known as Correggio, and that the same ripe, mellow beauty of contour, and the same warm, harmonious suavity of tone-colour are to be found in the art of both. The similarity is all the more interesting and remarkable because Allegri would seem to stand in very much the same relation to the great polyphonists of the preceding age as that in which Correggio stands to the great painters of the Italian Renaissance.

Another eminent master of the strict *a cappella* style of composition during this period was Francesco Foggia, whose work still maintains a place in the repertoire of the Catholic church, and Rome also produced a flourishing new school of church music, based to a certain extent on that of the Venetians, but possessing certain definite characteristics of its own. Its most noteworthy feature consists in the employment of a vast number of voices, and sometimes of instruments as well, beyond anything of which even Gabrieli had dreamt ; resulting in a massive, Baroque grandeur and brilliance which is the exact musical counterpart of the great colonnades of Bernini in the Piazza di San Pietro, the fantastic ceiling-paintings of Pozzo in S. Ignazio, and the innumerable sumptuous church façades and interiors of Sistine Rome. The greatest masters of this school were Antonio Maria Abbatini, who habitually wrote motets for as many as twelve, sixteen, twenty-four, and even forty-eight voices, and Orazio Benevoli who, amongst other works of gigantic proportions, wrote a mass which, in its enormous vocal and orchestral demands, has no parallel in all music save the great *Requiem* of Berlioz. The bare enumeration of the forces necessary for its execution would occupy at least half a page ; it is sufficient to say here that the score consists of over fifty staves.

Such achievements as these are apt to raise doubts in one's mind as to whether we have not so far formed a totally wrong conception of the history of music in the seventeenth century. It is at least certain that such works, whatever their æsthetic value may be, great or small, are historically much more important and more characteristic of the period, far more the kind of thing we should naturally expect from the age of Bernini, Giordano, Pozzo, Maderna, Fantini, Marini, Churriguera, and all the other literary and artistic *fantaisistes* of the Baroque period, than the thin, arid recitatives with figured bass on which the attention of musical historians has been hitherto hypnotically concentrated to the exclusion of almost everything else.

By the middle of the century opera had practically ceased to be a court spectacle in Italy and had become a popular form of entertainment, particularly in the North ; in Venice alone, for example, towards the end of the century there are said to have been no fewer than seventeen opera-houses of which at least eight were open at the same time. The inevitable consequence of this enormous vogue and popularity was that a more immediately attractive style of composition came into existence. The dreary desert stretches of recitative, which were the most conspicuous feature of the earliest operas, continually tend to decrease both in number and in size ; they are never permitted to last long enough for the public to weary of them, but are generally broken up into sections of smaller extent and interspersed with flowering oases of pure melody. Similarly, the choral element which had begun to play an important part in the operas of the Roman school, again tends to drop out and frequently disappears altogether, while the comic scenes become more frequent and important.

The leader of this new development, which was centred in Venice, was Ercole Cavalli, a composer of immense fertility (he is said to have written no fewer than sixty operas of which practically all survive in manuscript only), and the sole figure in the early history of opera whose gifts can be fitly compared, and not by any means to his disadvantage, with those of his great predecessor Monteverdi. He may not possess the same power as the latter of depicting dramatic situations and events, but he has a greater gift for characterization; and while Monteverdi excels in expressing the states of mind, and the abstract emotions experienced by the protagonists—fear, hope, love, hate, joy, sorrow, and so forth—Cavalli is more successful in the delineation of types and individuals. In fact it might well be claimed for him that he is the first portrait-painter and psychologist in music. For example, his frequent mezzo-soprano arias, written in the characteristically Venetian 6/4 and 3/2 barcarolle rhythms, suggest vividly a definite type of Venetian woman, such as Titian and Giorgione loved to paint, which may still be seen to-day in the narrow winding *calli* of the city of the lagoons. On the other hand it is certainly true that he does not possess anything like Monteverdi's sheer genius, his power and originality of conception, his superb daring of execution, his nervous force and almost demoniac intensity; but he almost certainly possesses an infinitely wider range of melodic invention, a greater ease and spontaneity of thought, and a more supple and polished technique. While Monteverdi is always scrupulously attentive to the meaning and proper accentuation of the text, Cavalli does not scruple to repeat words and phrases when it suits his musical purposes; in short he may be inferior to his predecessor as a dramatist, but his purely musical gifts are possibly greater. It is, moreover, worthy of note that the influence of the younger master is distinctly traceable in Monteverdi's later works for the stage, especially in the *Incoronazione di Poppœa*, by far his greatest opera, written for a Venetian theatre.

The second great master of the Venetian operatic school, Marc'Antonio Cesti, is in many respects the opposite of Cavalli. His greatest strength lies in a vein of tender and passionate melancholy, and he lacks entirely the robust vigour and clear-cut outlines of the latter, to whom he bears much the same relation as Bellini does to Rossini in later times. In Cavalli's work the balance between aria and recitative is more or less equal ; in that of Cesti the arias definitely predominate in number, length, and significance. In the operas of the former the musical interest generally coincides with the dramatic interest ; in those of the latter the situation is unfolded in somewhat dry and perfunctory recitative, and the musical development reserved for moments of dramatic repose. In fact he continually tends to sacrifice dramatic to lyrical expressiveness and, as one would naturally expect from a pupil of Carissimi, one finds in his work, to a far greater extent than in that of Cavalli, an attempt to effect a compromise between the conflicting claims of monody and polyphony. It should also be mentioned that while Cavalli was almost exclusively a composer of operas, a considerable part of Cesti's output consists of cantatas, some of which, paradoxically enough, give the impression of being more dramatic in conception than his operas.

The third master of the Venetian school of the seventeenth century was Giovanni Legrenzi. Very little of his work is accessible, unfortunately—even less than of Cesti—but from the little we know of it we can say that his most noteworthy characteristic would seem to reside in a more definite pre-occupation with the instrumental side of opera than is to be found in the work of any of his predecessors, with the sole exception of Monteverdi. By this time, however, the orchestral balance had entirely shifted. The large orchestra employed by Monteverdi in *Orfeo*, remarkable though it is, represents the last of the old order, the consummation of the sixteenth century tradition of instrumentation rather than the beginning of the new, as it has generally supposed to have been. In *Orfeo* the principal rôle was taken by the plucked instruments —lutes, *chitarroni*, *teorbi*, and the like—while the strings and wind instruments played a subsidiary part. In the operas of the Venetian school, however, the plucked instruments tend to disappear altogether, and the main weight of the accompaniment is henceforth confined to the strings. In this gradual process of the standardization of the modern orchestra, with the strings building the core and nucleus of the *ensemble*, Legrenzi played an important part. So far as the general qualities of his art are concerned, he is distinguished by the gaiety and vivacity of his style and his technical dexterity. As a melodist, however, he is decidedly shortwinded by the side of Cesti, and if the latter may be said to bear a distinct resemblance to Bellini, and Cavalli to Rossini, Legrenzi might justly be called the Donizetti of the seventeenth century.

While the foregoing Venetian masters are essentially secular and primarily dramatic composers, Antonio Lotti, a pupil of Legrenzi, was more important as a composer of sacred music, despite the fact that he wrote a large number of operas and other secular works. His four-part *Miserere* in D minor, a work of great power and expressiveness, may still be heard occasionally to-day, and is rightly regarded as one of the finest specimens of the *a cappella* style of composition belonging to the post-Palestrina age.   Antonio Caldara, also a pupil of Legrenzi, is one of the greatest figures of the first part of the eighteenth century, and one of the most unjustly neglected in the whole history of music.[1]   He was a composer of immense fertility, his output consisting of no fewer than seventy operas, thirty oratorios, as many masses, and a vast quantity of other works including violin sonatas, cantatas, madrigals, and church music of every description. Like Lotti, however, he was primarily a church composer, and his best works in this sphere are the equal of those of any of his contemporaries. His *Stabat Mater* and *Missa Dolorosa* in particular, are distinguished by a great intensity of feeling and harmonic power, while his sixteen-part unaccompanied *Crucifixus* is one of the most astonishing *tours de force* of contrapuntal art in existence, besides being a work of great expressive beauty.

Another great Venetian master of the same period as Caldara, namely Benedetto Marcello, is chiefly celebrated for his settings of the Psalms.   Before writing them he is said to have sought the company of Jews in order to learn from them the intonations of the synagogue music, and may therefore claim to be regarded as the first composer to make conscious employment of local colour. Another innovation for which he was responsible is the introduction of 5/4 rhythm in the final aria of his cantata *Senza gran pena*. Of greater artistic significance than such experiments, however, is the rare beauty which he achieved in his best works, the most noteworthy characteristic of which

---

[1]   He is not even mentioned in the most recent Edition of Grove's Dictionary of Music and Musicians.

consists in his long, flowing, melodic lines, of a strength and suppleness like that of finest Toledo steel.   A superb example of his art is to be found in the cantata *Didone*, a work of Baroque grandeur and nobility reminding one of the splendid and sumptuous art of his great contemporary and countryman Tiepolo, the painter.

Strongly contrasted with the foregoing masters is Baldassare Galuppi, a versatile composer whose greatest strength, however lay in the direction of comic opera—a *genre* which he may almost be said to have invented, and in which he excelled all composers of his time by virtue of his possession of an inexhaustible flow of melodic invention, and a comic verve and vivacity of treatment which still retain their charm to the present day.   Finally Antonio Vivaldi, known principally on account of his many violin sonatas and concertos, may be said to complete the list of the great masters of the second Venetian school.   No other tribute to the grace and elegance of his style is necessary than to mention the fact that Bach thought it worth while to take the trouble of arranging and adapting a large number of his concertos for different combinations of instruments, and that the influence of Vivaldi on Bach's style is always strongly in evidence, especially in the works of the Cöthen period.   The orchestration of his concertos is particularly remarkable for its fulness, and for the fine sense of differentiation of instrumental characteristics and capacities which it exhibits.

Towards the end of the seventeenth century, however, the main centre of musical activity in Italy had shifted from Venice to Naples, where an important school had arisen of which the first noteworthy figure was Francesco Provenzale. Very little is known of his work—indeed, previous to M. Romain Rolland's researches nothing was known of it at all—yet this little is nevertheless sufficient to reveal the existence of definite features, particularly a vein of characteristically warm, southern melody, and a strain of sombre and passionate intensity, that clearly differentiate it from the work of his contemporaries in other parts of Italy. Alessandro Stradella, on the other hand, gives the impression of being a transition figure, and a connecting link between the Venetian and Neapolitan schools.   If his name is more familiar to us than that of most of his colleagues during this most neglected of all periods of musical history it is not at all on account of his work, practically all of which lies scattered in manuscript in various libraries throughout Italy, but on account of the fact that he was murdered under more than usually romantic circumstances, and has consequently enjoyed the somewhat dubious distinction of having been made the hero both of an opera by one Flotow, which once had a considerable vogue, and of a novel by the late Marion Crawford. Nevertheless, even the few fragments of his works which have been printed would be sufficient to assure him a prominent place in musical history even if he had died quietly in his bed. One of his operas called *Il Trespolo Tutore*, is one of the first genuine comic operas ever written and probably is the first to contain an example of the *basso buffo* type of part which was to remain such a prominent feature of Italian comic opera up to the time of Rossini and Donizetti, and has recently received a new lease of life in the *Rosenkavalier* of Strauss. The humorous characterization of the part is certainly far in advance of anything else of the same kind at the time when it was written. In another opera of more serious type, *Floridoro*, he shows himself to possess a vein of rich impassioned melody similar to that of Cesti, but less effeminate and languid, and an occasional *volkstümlich* freshness and charm which are like a breath of fresh air after the hot and somewhat vitiated theatrical atmosphere of Venetian opera. His oratorio, too, *S. Giovanni Battista*, is perhaps the greatest landmark in the form between Carissimi and Handel. The texture of his accompanying parts and the invention displayed in his basses in particular, are remarkable, while his treatment of recitative is superior to that of the later Venetians such as Cesti and Legrenzi. In his music the increasing dominance of instrumental conceptions begins to make itself felt in the elaborate figurations and occasional large leaps which are to be found in his voice parts—a tendency which reaches an extreme stage of development with Bach and Marcello—and the *da capo* form of aria (A, B, A), which was to play such a large part in Neapolitan opera, becomes noticeable in his work for the first time, though isolated examples of its employment can no doubt be encountered elsewhere before him.

But it is in the music of Alessandro Scarlatti that the Neapolitan school, and indeed all the Italian schools of the seventeenth century, attain their highest point. Scarlatti is one of the great stylists of music and is excelled in this direction, if at all, by Mozart alone. Not a phrase of his mature work could possibly be improved upon ; not a bar is there that is not faultlessly wrought and finely polished until it glitters like a jewel. One finds, too, in his best work a power of building and moulding a long, extended melodic line into a perfect symmetry and proportion which is probably unequalled by any composer save Bach—for example, the aria *Farfalla*, from his cantata *La Pazzia*, has a melody sixteen bars long which is a perfect organism, and not merely a succession of four phrases of four bars each. At the same time he shares with the great German master the faculty for inventing short, pregnant motives and figures of accompaniment from which a whole long movement evolves, and many of his discoveries in this direction became the stock-in-trade of succeeding generations of composers ; in fact Scarlatti may truly be said to have coined the best part of the musical phraseology of his period, and to have stamped that of it which was already in circulation with his image and superscription. It is certainly true that in his hands and in those of his successors the dramatic side of opera suffers, largely as a result of his systematic employment of the *da capo* form of aria, which inevitably inhibits dramatic vitality and tends to reduce opera to the level of a concert ; but it is certainly not true, as has sometimes been said, that his art is inhuman and lacking in emotional appeal. For example the aria *Son pur*, from the cantata *Dove alfin*, has a grandeur and a poignance which are truly remarkable, and innumerable similar instances are to be found scattered in profusion throughout the whole of his vast output.

Scarlatti is one of the most important names in musical history, yet none of his work survives to-day, either in the opera-house or in the concert-hall. The opposite is true of his son Domenico, a figure of infinitely smaller proportions and artistic significance, whose harpsichord sonatas, nevertheless, are among the few works of the period, apart from Bach and Handel, that still retain a place in the modern concert repertoire. The great merit of these pieces lies in the fact that while they are first and foremost pianistic, they are pianistic in the best sense of the word—not mere idle displays of virtuosity, but works in which the substance of the musical thought is never devoid of intrinsic musical interest, apart from the medium.

In spirit, it may be mentioned, Domenico Scarlatti belongs rather to the succeeding age, to what we may call the Rococo rather than to the Baroque period. The grandiose, florid, and luxurious lines of the elder Scarlatti and his contemporaries tend to give place in his work to a more precise, delicate, miniaturist, epigrammatic style, in which one may seek in vain for any trace of human sensibility or emotion. Indeed, his dazzling brilliance and grace seem at times almost excessive ; one comes to long for a sombre, shadowy passage as one longs for a cloud to come and veil, if only for a brief moment, the hard, white glare of Italian summer skies. The very perfection of his art is largely the outcome of his inveterate limitations, and in this he strongly resembles Chopin, who bears much the same relation to his age that Domenico Scarlatti bears to his.

Another eminent master of the Neapolitan school is Leonardo Leo, perhaps the most richly gifted and versatile of all Alessandro Scarlatti's immediate successors. His output consists of some forty operas, both serious and comic, a vast quantity of sacred works, both *a cappella* and with orchestral accompaniment, and a considerable amount of music for organ, harpsichord, and various instrumental combinations. Unfortunately, apart from some of the church music, practically the whole of his work, like that of so many composers of the period, remains in manuscript ; and it is therefore impossible for anyone except a specialist in the period to form any definite first-hand judgment concerning it. The superb *Miserere* and *Dixit Dominus*, however, which are well-known, are sufficient in themselves to justify us in regarding Leo as one of the greatest masters of the Baroque style of church music in Italy.

His contemporary Francesco Durante is conspicuous among Neapolitan composers in his complete avoidance of the theatre. His music for the church is distinguished by its scholastic ingenuity, and by the noble severity and restraint of its style, while his cantatas and instrumental music frequently reveal a poignant expressiveness and a degree of harmonic audacity (see, for example the *Duetto da camera* " Fiero acerbo ", reprinted in Riemann's *Musikgeschichte in Beispielen*) which are not easily reconcilable with the conventional view of the Neapolitan school, and indeed, of all the Italian schools of the century—namely, that melody was for them the sole consideration to which all other elements of musical style were subordinated.   On the contrary, the work of both Scarlatti and Durante, to mention only two, abounds in harmonic interest, and Leo was among the most learned contrapuntists of the day. The reproach only holds good of the later members of the school such as Leonardo Vinci and Nicola Logroscino, whose activities were mainly confined to the domain of the *opera buffa*.

The fact of the matter is that a long-established prejudice against what we conveniently term Baroque art is responsible for a quite absurd under-estimation of the merits, and an equally disproportionate exaggeration of the defects, of almost all the composers with whom we have been concerned in the present chapter.   The very adjective " Baroque ", like " Gothic " in the eighteenth century and " Impressionistic " in the nine-teenth, was originally a term of reproach ; but while the others have outlived their derogatory associations, Baroque alone still continues to be employed in a disparaging and condemnatory sense.   In other words it is used to denote only the least worthy aspects of seventeenth century art instead of being applied, as it should be, to all the art products, both good and bad alike, of a particular period, which possess certain clearly recognizable and easily definable stylistic qualities in common.   Baroque art, in short, like Gothic, Impressionistic, Romantic, Classic, or any other kind of art, can be good as well as bad ; the painting of El Greco, Rubens, and Tiepolo, the plays of Corneille, Calderon, Racine, the music of Bach and Handel, to mention only a few names at random, are, stylistically considered, no less Baroque than the inferior art to which the use of the term is generally restricted, with derogatory implications which are often quite undeserved.   In fact, precisely the same qualities which we affect to admire in some artists of the period we affect to despise in others who, if not as great, are in many cases worthy of respect and admiration.   The difference between the two categories is more often one of degree, not of kind, than wo are willing to recognize.   For example, there are works of Scarlatti, Marcello, Lotti, Caldara, Leo, Durante, to mention only a few, which might easily pass for works of Bach, and are the equal of any that have been written except by the very greatest masters of all time.   It is to be hoped that the gradual break-down of the prejudice against Baroque art which is to be observed in the best literary and artistic criticism of to-day will in due time communicate itself to music, and result in the rehabilitation of these and many other undeservedly neglected masters—all the more so because it is undoubtedly a fact that it was in music that the Baroque ideals found their most convincing and characteristic expression. The necessity of securing material stability and balance which inhibited the free exercise of fantasy on the part of both architect and sculptor, the necessity of maintaining some semblance of contact with life and actuality incumbent upon both poet and painter, were both alike inoperative where music was concerned. The frequent absurdity of Baroque architecture, painting, sculpture, poetry, and drama, does not reside in the inherent falsity of their artistic ideals *per se* so much as in the fundamental unsuitability of the *media* employed to express them. The medium of sounds, on the other hand, was peculiarly fitted to their expression, if only because in music, which affords no possibility of a direct comparison with reality, there is no absurdity ; and possessing as it does the most disembodied, abstract and non-material medium of all the arts, it is admirably adapted to the realization of the most extravagant fantasies of construction. Consequently, the unbridled exuberance, the heroic vitality, the profusion of ornament, the audacity of conception, which are the hall-marks of all Baroque art, good and bad—these are all qualities that can be given a fuller scope and a more adequate and convincing embodiment in music than in any other art.

Again, we have already seen that music was the art best fitted to interpret the ideals of the early Catholic Church, and it is equally true that it is also the art that was best able to express the Catholic Reaction against the pagan humanism of the Renaissance. Baroque art, whether sacred or secular, is the art-expression of the spirit of the Counter-Reformation, and music is the Baroque art *par excellence*. And the source of inspiration of the whole period, of all its art, literature, and music, was Spain. The Counter-Reformation itself was largely a Spanish creation. Loyola, the founder of the Society of Jesus which played such an overwhelmingly important part in the movement, was a Spaniard, its greatest saints, Theresa and John of the Cross were Spaniards, Spanish cardinals and theologians played the leading rôles in the Council of Trent, Gongora was the central figure in the Baroque movement in literature to which he gave his name, El Greco was its greatest painter, and Churriguera was the completest exemplification of the same tendencies in architecture.   Likewise, the whole spirit of Southern Baroque music was predominantly Spanish, but since Spain, for some unknown reason—perhaps for no reason at all—produced no great musicians of her own after the death of Victoria, it is only natural that the region which gave the most complete and perfect expression to the Baroque ideals in music should be the kingdom of Naples, then a mere province of Spain, ruled from Madrid by a Viceroy, and wholly dominated by Spanish culture and artistic influences.

CHAPTER X

Northern Schools of the Seventeenth and Early Eighteenth Centuries

While these developments were taking place in Italy, the operatic impulse had penetrated into other countries. Cavalli was commissioned to write a work for the Paris stage, and a short time later Giovanni Battista Lulli, a Florentine, took up his residence in the French capital, and speedily succeeded in obtaining a virtual monopoly as purveyor of music to the King of France, Louis XIV, who then occupied the throne. The peculiar conditions prevailing at his court played an important part in deciding the form which French opera was destined to take. At that time all the arts, all forms of activity whatsoever were almost entirely devoted to the glorification of the king and to the gratification of his tastes, sentiments, and desires ; and the music of Lulli, like the architecture of Louvois and the painting of Lebrun, was primarily little more than an instrument of flattery, another artistic medium for the payment of fulsome tributes to the radiant and transcendant virtues of the Roi Soleil. The subject-matter of his operas and ballets was often chosen by the king himself who, although he had no ear for music and an execrable voice, was in the habit of joining in when rhapsodies in his honour, thinly disguised as allegory, were introduced.

It could hardly be expected that great art could possibly arise or flourish under such servile and humiliating conditions ; indeed, the marvel is that Lulli was able to achieve as much as he did. His greatest strength lay in the instrumental sections of his operas, particularly in the overtures which in his hands attained to a much higher stage of development than in Italy. On the other hand he lacks entirely the spontaneous lyrical gift and melodic invention of his Italian contemporaries. In his avoidance of mere sensuous beauty, and in his minute and deferent attention to the exact declamation of the text, he betrays his Florentine origin and his allegiance to his native ideals of music-drama.   Apart from his overtures, however, the musical interest of his work is so slight as to be practically non-existent to-day.

François Couperin, misleadingly termed " le Grand ", has of late years come in for a great deal of uncritical adulation on account of the Chauvinistic attempts on the part of modern French musicians, such as Debussy and Ravel, to show that he is their spiritual ancestor. It may be conceded that his harpsichord pieces show a fine sense of instrumental values and possess a faded, old-world charm and a quaint, rococo gravity, reminding one of china shepherdesses and similar antiques and properties of the period, but it is seldom anything more than boudoir music, of which one speedily tires. A more robust and sympathetic personality is to be found in Jean-Marie Leclair, a composer of violin music which invites and well sustains comparison with that of any of his Italian contemporaries. His work is invariably characterized by originality of thought and remarkable expressive power, and he is considerably in advance of his time, from a technical point of view, by virtue of his extensive and resourceful employment of double-stopping.

In England during the seventeenth century there is only one composer who need concern us here, namely Henry Purcell ; indeed, he is the only Englishman of any period who is accepted as a composer of the first rank by the rest of the world.   In this country, however, the comparatively recent revelation of the splendours of the great Tudor and Stuart schools, which has not yet extended to the Continent, has brought about a considerable reaction against Purcell which has perhaps been allowed to go too far. It is one of the ineradicable vices of musical criticism, to a great extent of all criticism, that it seems unable or unwilling to exalt one great artist save at the expense of another. It may readily be admitted that the standards of musical taste and the artistic ideals in general of Purcell's age stood on a very much lower level than in that of the Elizabethans, and that consequently those of his works that are only the reflection of the ideals and fashions of the period are so manifestly inferior to the similar works of Byrd and his contemporaries as to be almost completely negligible. In others again, side by side with beauties of the highest order, we come upon passages so trivial and empty that it is difficult to understand how they could have been written by the same man.   The fact remains, however, that in those works in which he rises above the standards of his age, he reaches to a level that only the very greatest composers of the century were capable of attaining, and it is by these alone that he should be judged. One of them is his only opera *Dido and Aeneas*, which by itself outweighs in musical significance the entire output of a Lulli, and it must also be held to compare more than favourably with any single production of the Italian schools.   One could easily make up a bouquet of airs and recitatives out of, say, Cavalli's sixty or more operas, which might conceivably put Purcell's solitary effort in the shade, but it is certainly very doubtful, to say the least, whether any single complete work of the Italian master could be worthily placed beside it.   For whatever the merits of the Venetian—and they are great and many—it cannot be denied that the excessive length of his operas effectively precludes the possibility of their successful revival to-day.   *Dido and Aeneas*, on the contrary, largely on account of its comparatively modest dimensions, can, and does, still stand the test of performance under modern conditions, despite the formidable handicap entailed by a weak and foolish libretto.   It is, indeed, perhaps the earliest opera in musical history of which this can truly be said.   Furthermore, finely chiselled and concise though each number of the Venetian, or even the Neapolitan, operas may be, it cannot be denied that they are, considered as wholes, completely formless, and are seldom anything more than interminable strings of arias and recitatives of very similar type ;   whereas *Dido and Aeneas* has definite shape and form, besides possessing greater variety and resource of treatment.   In dramatic power it is excelled by the *Orfeo* of Monteverdi alone among operas of the seventeenth century, while of its intrinsic musical beauty it is impossible to speak too highly ;   alike in melodic, rhythmic, harmonic, and instrumental interest, it successfully challenges comparison with the best work of the period in any form, and in any country.

Purcell's achievement in other directions is of scarcely less importance.   His *Te Deum* and *Ode for St. Cecilia's Day* are amongst the finest choral works with orchestral accompaniment of the pre-Handelian period, and his sonatas for two violins, bass, and harpsichord, in which he modestly declares himself to have only "faithfully endeavoured a just imitation of those of the most famed Italian masters", are so far in advance of their alleged models that it is difficult to believe that they were not composed at least fifty years later than they actually were.

But it is perhaps the hitherto unknown and only recently published *Fantazias* for strings, in three, four, and five parts, that constitute his most interesting and valuable contribution to the literature of chamber-music. As Mr. Warlock justly observes in the preface to his edition of them, "despite their startling originality, the *Fantazias* are essentially in the tradition of the Elizabethan polyphonists"; yet at the same time one is constantly encountering passages and progressions in them that one would have imagined could only have been written by Bach himself, were it not for certain strongly marked idiosyncrasies and mannerisms which could not possibly belong to any composer but Purcell. These works then, apart from their intrinsic beauty, are of great significance in that they strikingly reveal the essential underlying continuity between Gothic and Baroque; between the old polyphonic art of Byrd and Palestrina, and that of Bach and the other great masters of the latter part of the seventeenth and the first half of the eighteenth centuries. The former is sacred, modal, and vocal, that of the latter secular, tonal and instrumental, but fundamentally they are one and the same style. And in the same way that Byrd, although he may be surpassed by other composers of his time in each single aspect of his activities, considered all-round has no rival in the sixteenth century; so Purcell, by virtue of his high achievement in both vocal and instrumental music, in both lyric and dramatic forms, in both sacred and secular traditions, stands out from among all the masters of his age.

It is a remarkable fact that up to the close of the sixteenth century we have witnessed the rise and development of many great schools, Italian, Flemish, English, French, Spanish, and that the one great country in Europe that has so far contributed nothing of importance to the history of music is Germany. It is true that here and there individuals of Teutonic nationality had achieved great eminence, such as Heinrich Isaac, Jacob Gallus (Handl), Leo Hassler, Ludwig Senfl, and others, but they formed no independent, autonomous school. They were only eminent members of foreign schools, Flemish or Venetian, and stylistically indistinguishable from the native members of them.   It is also true that there were certain technical traits in the work of some of the German members of the Flemish school, such as Adam von Fulda, which seemed to foreshadow the possible emergence of a specifically German school— particularly in the tendency occasionally to be met with to write a melody in long notes in the uppermost part with subsidiary, contrapuntal embroideries in the lower voices—but this in itself hardly constitutes sufficient grounds to warrant the discriminating appellation of a German school, and in any case it was not a characteristic that succeeded in maintaining itself for long.   The first composer to succeed in evolving a genuinely and unmistakably Teutonic style in music was Heinrich Schütz, despite the fact that, like his fellow-countrymen Hassler and Gallus, he began his artistic career as a member of the Venetian school, and as the pupil and disciple of Giovanni Gabrieli.   He wrote one opera, *Dafne*, the music of which has entirely disappeared, and madrigals and other choral works in which the influence of both Gabrieli and Monteverdi is paramount ; but his most important works are his oratorios such as *Die Si ben Worte Jesu Christi*, the *Historia der Auferstehung*, and particularly his *Matthaüs Passion*—the direct ancestor of the Passion Music of Bach—from all of which the former traces of Italian influences are eliminated.

The most striking characteristic of Schütz's mature art lies in its expressive depth, of a kind wholly new to music, and recognizably German.   The expressiveness of the great Italian masters is always essentially objective, a rendering into tone of emotions only intellectually or imaginatively experienced ; in the music of Schütz, on the contrary, and in that of all typically German composers, one feels that the emotions have been inwardly and subjectively experienced by the composer himself.   It is interesting to speculate to what extent this quality of self-revelation and self-confession, which only comes into music—and into the other arts as well—after the Reformation, and is only to be encountered in the art of those countries which embraced the Lutheran or Calvinistic creeds, is to be attributed to the discontinuation of the Catholic practice of confession, and to the consequent emergence in art of emotions denied their habitual outlet or *catharsis*.

In the art of Schütz every means of securing musical interest is ruthlessly sacrificed to his expressive purpose, with the result that he attains to a stark, elemental simplicity and a mystical grandeur and solemnity that are quite unlike anything else, and are among the most affecting things in all music. He also possesses a highly personal harmonic style, of which the distinguishing mark is a strong predilection for chords containing the interval of the diminished fourth, which frequently imparts a strangely poignant quality to his writing. It is incidentally interesting to note that Schütz became deaf in his old age, and that it is therefore probably no mere coincidence that we should encounter in his later work the same mysterious, inner radiance, the same abstract, disembodied quality of thought, the same note of wistful and tender resignation, that we find in the later work of Beethoven.

Schütz's one opera, as we have already said, has disappeared, and it was not for a long time, namely, towards the end of the century, that German opera came into being ; and in the same way that Lulli brought the operatic form from Italy to France, so Agostino Steffani, a Venetian, transplanted the seed to Hamburg. There was naturally, however, nothing specifically German about his art, and it was left to his pupil and successor Reinhard Keiser to evolve a style which, though still recognizably Italian in essentials, gradually came to acquire in his hands certain definitely national characteristics. These show themselves more particularly on the instrumental side of his compositions, to which he pays a greater degree of attention than any of his Italian colleagues ; indeed, the variety and resourcefulness of his scoring are quite remarkable considering the time at which he wrote. In his *Octavia*, for example, we find an aria accompanied by four bassoons, and in his *Orpheus* a scene in which strings and oboe are employed is followed by one demanding no fewer than five flutes. He also anticipates Meyerbeer by a century and a half in accompanying an aria with a single *obbligato* instrument, and he makes a more extensive use of horns, trumpets, and drums than any of his contemporaries. At the same time Keiser possesses a remarkable talent for musical characterization, especially of a comic order, and a spontaneity of melodic invention unsurpassed even by Cavalli, Scarlatti, or any other composer of this exceptionally prolific age. He is said to have written no fewer than one hundred and sixteen operas, to say nothing of a considerable quantity of miscellaneous works as well ; and in the latter part of his life hardly a year passed without the appearance of three, four, and sometimes even five new operas from his pen, all distinguished as much by their brilliance and refinement of workmanship as by their dramatic felicity and inexhaustible wealth of musical ideas.

Johann Jacob Froberger, the first great German composer of key-board music, was a pupil of Frescobaldi, from whose art he succeeded in distilling a distinctively German style in the same way that Schütz had from that of his master Gabrieli. His organ music is chiefly remarkable for the fine understanding it exhibits of the capacities and limitations of the instrument, and for a considerable advance in formal cohesion compared with the work of his predecessors in this field of composition. This is particularly exemplified in his fondness for subjecting a melody to various rhythmical variations and distortions in the course of a movement, by means of which he obtains both unity of thematic material and variety of treatment at the same time —a device already tentatively employed by Frescobaldi and Sweelinck, and anticipating by nearly two centuries Liszt's idea of theme-transformation as found in his symphonic poems. If in style generally his organ music shows him to be a follower of Frescobaldi, his clavier compositions, on the other hand, show him in the rôle of an innovator and a pioneer. If not actually the inventor of the *Suite*, consisting of a series of dance-movements such as the *allemande. courante, sarabande*, and *gigue*, he was nevertheless the first to raise it to a high standard of artistic excellence, and even occasionally to make it the vehicle for the expression of profound emotions. Examples of this are to be found in the lament for the death of Ferdinand IV in the form of an *allemande*—a piece strangely anticipatory of the slow movement of the *Eroica Symphony* of Beethoven—and in the very similar *Tombeau fait à Paris sur la mort de M. Blancheroche*, also a piece of great beauty and expressiveness.

Lacking something of Froberger's rugged power and depth of feeling, Johann Pachelbel, his greatest immediate successor, excels by virtue of his remarkable command of contrapuntal resource, and by the easy brilliance and smooth grace of his style. He is particularly noteworthy for his cultivation of the choral prelude, a form consisting in a kind of musical disquisition on an old choral melody, as a sermon is based upon a Bible text, which attained a great vogue in Germany in the course of the seventeenth century. The origin of these choral melodies, which play as important a rôle in Protestant church music as Gregorian chant plays in that of the Catholic church, is briefly as follows. In the early days of the Christian cult, it was customary for the congregation to take an active part in the singing of the liturgy, and it was not until the Gregorian reform was carried through in the sixth and seventh centuries that the musical part of the service was exclusively confided to the clergy. In Germany, however, this innovation was not established in its entirety, and the congregation still continued to take part occasionally in the service. This practice gave rise to the presence of verses in the vulgar tongue, largely translations of the original Latin texts, which were interpolated here and there ; with the result that, when the Reformation came, a nucleus of German sacred lyric already existed to which Luther and his co-workers composed and adapted music which was sometimes a fragment or reminiscence of Gregorian chant, sometimes a popular melody, sometimes a blend of both. It was these melodies, then, that served as the basis of the choral prelude, and made their influence felt throughout the whole field of Protestant church music, even when they are not actually present.

Pachelbel's greatest successor in the direction of the choral prelude was Dietrich Buxtehude, a Danish composer, by whom the form was raised to an unexampled pitch of elaboration, and enriched with every conceivable device of contrapuntal and decorative resource at his disposal. In his hands, indeed, the theme is frequently so varied and adorned with arabesques as to become totally unrecognizable, and even when presented textually it is often hidden from sight altogether under the exuberant welter of ornamentation with which it is surrounded, in the same way that in the sermons of the great divines the scriptural text serves only as a point of departure for a disquisition upon the nature of the universe. Nevertheless, it is Baroque music in the grand style at its very best. He shone also in other forms, however, such as the *passacaglia*, *chaconne*, *fugue*, and *prelude*, and in some of his work he wrote in a clearer and more sober homophonic style, showing himself to be as great a master of harmonic as of contrapuntal writing.

Finally, all these various tendencies and artistic manifestations which we have been considering in this chapter and in the last—in other words, the whole of the music of the seventeenth century—are carried to their logical conclusion and highest point of perfection by two great German masters, Johann Sebastian Bach and George Frederick Handel, whose names are so indissolubly interconnected with each other that it is almost impossible to follow any other method in attempting to appraise their achievement than that of Plutarch in his Parallel Lives ; no other can so well bring out the differences as well as the resemblances between them, or better reveal the essential and characteristic qualities in the art of each. It need hardly be said, of course, that to treat them both adequately would require at least a whole volume as large as the present one, and that consequently it is only possible to indicate here a few of their more salient features.

It is a remarkable fact which is of great symbolic significance that these two masters, born in the same country and in precisely the same year, never met each other in actual life, for the same phenomenon is to be observed in their work. It is as if they had agreed, like two conquerors, to share the whole world of music between them, and by mutual consent never to intrude on each other's domain ; it is as if a sharp line of demarcation had been established between their respective spheres of influence by the Spirit of Music, like that drawn by Pope Alexander VI, allotting one half of the New World to Spain and the other half to Portugal.

The sovereignty of Handel extended over the whole range of dramatic music, both opera and oratorio ; Bach, on the other hand, wrote no opera and, strictly speaking, no oratorio, for his Passion Music belongs to an entirely different tradition. In the work of the former the southern Italian forms are consummated, his operas and cantatas being a culminating point of the Neapolitan school of his time, while his oratorios and concertos are the logical development and extension of those of Carissimi and Corelli respectively. The work of Bach, on the contrary, is more specifically German, and fundamentally based upon the chorale and on the organ tradition of Pachelbel and Buxtehude ; in so far as an Italian influence is to be perceived in his art, it is that of the north, and of Venice in particular, both directly through Lotti and Vivaldi, and indirectly through Schütz and Sweelinck.   The music of Handel, even his instrumental work, is predominantly vocal in both line and colour ; that of Bach, even his vocal writing, is definitely instrumental in character.   Even at the point where their vast territories seem to merge and intersect, namely, in the musical interpretation of Holy Scripture and its truths, a clear-cut line of demarcation can still be perceived between the two.   The oratorios of Handel, with the single exception of the *Messiah*—in which, however, the personality of Christ is only touched upon in the vague, allusive manner of the prophets—deal exclusively with the Old Testament, and conjure up before us vivid presentments of the heroic figures of Judaic antiquity : splendid living portraits in sound of Saul, of Esther, of Judas Maccabaeus, and the rest.   The Passions of Bach, on the other hand, are a musical interpretation not only of the events but of the inner spirit of the New Testament : he recreates in tone the personality and acts of Christ as it had never been done before and never has been done since by any musician, and by very few artists of any kind.

In the fundamental nature of their respective individualities and methods of work they also differ from each other as completely as it is possible for two artists to do.   Handel was a somewhat careless and unequal writer, and if he survives to-day in our concert-rooms practically by virtue of one single work, the *Messiah*, the reason is to be found in the fact that, although almost all his other works are full of the most admirable sections, these are found side by side with others so markedly inferior as to be almost commonplace.   All his works, in fact, with the one notable exception already alluded to, are mere centos—gigantic improvisations, thrown off with effortless rapidity in heedless profusion and pieced together with the utmost nonchalance, in which sublimity and triviality, inspiration and mere hack journeyman's work are strangely intermingled.   Bach on the contrary, despite his equally gigantic output, was evidently a slow and painstaking worker.   He may have actually written his music down with great rapidity, but it is impossible to doubt that each work must nevertheless have been the outcome of a long period of intensely concentrated thought and spiritual gestation.   While Handel's scores are frequently so sketchy and hastily written that it has often been found to be impossible to perform them satisfactorily as they actually stand, without some measure of alteration and adaptation, Bach's works are almost invariably carefully realized and executed, perfectly finished in detail, and can for the most part be performed to-day without the alteration or addition of a single note. In fact we may say that Handel's vast output resembles the ruins of Pompeii, in which an occasional building here and there has miraculously escaped total destruction by the ashes and cinders of oblivion, but that the work of Bach is a musical Herculaneum, hermetically sealed up by the lava of contemporary neglect, which has remained intact throughout the ages, and has only recently been unearthed, to the wonder and admiration of men. Handel to-day is paying the penalty for his instantaneous success, recognition, and popularity, and for the homage of the age for which he wrote ; Bach now, at long last, reaps the reward of writing, not consciously perhaps, for posterity—probably no great artist ever does—but for himself alone, or, what is very much the same thing, *ad majorem Dei gloriam.*

Handel's uncanny faculty of assimilation is perhaps his most striking and noteworthy characteristic. If it were true, which it most assuredly is not, that the greatest artist is he who best and most completely expresses the spirit of his age in forms which he has unquestioningly accepted from his predecessors, then Handel must be accounted the greatest composer who has ever lived. He invented little or nothing ; he is like a vast mirror, reflecting objectively and impersonally the whole of the life and thought of his time, or like a gigantic chameleon reacting to every influence and every artistic environment with which he came into contact—to such an extent, indeed, that he frequently did not scruple to utilize the work of other men as a kind of quarry whence he might draw any material that suited his purpose. In the well-known instance of his *Israel in Egypt*, no fewer than sixteen out of the thirty-nine numbers are built on, or employ, themes and even entire movements of other composers. On account of this Handel has often been reproached with plagiarism, and the charge cannot, of course, be denied or refuted, although admirers and apologists without number have tried to do so. This habit of his, nevertheless, of drawing upon the work of others has undoubtedly been misunderstood to a great extent ; certainly far too much stress, both ethical and artistic, has been laid upon it.   Mr. Shaw, in his *jeu d'esprit*, " The Dark Lady of the Sonnets ", has drawn an amusing picture of Shakespeare jotting down in a notebook phrases culled by him from the conversation of ordinary people, which he eventually made use of in his plays ; and it is probable that Handel's appropriations were of a very similar kind, equally innocent from an ethical standpoint and justifiable from an artistic one.   It is one of the surest signs of a second-rate artist or an amateur to scruple to make use of suggestions made by others if they should happen to answer his purpose. The sole preoccupation of the genuinely disinterested artist should be the work of art, and not his own reputation or *amour propre*, and if he is fortunate enough to find an idea in the work of another artist which will help to make his own work better, or one which is so admirably adapted to his purposes that it would be impossible for him to find anything more suitable himself, he should not allow his æsthetic requirements to be subordinated to any considerations concerning the ethics of property.   It is an interesting fact, moreover, that Handel stole—if indeed we can call it stealing—almost exclusively from composers of the second rank, and that he very seldom used such material unaltered, but practically always improved upon it.   It is perhaps not too fanciful to suggest that he would almost seem to have regarded such hints and suggestions as he received from the work of others as the musical equivalent of Pirandellian " characters in search of an author "—ideas in search of a composer, in fact, to which he imparted the full significance and vitality that had been denied them by their original begetters.   It is, moreover, interesting to note that he was one of the original founders of the Foundling Hospital, for some of his scores are like musical foundling hospitals, charitable institutions in which the neglected waifs and strays of other and lesser men are tenderly cared for, and given the opportunities for development and self-expression which they deserved and had not received at the hands of their neglectful parents.

Handel, then, we may say, was essentially a vast, impersonal mouth-piece, through which the voice of his age finds expression ; he was to a great extent absorbed by other people's styles, and became the servant of their ideas.   With Bach, on the contrary, it was the forms and idioms of the age that were only a vehicle for the expression of his own intensely individual ideas ; he absorbed all styles, instead of being absorbed by them like Handel, making them his own by virtue of the highly personal thought he poured into them. Handel is the sum-total of his age, with all its qualities and defects, but Bach belongs to no age and cannot be placed in any category or pigeon-hole whatsoever. He is the greatest problem of musical criticism and æsthetic. None of the elaborate systems of weights and measures we employ in dealing with lesser men are applicable to him : he is too big. Every generation sees a different aspect of him ; all schools, however opposed in tendency, unite in claiming him as their master. From Mendelssohn to Stravinsky there is no composer who does not, theoretically at least, seek to follow in his footsteps, and even the " jazz " merchants, with sublime effrontery, do not hesitate to invoke his august name in justification of their beastly activities. Every one, in fact, can find in Bach precisely what he wishes to find, because everything is contained in him. We can call him a classic, or a romantic, if we choose, but he is both and neither. One can justly regard him as the most abstract of musicians, the most exclusively preoccupied of all composers with problems of form, texture, and design, to the exclusion of all other considerations ; we may with equal justice claim him to be the most persistently literary and graphically pictorial of composers. From one point of view no one was ever more indebted to tradition and to the conventions of his time, yet equally none is more profoundly individual. He is at once the most remote in spirit from the present age, and at the same time the most inexplicably akin to it. It would be an easy task to collect some hundred passages or isolated progressions from his works which are so " modern " in both feeling and in manner that they might have been written to-day, yet the majestic calm and tranquillity of his art is at the opposite pole to the modern Zeitgeist. No composer who has ever lived is so introspective, so full of deep emotion, yet none is more impersonal and aloof. In some parts of his work we encounter an Olympian objectivity, a truly classic calm and sublimity such as we find in Homer or in Aeschylus ; again in others we find a poignancy of emotional expression that has no parallel in any music save possibly that of the later Beethoven. No composer is more systematic and methodical—one might almost say mechanical—in his procedure, yet none is more frequently inspired or more liable to do the unexpected. His very style eludes analysis or definition ; we can equally well regard his harmony as the outcome of his contrapuntal thought, or his counterpoint as the result of his harmonic conception.

No man ever put more of himself into his works, yet his personality remains a complete enigma to us. The man who created this whole world of art, the mere study of which in its entirety is itself almost the task of a lifetime, was only a humble church organist, playing his instrument in church every Sunday and teaching choir-boys during the rest of the week. There is indeed something almost mythical about him. If he had lived two thousand years ago we should confidently say, as it has been said of Homer, that he never existed, and that his name was merely a convenient kind of label used to denote the collective activity of innumerable anonymous creators throughout the ages. We should have found striking corroboration of this theory in the fact that, such was the great prestige of the Bach family in music, that the name Bach in the seventeenth century, in his native country, was synonymous with " musician ". As it is, however, there is too much historical evidence to show that he actually existed and actually wrote the works that bear his name. It has consequently been deemed necessary to evolve a more mystical form of the same theory, and to suggest that Bach was a mere impersonal force, functioning unconsciously and almost in spite of himself. Dr. Schweitzer, for example, dogmatically asserts—on what authority it might perhaps be indiscreet to enquire—that " Bach himself was not conscious of the extraordinary greatness of his work.—No one was less conscious than he that his work was ahead of his epoch ", the idea being, presumably, that if he had been aware of it he would have gone about the world proclaiming it to every one, or would have plagued all his friends, in the manner of Wagner, with letters and treatises in order to prove it to them. But apart from the somewhat impertinent assumption that Bach was unable to perceive what we ourselves are perfectly well able to see, is it not inherently improbable, to say the least, that an artist in whose gigantic output it is virtually impossible to put one's finger on a single imperfectly realized work, should be entirely lacking in the critical faculty that would enable him to discern his worth ? We know from experience, on the contrary, that the artist who is so lacking in self-knowledge and self-criticism as to be unconscious of his own greatness, is invariably unequal in his achievement and uncertain in his direction; and that he produces good and bad work alike without seeing the difference between them, like Schubert, for example.

With Beethoven, who alone can be compared to Bach in stature, we are always conscious that it is a man who has written his music, a man infinitely greater than ourselves, but nevertheless cast in the same mould, subject to the same infirmities, to the same unalterable conditions of life and artistic creation.   Even he is often unequal to the problem he has set himself.   In the *Missa Solemnis* and in the *Ninth Symphony*, like Jacob after wrestling with the Angel of the Lord at the ford, he often goes halt and lame.   It is never so with Bach; his hand never falters, there is no slackening of grip. How are we to account for this superhuman mastery, this fault-less perfection of utterance?   Were his works dictated to him by some god or dæmon?   Was he some Faust of music who sold his soul to the devil in exchange for artistic omnipotence? Was he a musical alchemist who had discovered a kind of philosopher's stone, some formula of construction which enabled him to transmute the basest material into purest gold? Any such explanation seems more natural and comprehensible than that any ordinary mortal could have created such a work; no theory could possibly be too wild or strange which sought to account for the existence of such a miraculous phenomenon.

CHAPTER XI

THE MUSIC OF THE EIGHTEENTH CENTURY

ENOUGH has been said in the course of the two preceding chapters to show that the salient feature of the music of the seventeenth century does not consist, as it is commonly supposed to do, in the supersession of a polyphonic mode of thought by a harmonic one, but rather exactly the opposite : namely, in a rebirth of counterpoint, a second wave of polyphony after the backwash of the Renaissance—tonal, secular, and instrumental this time rather than modal, sacred, and vocal—and culminating triumphantly in the art of Bach and his contemporaries, whose fugal forms are quite recognizably only the consummation and last consequence of the canonic art of the Flemish masters. The Florentine movement, to which so much attention is wrongly paid and so much significance wrongly attributed, was merely a short-lived reaction between two fundamentally similar and closely allied tendencies, the Gothic and the Baroque, and an unsuccessful attempt to anticipate the revolution that was only to come about a century and a half later, and to which we must now turn our attention.

Towards the middle of the eighteenth century, or even a little earlier, a profound alteration in taste is perceived in all the arts. Indeed, we find ourselves suddenly in an entirely different world from that of the previous century. The sometimes magnificent and frequently excessive exuberance of the Baroque, exemplified in the Jesuit churches, the sculpture of Bernini, the poetry of Marini, Gongora and their followers, and in the music of Scarlatti and his school, gradually gives way to a new style in which order, proportion, restraint, and logic are the prevailing characteristics. The cultural centre of activity which in the Gothic period was Flanders, at the time of the Renaissance was Italy, and in the Baroque age was Spain, now shifts to France ; and if we may say that Gothic is the art of the cathedral, Renaissance the art of the palace,

Baroque the art of the theatre, so Rococo as we may call it, revolves around the Paris salon.

The first musician to play a leading rôle in this transformation of taste was Jean Philippe Rameau, one of the most important figures in the history of music. Indeed, it would not be going too far to say that he occupies much the same place in it that his countryman Descartes occupies in the history of philosophic thought; for if Descartes is the father of modern philosophy, Rameau might with justice be called the father of modern, or at least eighteenth century music. In exactly the same way that the former sought to substitute a balanced, logical and reasoned system of thought in which all the constituent propositions are closely related and inter-dependent as in the books of Euclid, for an undisciplined conglomeration of scientific opinions and religious prejudices, so the latter aimed at the supersession of the largely empirical and unsystematized technique of the Baroque composers by a severely logical, co-ordinated, cut-and-dried system of harmony. "Music", he declared, "is a science which should have definite rules—a physico-mathematical science"; and to such an extent was he convinced of the necessity for scientific methods that he once observed to his friend Chabanon that he regretted having devoted so much time and labour to composition which would have been better spent in purely theoretical activities. As it is the list of his writings is almost as long as that of his musical works, and when we learn that he wrote practically no music at all until he had passed his fortieth year, with the exception of short pieces for the *clavecin*, it becomes clearly evident that he was first and foremost a theorist and a legislator of music, and only secondarily a composer. In any case it is at least certain that his achievement in the former capacity was the more important of the two. Rameau, the composer, is rather the successor of Lulli than the forerunner of Haydn and Mozart, belonging to the seventeenth rather than to the eighteenth century, the last of the old order rather than the first of the new. Moreover, despite the undoubted grandeur and virility of much of his music, his constant tendency towards abstraction, and his reliance on calculation and reflection in preference to artistic instinct, robs it of all spontaneity and charm, and is responsible for the somewhat forbidding air of dryness and austerity from which it is never entirely free. In orchestration he may be conceded to have made bold and fruitful innovations, but apart from this one aspect of it his music has little intrinsic appeal to us at the present day.

Rameau the theorist, on the other hand, is of truly epoch-making significance, and exercised a profound influence on music which lasted for nearly two centuries and is only now waning. The essence of his doctrine is summed up in the revolutionary *dicta* to the effect that "it is harmony, not melody, which guides us", and "no combination of melodies can sound well unless their movement is governed by harmonic considerations and exigencies". This, it need hardly be observed, virtually amounts to a modern restatement of the ancient Greek doctrine of the paramount importance of harmonic conceptions, and the consequently secondary rôle of pure melody which had been the guiding principle of western music since Gregorian chant. Rameau was further led to postulate the existence of chords as absolute independent entities, detachable from all context, devoid of any melodic implications, and susceptible of scientific analysis and classi-fication. This conception of harmony is still current to-day, and is responsible for most of the worst music ever written. More than any other man Rameau was responsible for bringing about the substitution in modern times of harmonic criteria for those of counterpoint, and of more or less arbitrary laws, rules, and reasons, for the free, unrestrained and spontaneous exercise of creative fantasy. To him is also due the definite establishment of the major and minor scale system with the latter varying in ascent and descent, for the enthronement at the centre of his harmonic system of the trinity of tonic, dominant, and subdominant, and for his invention of the abstraction called the fundamental bass and the principle of inversions. Rameau, in a word, was the father of modern text-book harmony, and of all the pestilential heresies to which it gives rise.

As we have already said, these sweeping changes that he introduced are the result of his theory rather than of his practice, which was comparatively timid and conventional. The first composer of note to put the new principles into execution was Carl Philipp Emanuel Bach, son of the great Johann Sebastian. It is exceedingly difficult for us to-day to arrive at an exact and just appraisement of the value of this composer's work.   The prominent position that he is generally accorded in histories of music is almost entirely due to his activities as a pioneer, and in particular to the part that he played in the formal evolution of sonata form, of which he is often held to be the inventor.   This is, however, to a great extent untrue—it is certainly at least an exaggeration.   He may be allowed to have conceived his movements more as organic wholes and less as pattern-sequences of unrelated episodes, than any of his predecessors, but that is about all ; the form was already in existence before his time, both in its general planning and in most of its details.   But if his importance in this direction has been somewhat exaggerated, hardly sufficient emphasis has been laid on his stylistic innovations, which are often of exceptional daring and originality.   Occasional moments in his work, indeed, strikingly presage many of the procedures not only of Haydn and Mozart, but of Beethoven even ; examples of which are to be found in the dramatic, explosive alternations of *forte* and *piano* in the *C minor Fantasia*, in the thematic material and its treatment in the *D minor piano concerto*, reminding one of the *Ninth Symphony*, in the recitative passage of the *F major sonata* in which the germ of a similar passage in Beethoven's *D minor sonata* Op 31 is clearly to be seen, in the *rondo* of the third sonata of the 1780 set, anticipating a familiar passage in the *Fifth Symphony*, and in his continual employment of rests and pauses as a means of expression.   Nevertheless, although many, if not most, of the separate ingredients of the styles of his great successors are to be found in his music, they are never welded together into a whole, and are seldom made the vehicle of any expressive purpose.   Side by side with these extraordinarily interesting and suggestive moments one finds long stretches of the most superficial, conventional, and uninteresting music, entirely devoid of significance.   In fact it would seem that his art possesses the same features as that of his great successors in the same way that a commonplace father may possess the same features as his gifted children, but that is all.   On the other hand, it would be wrong to attach too little importance to the man who elicited from both Haydn and Mozart the tributes which have been recorded.   " Everything that I know I have learnt from Emanuel Bach ",-said the former on one occasion, and the latter is reported to have said, even more emphatically, " Bach is the father, we are the children ; those of us who can do a decent thing learnt how from him, and whoever will not admit it is a scoundrel ".   On the whole, then, we shall probably be right if we regard Emanuel Bach as one of these artists, common in periods of transition, who suggest more to others than they are themselves capable of realizing, and who often make discoveries and innovations, the possibilities of which they are themselves completely unaware of.

Rameau, then, was the prophet and forerunner of the new principles, although his work shows few traces of their application.   That of the younger Bach, on the other hand, definitely does, though not without a considerable admixture of the old.   Indeed, in one aspect of his work he is still to a great extent the inheritor of the old contrapuntal tradition ; only late in life did he succeed in throwing off its influence completely, and by that time younger masters had already been writing in the new style, and might well have influenced him in turn. At the time of his death, for example, in 1788, Haydn was fifty-six years of age, Mozart thirty-two, and other older masters, more strictly his contemporaries, had for a long time been active in the new paths.   Of these the most important are the composers of the school of Mannheim, to whom, rather than to the younger Bach, is due the credit for being the first to achieve a style from which almost every trace of Gothic or Baroque elements had been completely banished.

The court of Mannheim during the reign of the Elector Karl Theodor, in the middle of the eighteenth century, was undoubtedly the most brilliant cultural centre in Germany, possibly even in the whole of Europe at that time, and every branch of artistic and scientific activity was represented there by its most distinguished practitioners, both native and foreign.   More especially, however, was it renowned for its music and musicians.   Operas and concerts of both sacred and secular music, performed by the finest singers and instrumental virtuosos in Europe succeeded each other in ceaseless profusion throughout the entire year, and the permanent orchestra was reputed to be the finest to be found anywhere.   In the summer months the court adjourned to Schwetzingen, where the electoral prince possessed a magnificent palace set in the midst of splendid grounds containing Chinese gardens, English hermitages, French rose-arbours, Italian orange-groves, interspersed with grottoes, Greek temples, artificial lakes, and filled with innumerable statues of marble, stone, and bronze.   Sometimes the orchestra would be distributed in boats on the river Neckar, or concealed in thickets for the return from the chase ; and in the bathing pavilion of the Hesperides gardens every evening elaborate concerts were held, so that one might almost imagine, to quote the words of Schubart, " that one had been transported by magic to an island in which everything had been transmuted into sound, and where nymphs, sylphs, gnomes, and salamanders made concerted symphonies of water, air, earth, and fire-music together ".   In the more prosaic and sober words of Dr. Burney (" The Present State of Music in Germany ") : " To anyone walking through the streets of Schwetzingen during summer, the place must seem to be inhabited only by a colony of musicians who are constantly exercising their profession ; at one house a fine player on the violin is heard, at another a German flute, here an excellent hautbois ; there a bassoon, a clarinet, a violoncello, or a concert of several instruments together.   Music seems to be the chief and most constant of his Electoral Highnesses amusements ; and the operas and concerts to which all his subjects have admission, form the judgment, and establish a taste for music, throughout the Electorate ".

It is only natural that such ideal conditions and opportunities should have given birth to a native school of composition which, although it produced no masters of the very highest rank, nevertheless reflected the spirit of the eighteenth century more completely and perfectly than any other.   The distinctive features of the music of this Mannheim school consisted in the virtual abandonment of the figured bass, and the reduction to a minimum of the canonic and fugal elements which are still to be found to a certain extent in the music of the younger Bach ; resulting in the creation of a style in which delicacy of tone-colour, subtlety of dynamic light and shade, effortless ease and grace of melody, and a harmonic brilliance and refinement, are the distinguishing traits—a style, in a word, which was the precise musical equivalent of that of the great French painters of the period, Watteau, Boucher, and Fragonard, and the finest musical flower of the culture and civilization of the eighteenth century.

The first composer of this school in whose work these characteristic qualities are to be found at their best was Johann Stamitz, and his most important colleagues and followers, only little less in stature than their master, were Richter, Cannabich Holzbauer, and Schobert. Although, as we have already said, they were none of them composers of the very highest rank, it would be a mistake to regard them as being important only in so far as they prepared the way for Haydn and Mozart. The consummate elegance and grace of Stamitz's melodies, in particular, his masterly thematic treatment, the perfect polish and refinement of his detail, are sufficient to entitle his work to recognition on its own merits, apart from all mere historical considerations, and the same is true in lesser degree of his followers. Their main fault consists in a certain lack of vitality and a suggestion of preciosity and effeminacy.

While these important developments were taking place in instrumental music in Germany, analogous tendencies were manifesting themselves in Italian opera in response to the dictates of French taste. Under the long predominance of the Neapolitan school of operatic composers and their principal librettist Metastasio, the opera had gradually crystallized into a rigid and sharply defined form with conventions, both literary and musical, which had to be strictly observed throughout. For example, every opera consisted of three acts in which six principal characters, constituting three pairs of lovers, appeared ; the first soprano and the principal male singer each sang five airs—an *aria cantabile*, an *aria di portamento*, an *aria di bravura*, an *aria mezzo carattere*, and an *aria parlante* ; the same character was not allowed to sing two arias in succession, and no two arias belonging to the same category could follow each other immediately ; each scene had to end with an aria, and the first and second acts with arias of greater importance than were to be found elsewhere ; in the second and third acts two places had to be reserved, one for an orchestrally accompanied recitative, the other for an elaborate duet sung by the principal pair of lovers, and so forth. It is of course, customary to heap scorn and ridicule on such rigid conventions, and to complain that their universal acceptance inevitably robbed opera of all semblance of approach to reality and of every vestige of dramatic interest, reducing it to the level of an elaborate costume-concert. Such a criticism, however, shows a confusion

of two issues : realism and drama are not necessarily synonymous and interchangeable terms, and the acceptance of definite
formal conventions does not inevitably entail the loss of dramatic
interest. The Metastasian opera is only very slightly more
stereotyped and conventionalized than Greek drama or classical
French drama, and certainly not more so than musical forms
such as sonata or fugue, in which a high level of musico-dramatic
interest is often attained ; and in this musical sense of the word
Neapolitan opera is frequently very much more dramatic
than people who have never examined it are willing to admit.
In the eyes of the Neapolitan operatic composers, opera
was a musical form, just as the symphony, sonata, fugue,
mass, or motet, are musical forms, and therefore just as
much subject to musical laws and strict formal discipline
as they are. The libretto was therefore framed in accordance with the musical requirements, instead of the music
in accordance with the literary requirements, but that does
not necessarily mean that dramatic considerations were
entirely neglected.

So far as realism is concerned, the criticism is just ; anything
more unreal than the opera of the seventeenth and early
eighteenth centuries could not possibly be imagined. This is
not necessarily a fault, however, for it might well be questioned
whether opera ought to aim at giving an impression of reality,
and whether its greatest strength and appeal do not rather
consist in its utter unreality and unlikeness to every-day life
—in its ideality in fact. It might indeed be questioned
whether even the most realistic opera can ever be anything but
a monstrous and ridiculous caricature and perversion of
actuality. The operatic composers of the Baroque period
accepted unreality as a necessary and unescapable condition
of the form, and preferred to emphasize it, making it thereby a
virtue and a strength, instead of trying to dispose of it—an
utterly impossible undertaking—and thereby making it a
defect. So long as there is no possible comparison with
actuality there can be no absurdity, and when we find that in
Cavalli's *Eliogabalo*, for example, the three heroes' parts are
taken by three *castrati*, and that a woman's part was sung by a
tenor, or that in Gluck's early *Nozze d'Ercole* the part of
Hercules was taken by a woman, we are much less conscious of
absurdity than when the egregious Lieutenant Pinkerton in

Madame Butterfly asks his friend whether he will have a milk-punch or a whisky and soda.

However congenial the Metastasian conception of opera was to an age like the Baroque and to a country like Italy, in both of which musical values were paramount, such a form of stage work was little short of an outrage in the eighteenth century and in France, both of which were entirely dominated by literary ideals and subject to the aesthetic dogmas enunciated by the Encyclopædists and other literary pontiffs. The catchword of the period, as of most highly refined, artificial, and sophisticated periods, was " back to nature ", and the function of music, as of all the other arts, was conceived to be the imitation of reality. In the words of a contemporary poet :

> La musique doit, ainsi que la peinture,
> Retracer à nos yeux le vrai de la nature.

It is obvious that neither the highly artificial and conventionalized opera of Lulli and Rameau, nor the Metastasian *opera seria*, could satisfy this characteristic craving of the eighteenth century for realism, imitation of actuality, and *le vrai de la nature*. The only form of dramatic music in existence which did to a great extent fulfil these requirements was the *opera buffa* of the Neapolitan school, of which the most eminent masters were Leo, Logroscino, Vinci, and especially Pergolesi, whose delightful *Serva Padrona* is the best-known example of the form, and is still to be heard to-day.

It has been suggested that the great and enduring reputation that this last-named composer, alone among all his colleagues, has continued to enjoy ever since his death right up to the present time, is entirely undeserved, and is attributable less to his merits than to the fact of his early death at the age of twenty-six, under somewhat romantic circumstances. In the words of Professor Dent, an acknowledged authority on the period, " Pergolesi is inferior to Leo and Logroscino in comic opera, and indeed could only be considered a great composer in any department by critics who were entirely ignorant of the works of his predecessors and contemporaries ". Now it is certainly true that his pre-eminence is not so great as to justify his enormous vogue and reputation when compared with the total neglect of the other masters mentioned above, but Professor Dent would seem to be going rather too far in the opposite direction when he suggests that Pergolesi is manifestly inferior to them. Even critics not entirely ignorant of the works of his predecessors and contemporaries may still be permitted to consider that, despite the great merits of his rivals which certainly deserve a far greater measure of recognition than they generally receive, both the *Serva Padrona* and the equally famous *Stabat Mater* of Pergolesi are, in their different ways, among the finest achievements of the first half of the century, and are fully entitled to the admittedly somewhat fortuitous and accidental renown which has been accorded them through the unaccountable vagaries of insufficiently informed criticism. His *Trios* also, for two violins and bass, apart from their intrinsic merit, are of great historical interest as being among the first chamber-music works to point the way to the formation of the characteristically eighteenth century style of Haydn and Boccherini.

The style of writing that distinguishes the work of Pergolesi and his greatest successors, such as Cimarosa and Paisiello, presents a striking contrast to that of Scarlatti and his school; the long, flowing, richly embellished melodic curves, the stately and majestic rhythms, the elaborately wrought polyphonic texture of the latter, give place to dapper, clear-cut lines, swift and vivacious *tempi*, and a definitely harmonic outlook, while the long *ritornelli* which tended to hold up the action of the operas of the older school are eliminated, and the number of *da capo* arias greatly reduced.

The instantaneous and sensational triumph of *La Serva Padrona* and other similar works when they were performed by a troupe of Italian players at Paris in 1752 led to the famous *Guerre des Bouffons*, waged between the supporters of the new Italian opera and those of the old French school of Lulli and Rameau, which ended in the complete triumph of the new art. Brilliant and fascinating though it was, however, it was soon perceived that the *opera buffa* was too slight and unpretentious a form to fill by itself the place hitherto occupied by the old *opera seria*. An attempt was therefore made to reform and revitalize the old form in accordance with the new æsthetic requirements of truth to nature and the imitation of actuality.

The entire credit for this reform is generally given to Christoph Willibald Gluck, but this is to a great extent a misconception. His ideas set forth in the lengthy preface at

Alceste (1767), to the effect that the function of music in opera is to support the poetry, that it should have no independent existence apart from the text, that no opportunities should be given to the singers of indulging in vocal displays to the detriment of the dramatic interest, that the *da capo* aria is undramatic and must therefore be abolished, that accompanied recitative should take the place of the *recitativo secco*, that the overture should bear a definite relation to the drama which is to follow, and should prepare the listener's mind for it—all this, as Mr. Ernest Newman (in his study of " Gluck and the Opera ") and others have conclusively shown, is little more than a restatement of current æsthetic doctrines, and an attempt to put them into practice.   But what is still more important and less generally recognized is the fact that there was no single point in his programme in which he was not anticipated by some composer of the Neapolitan school. Metastasio himself was the first to declare that " when the music in union with drama takes precedence, then both drama and the music itself suffers in consequence ", and the great abuses on the part of the singers which undoubtedly prevailed in the Italian opera of the time were not the fault of composers so much as of audiences which not merely tolerated but encouraged them. In the work of the best Italian composers immediately before and contemporary with Gluck there are actually singularly few concessions made to the singers except in the *arie di bravura*, which were, however, of comparatively infrequent occurrence, and were generally introduced in such a way and in such parts of the work that the action did not greatly suffer. Again, in the operas of Niccolo Jommelli, for example, we frequently find that the old *da capo* form of aria is abandoned in favour of the *cavatina*, or one-part, and two-part aria ; and already in the work of Hasse, a German member of the Neapolitan school, a notable increase is to be observed, both in number and importance, of orchestrally accompanied recitatives—a tendency which is carried to even greater lengths by some of his successors. In the whole of the second act of Jommelli's *Demofonte*, for example, (1764), *recitativo secco* occurs only in two comparatively unimportant scenes. Finally, a definite programmatic tendency can be clearly discerned in some of the overtures of Tommaso Traetta.

The so-called reform of Gluck, then, so far from being an

M

isolated phenomenon, due solely to his initiative and confined to his work alone at the time, was not only the outcome to a great extent of literary and æsthetic theorizings on the part of innumerable writers in France, Italy, and Germany, but also the complete and consequential development, merely, of the practice of many Neapolitan masters such as Hasse, Jommelli, Traetta, and even to a certain extent his rival Piccinni. The only crucial difference between, say, the *Orfeo* of Gluck, and the average Neapolitan opera, consisted in the rejection of the old Metastasian formal conventions, but this innovation was not due to Gluck, but to his librettist Calsabigi, who wrote his text before the former had conceived his project of reform.

That neither the aims of Gluck nor the artistic outcome of them were so widely different from those of some of his Italian rivals is shown by the fact that his contemporaries did not by any means place him in a category by himself. Writers such as de la Cépède, Ange Goudard, Heinse, and others, all speak of Piccinni, Sacchini, and Traetta in the same breath with him, as exemplifying similar tendencies ; Heinse indeed, specifically refers to Traetta as the father of Gluckian opera, and Grimm, the bitterest opponent of Gluck in Paris, disliked the work of Traetta and Jommelli just as much as his.

That this comparative identity of aims and methods is not generally recognized to-day is simply due to the fact that the work of the Neapolitan composers in question is somewhat inaccessible and almost completely unknown, whereas that of Gluck is familiar to all. Certainly no one even superficially acquainted with the art of Jommelli and Traetta could possibly say, as does M. Tiersot in his monograph on Gluck, that Piccinni imitated his rival in Didon—" pour y réussir il n'avait pas hesité à se conformer aux principes d'art qu'il était venu combattre ". Rather is it exactly the opposite ; in order to succeed, Gluck did not hesitate to make good use of suggestions which he found in the work of other masters such as the two mentioned above, of whom Piccinni was, like Gluck himself, only a logical successor. Not that there is any reason why he should hesitate to do so ; the only point is that great injustice has been done to other men only very little, if at all, inferior to him. Indeed, one might even go so far as to say that while Gluck may readily be conceded to have excelled them all in the realization and expression of a dramatic situation, he is often markedly their inferior from a purely musical point of view· For it cannot be denied— is, indeed, generally admitted—that Gluck's workmanship is often awkward and clumsy, and that he was singularly deficient in melodic invention and in both contrapuntal and harmonic resource. Even in the matter of orchestration, in which Gluck's greatest strength undoubtedly lies, he was anticipated to a great extent by Jommelli, whose scoring was frequently of a quite remarkable daring and complexity. The orchestra he disposed of during his stay in Stuttgart, for example, in 1758—four years before Gluck made his first decided step in the new direction with his *Orfeo*— consisted of thirty-eight players, and in 1767, the year of *Alceste* and its famous preface, of no less than forty-seven, both figures being exclusive of brass instruments, the number of which varied considerably according to the composer's requirements.

While no one in his musical senses, then, would for a moment dream of denying the majesty and grandeur of Gluck's conceptions, the truly Attic nobility and simplicity of his style in general, and his fine sense of orchestral colour in particular, to say nothing of his dramatic power and felicity, his possession of these admirable qualities should not be allowed to blind us either to his manifest faults and shortcomings, or to the equally great merits of his rivals, whose main strength, perhaps, lies in their possession of a vein of impassioned lyricism, and an intensity of emotional utterance which Gluck entirely lacks save occasionally in the expression of horror, anguish, hate, and similar states of mind. His inability to rise to any great lyrical heights is shown by his " Paris and Helen," which is a complete failure.

That composers of such incontestable greatness and of such lofty ideals as Jommelli and Traetta should be referred to in what purports to be the outline of a history of music, as belonging to " the dreary succession of contented mediocrity " (Sir Henry Hadow, " Music ". Home University Library) could only be excused on the grounds that it had perhaps never occurred to its distinguished writer to examine their music before writing about it—if indeed that is an excuse at all, and not, as it would be in any less discredited branch of activity than musical criticism, a reproach. It is certainly not an opinion that is held by any of those who have made a close study of this music, or even by those who, like the present writer, have a comparatively superficial knowledge of it.   And that such a noble and highly gifted artist as Piccinni, of all people, should be held up in musical histories to derision and contempt, and regarded as the typical representative of all the most pernicious tendencies in operatic art, is probably the cruellest injustice and the most glaring example of shallow prejudice and ignorance in the whole history of musical criticism. Gluck is incontestably a great musical dramatist, but as a musician pure and simple he is equally incontestably the inferior of his great rival—at least in the eyes of anyone who is willing to take the trouble of looking at the music for himself, and has the courage and capacity to form his own judgment independently of the overwhelming consensus of uninstructed opinion. As the eminent German musicologist, Professor Kretzschmar, says in his important study entitled " Aus Deutschlands italienischer Zeit " : " Wir unterschätzen die Kunst der Neapolitanischen Schule. . . . Man könne geradeswegs behaupten dass die Mehrzahl der heutigen Gegner der Neapolitanischen Schule von ihr nichts kennen, als die Arien der Königin der Nacht und anderer Mozartscher Stücke, dazu noch etwa ' Tod Jesu ' (of Graun) und einige schwächere Sologesänge Gluck's."

CHAPTER XII

The Viennese School

Despite the fact that France produced no creative artist of the highest rank, with the possible exception of Rameau—who, however, as we have already observed, belongs in spirit to the preceding age—Paris remained the centre of operatic activities throughout the greater part of the eighteenth century. The most important developments in the field of instrumental music, on the contrary, took place in Austria, although actually out of the four great masters who constitute the chief glory of the so-called Viennese school, only one can properly be said to belong to that city or even to be an Austrian in the strict sense of the word, namely Franz Schubert Of the others, Joseph Haydn was a Croatian peasant by birth, Wolfgang Amadeus Mozart, though a native of Salzburg, was essentially a cosmopolitan, Ludwig van Beethoven was a German of Dutch descent, and the extent to which they constitute a school has been greatly exaggerated They wrote in the same forms, but treated them entirely differently ; they employed to a great extent the same vocabulary, but they expressed widely divergent ideas and emotions.

It is necessary to emphasize this fact at the outset on account of the characteristic tendency of musical historians, which we have already encountered so often, to regard music as if it were a collective and almost impersonal activity like one of the sciences, in which each successive genius stands on the shoulders of his predecessor and sums up in himself all previous knowledge and experience, adding to it something of his own which is likewise in its turn taken over, extended, and carried to a higher pitch of perfection by his successors. This tendency is nowhere more in evidence than in dealing with the masters of the Viennese school, and nowhere has it led to such false conclusions. Haydn, the first of the illustrious line, has particularly suffered from it, and has gradually come to be regarded by most people as a mere forerunner of Mozart, in whom all his characteristic qualities are presumed to be contained and perfected. The individualities of both have in consequence been diminished, obscured and confounded in such a way that they have become almost indistinguishable from each other, whereas it is only in small and unimportant matters that they are at all similar.

Haydn is no more included in Mozart than Mozart is included in Beethoven. That they both did to a great extent write in the same idioms and forms, as we have already said, is true enough ; that each in turn learnt a great deal from the other is equally undeniable. There are even whole works, or at least whole movements that one might legitimately hesitate to ascribe definitely to either one or other of them, and even then the chances of one's being right or wrong would be about equal. Nevertheless this does not alter the fact that the collective impression that their respective outputs convey is one of complete and profound dissimilarity. Haydn's style is altogether broader and more robust ; on the other hand he seldom, if ever approaches Mozart in subtlety and refinement of detail. The latter aims constantly at the utmost symmetry of design, as exemplified in the four- and eight-bar phrase ; the former, on the contrary, often writes phrases consisting of an odd number of bars—three, five, seven, and even nine. Mozart never rests content until he has refined and polished each sentence till it glitters like a jewel ; Haydn writes in a less epigrammatic and, in his slow movements particularly, more rhapsodic manner. In quartet and symphony Haydn sometimes constructs his movements on a single main theme, sometimes on several, whereas Mozart almost invariably employs the ordinary strongly contrasted first and second subjects.

The difference between the two masters, however, is not confined to mere questions of style and form. Their personalities are wholly distinct, and in their artistic tendencies they are in many important respects entirely opposed to each other. Mozart is always a typical child of the eighteenth century, and seldom succeeds in getting far away from the atmosphere of the *salon*. Needless to say, this is not necessarily a defect any more than it is a virtue ; great art is great art whether it springs from the *salon* or the countryside, the church or the theatre. The fact remains that Mozart is perhaps the only composer of whom it could be said, without any fear of contradiction, that there is not a single work of his which reveals the slightest trace of a feeling for nature. By this it is not merely meant that he consistently refrains from indulging in onomatopoeic imitations of natural phenomena, such as the rustling of leaves, the rippling of brooks, and so forth, but something much wider, deeper, and more fundamental—an attitude of mind, in fact. Haydn, for that matter, rarely indulges in realistic suggestions —in his instrumental music at least—yet his work always seems to possess a robustness and a fresh, open-air quality which are entirely lacking in that of the younger master and are, indeed, rare in eighteenth century art of any kind. These qualities have generally been attributed to the fact that many of his melodies reveal a striking resemblance to, and are even in many cases identical with, Croatian folk-songs, from which it has been argued that he was in the habit of making use of popular melodies as the thematic basis of his works, though actually it is just as likely that the peasants stole his tunes as that he stole their's. The point is, however, that whichever way you choose to look at it, there remains a definite relation between the music of Haydn and folk-song. You will not easily find peasants singing themes from the symphonies and quartets of Mozart, or of any other composer of the eighteenth century. Haydn is the first composer to give us a sense of contact with the soil, and to bring a breath of fresh air into the patchouli-scented atmosphere of the French *salon*.

With Haydn we cross the threshold of an entirely new world. It is only necessary to compare his art with that of his immediate predecessors, such as the younger Bach or Stamitz, in order to see what a profound gulf of separation lies between him and all other composers of his time. Haydn is the first democrat in music, writing neither for the edification of the religiously-minded nor for the dilectation of the hyper-cultured denizens of the court or *salon*, as in former times, but solely in order to gratify the aesthetic tastes and desires of the ordinary man, or, to put it in his own too modest words, in order that " the weary and worn, or the man burdened with affairs, may enjoy a few moments of solace and refreshment ". It is this quality in Haydn's art that constitutes his most enduring title to immortality, not his impersonal contribution to the evolution of symphonic form, on which such great emphasis is generally laid, and which has always been greatly exaggerated on account of our comparative ignorance, until quite recently, of the work of the Mannheim school.

If there is, as we have suggested, something Homeric about Bach in the objectivity and universality of his art, and in the mystery that surrounds his personality, it is perhaps not too fanciful to trace in Haydn a distinct affinity to Hesiod, whose employment of quaint, allusive, and homely phraseology derived, probably, from peasant poetry and speech, is strikingly analogous to the former's employment of folk-song idioms. In the work of both musician and poet the humble peasant of the fields is exalted above the warrior, the pastoral takes the place of the epic, and we leave the Gods of Olympus and the heroes of Troy for the simple work-a-day life of the countryside. One finds precisely the same quality of unaffected simplicity and sincerity, the same naïvety and kindliness, the same homely and slightly provincial wisdom, the same rustic *gaucherie*, in the music of Haydn as in the *Works and Days* of the old Greek poet. On the whole, too, Quintilian's verdict on Hesiod, that " he rarely rises to great heights . . . and to him is given the palm in the middle-class of speech ", is applicable also to the greater part of Haydn's work. It is not entirely true of his whole output, however, nor of that of Hesiod, for that matter. The grandeur and elevation of parts of the *Creation*, for example, affording a striking parallel to the solemn if somewhat uncouth strains of Hesiod's *Theogony*, reveal an aspect of Haydn's art which is apt to be overlooked ; and even in his instrumental music we are continually coming across deeply expressive passages of a kind which we associated more readily with the nineteenth than with the eighteenth century. The truth is that Haydn is something of an enigma, and not by any means merely the placid, genial, old *perruque* that he is popularly conceived to be. It is, of course, a conception of him that is justified by most of his music, but not by all, certainly not by his best. As he himself said, " some of my children are well-bred, some ill-bred, but here and there there is a changeling among them ".

Apart from the two late choral works, *The Seasons* and *The Creation*, Haydn's strength lay entirely in the direction of instrumental music ; his many operas are of no interest to us to-day, largely on account of their complete lack of psychological interest and dramatic vitality. Mozart, on the other hand, despite his unquestionable greatness as a symphonist, and indeed in all directions, was primarily a composer of operas. It is impossible to doubt that it was only the force of the circumstances in which he was placed that prevented him from devoting his entire time and energy to the production of works for the stage. As he himself wrote to his father in 1778, " you know my greatest longing—to write operas ", and again later, " I have an unspeakable desire to write another opera—if I only hear an opera mentioned, if I only go inside a theatre and hear them tuning up, I am quite beside myself—I am envious of everyone who writes an opera ; I could positively cry with vexation whenever I hear or even see an aria ". It is at least certain that Mozart, if he has not actually been surpassed by Haydn and Beethoven in the field of instrumental music, has at least been equalled by them ; in opera, however, he is unique. There is no one who can possibly be compared with him in this direction, and it is consequently by his achievements in this form that he can be most conveniently judged.

Mozart's whole conception of opera was diametrically opposed to that of Gluck and all other so-called reformers, both previous and subsequent, from Peri and Caccini to Debussy. While Gluck in his preface to *Alceste* proclaimed the doctrine that it was the function of music to support the poetry, and said that when he sat down to compose he tried above all to forget that he was a musician, Mozart explicitly declared that " in opera poetry must be the obedient daughter of music ", and invariably subordinated the literary to the musical interest whenever the two threatened to become irreconcilable. In other words, his sympathies were with the Italian rather than with the French school ; he was on the side of Piccinni rather than on that of Gluck. It is true that he was for a time considerably influenced by the latter, in *Idomeneo* particularly —the first of his great operas—but it was only a transitory influence which disappears entirely from his mature work.

Yet it would be a great mistake to suppose that Mozart's conception of opera and his emphatic rejection of the Gluckian ideals, necessarily involved a neglect of the interests of drama. He achieved a different kind of dramatic interest from that achieved by Gluck, and the difference between the two masters is in essence the difference between the two schools or traditions, Italian and French, to which they respectively belonged. In a word, Gluck is primarily concerned with the musical realization of situation, plot, and action ; Mozart concentrates rather on the depiction of characters and their interaction on each other. In sheer dramatic power Gluck is probably superior to Mozart, but he had nothing like the same talent for psychological characterization. The personages in Gluck's operas are like superb Greek statues, types rather than individuals, carved in an expressive attitude, but fixed and rigid, as in the Laocoon group ; they undergo no change or modification throughout the entire work. With Mozart, on the other hand, music becomes a psychological language of a subtlety and incisive power to which that of mere words cannot be compared. His creations are flesh and blood, as real and living as the creations of any novelist, and there seems to be no doubt that they took shape in his mind before the text of the opera was written. His characters develop as the work progresses ; every musical number serves to throw a fresh light upon them and to fill in the picture we have formed of them. Gluck, on the contrary, was entirely dependent on his librettist for his conception, and his powers of characterization, such as they were, were confined to monologues and soliloquies ; he was totally unable to particularize the psychological reactions of different people in the same situation, either in opposition or in agreement. Mozart's powers in this direction were astonishing and have never been equalled or even approached by any other composer. As a magnificent example of this it is only necessary to mention the quartet from *Don Giovanni*, " Non ti fidar ", in which the same musical motive is varied in such a way as to express perfectly the conflicting emotions of four separate individuals. To achieve such a miracle as this, and yet at the same time to write music which, all dramatic and psychological considerations apart, is equal in intrinsic beauty to the finest ever written in any musical medium whatsoever, is a feat almost without parallel.

And yet, in spite of all this, Mozart, unquestionably one of the subtlest and profoundest minds that has ever occupied itself with music, is commonly regarded, like Haydn, but with even less justification, as an artless and innocent child of nature to whom the heights and depths of human experience were unknown or inaccessible. The source of this grotesque misunderstanding is probably to be sought in the almost miraculous circumstances of his artistic career. The infant prodigy has been allowed to eclipse the great composer in the minds of most people, who are apt to take it for granted that because he started writing music at the age of four, his subsequent work was equally miraculous in origin, and equally unrelated to psychological experience or mental development ; he has been conceived and portrayed more or less as a kind of musical machine, pouring forth marvellous works in heedless and effortless profusion, almost unconsciously. We need go no further than his correspondence and conversation for a refutation of this opinion.   " It is a mistake to think that the practice of my art has become easy to me—no one has given so much care to the study of composition as I have. There is scarcely a famous master in music whose works I have not frequently and diligently studied ", and he expressly mentions the quartets dedicated to Haydn as being " the fruit of long and painstaking labour ".   Besides, it is not generally realized that there is as wide a gulf between his early and his late work as there is between the early and late work of almost any other composer. Although his powers certainly developed with astonishing rapidity, his actual process of development differed in no way from that of the normal artist.   As Professor Dent observes in his book on Mozart's operas, "there is nothing remarkable about *La Finta Semplice* except that it was the work of a boy ", and this applies to all his earliest works : even such a comparatively late work as the *Entführung aus dem Serail*, though full of the most delightful and fascinating music, is only greater in degree, not in kind, than the music of many of his predecessors and contemporaries. The later Mozart is unique ; the music of the *Entführung*, on the other hand, might quite conceivably have been written by Cimarosa and Paisiello at their best, in collaboration. It was not until he reached about his twenty-fifth year that he began to write the music which was to ensure his immortality. That is early enough, no doubt, but certainly not without precedent in the history of art.

Short as it was, in fact, his career can be clearly divided into three distinct periods, like that of so many great artists—allowing, of course, for a certain amount of overlapping. The first is the period of the infant prodigy, lasting up till about his sixteenth year, during which his work consists almost entirely of imitations of the accepted masters of the day, such as Emanuel Bach, Jommelli, and Stamitz. Many of them are admittedly beautiful, but, as we have already said, they are remarkable more on account of his age than for their intrinsic qualities. Then, after a few works among which the G minor symphony (K. 183) is the most important, and in which signs of individuality and maturity are apparent, a curious phase sets in which can only be understood and explained as the result of a profound psychological change and inner disturbance. In this second period Mozart would seem to have altogether ceased to take himself and his art seriously. Most of the music — not all—that he wrote between, roughly, his eighteenth and his twenty-fifth years is fluent, conventional, brilliant, but completely cynical, written with his tongue in his cheek ; and it is interesting to observe that this phase corresponds with the most bitter experiences of his life, and with the time when he was subjected to the utmost indignity and humiliation by his patron, the notorious Archbishop of Salzburg, and rejected by the woman he loved in favour of some miserable strolling player. A significant index to his state of mind at the time is found in his correspondence belonging to the year 1778 : "Frequently I fall into a mood of complete listlessness and indifference ; nothing gives me any pleasure ".

The works of this period consist largely of concertos, wayward and nonchalant in form, full of charming ideas which he hardly takes the trouble to work out, and serenades and *divertimenti* for various and frequently unusual combinations of instruments which, for all their grace and sensuous beauty, are little more than what the Germans call *Galanteriekunst*, intended as mere accompaniments to the arch-episcopal table and conversation. The most psychologically interesting example of the music of this period is probably the *Divertimento* for two flutes, five trumpets, and four kettledrums. When we remember that Mozart disliked the sound of the trumpet to such an extent that it actually caused him physical pain, and that he also had an aversion for the tone-quality of the flute, what depths of cynical perversity and disgust this fantastic choice of medium inevitably suggests !

To an acute contemporary observer it must have seemed that Mozart had gone the way of most infant prodigies, and that nothing more was to be expected of him. And in a sense he would have been right. The infant prodigy did indeed die in this period of suffering and unspeakable humiliation, but the composer of genius was then born. His break with Salzburg was symbolically significant—it was a severance of the navel-string that bound him to the past and to the artistic ideals of his predecessors and contemporaries. From that moment onwards dates his independence not only as a man but also as an artist. The set of six string quartets dedicated to Haydn, the three famous symphonies in E flat, C, and G minor, and above all the great operas, *Figaro*, *Don Giovanni*, and *The Magic Flute*, are unlike anything else in the whole of music— unique and unapproachable. The difference between such works as these and the rococo *Galanteriekunst* of his middle period is the difference between the work of a great genius and that of an exquisite but disillusioned talent. They belong to entirely different worlds.

It is significant to note that this miraculous efflorescence coincides with an intensive course of contrapuntal study which Mozart undertook in 1782, and was heralded by a series of works such as the *Fugue in C minor* for two pianos, a mass in the same key, an unfinished suite for piano, a three-part fugue for piano, the *Allegro and Andante* in F, and other works in which contrapuntal devices play the most important part. The fruits of this severe discipline are to be found everywhere in the great music of his last period—one need only point to such conspicuous instances of it as the last movement of the G. major quartet, the last movement of the *Jupiter Symphony*, the *Magic Flute Overture*, and the duet for armed men in the same work, based on an old German chorale melody accompanied by an elaborate scheme of contrapuntal imitation in the style of Bach—and altogether it is probably not going too far to say that the superlative greatness of the music of Mozart's last period is in large measure the direct outcome of his adoption of a more polyphonic style of composition than he had hithorto employed. It is at least certain that the prevailing fault of the music of the eighteenth century, generally speaking, was its constant tendency towards insipidity and effeminacy, as a result of its excessively homophonic character. Even a great deal of the early and middle period work of Mozart himself is not exempt from this criticism.

To attempt to define or explain the peculiar quality and the spiritual content of Mozart's finest work is to undortako a task the accomplishment of which is beyond the scope of mere words. In. all music, in the whole range of art even, it is impossible to find any parallel to its combination of qualities generally regarded as opposites, or at least mutually exclusive in practice, and without the corresponding faults which these qualities generally bring with them : depth without turgidity and clarity without shallowness, subtlety without perversity and simplicity without insipidity, strength without roughness and sweetness without sickliness. And if we miss in it the familiar Promethean gesture of defiance, the dramatic alternations of doubt and faith, of triumph and despair, which we find in the best-known works of Beethoven and which we have been taught, wrongly, to regard as the acme of spirituality, its comparative serenity and tranquillity should not be regarded as the unquestioning acceptance of a child-like and immature mind, but of one who has been tried and proved in fiercest fire. And while there is no music which seems to the undeveloped mind so direct and obvious, even to the point of triteness, there is nevertheless a degree of power and subtlety behind the transparent surface qualities that we only come to appreciate after a long time.

Indeed, it would almost seem that an attitude of more or less contemptuous indifference towards Mozart is a necessary preliminary to the true appreciation of him. In the preface to his life of Mozart, addressed to his friend Hartenstein, Jahn writes that " we coincided in our experience that at a certain stage of our mental development Mozart's music had seemed cold and unintelligible to our restless spirits—turning to him in later years-we were amazed alike at the wondrous wealth of his art, and at our former insensibility to it ". It is very doubtful whether anyone who has not passed through a similar experience can really understand Mozart, and certainly by none is he less understood than by those of his vociferous admirers to-day who affect to despise profundity, who worship superficiality, and seek to use him as a stalking-horse in order to combat the great art of other masters which they cannot even pretend to understand.

Strange though it may seem to us to-day, Mozart was commonly regarded, during the greater part of the last century, as a mere forerunner of Beethoven, in the same way that there is still a tendency to regard Haydn as only the forerunner of

Mozart. It has been one of the salutary consequences—perhaps the only one—of the recent reaction against Beethoven, that his great predecessor has now come into his own and has received his due as an individual and independent personality instead of as an impersonal link in a more or less imaginary evolutionary chain. Actually, Mozart stands distinctly apart from both Haydn and Beethoven, in style as well as in mentality, and bears a closer relationship to the Mannheim school than to the former ; and if one must at all costs find him a " successor ", it is not Beethoven by any means who stands nearest to the vacant throne, but Ludwig Spohr, whose style and characteristic chromaticism in particular is obviously derived from that of Mozart to a much greater extent than the art of Beethoven is. Indeed, that the early work of Beethoven should be glibly spoken of as " Mozartean " is an astonishing critical aberration. In the first place, Beethoven's early period is very much more original and personal than it is generally given the credit for being ; and in so far as it is indebted to predecessors it owes infinitely more to Haydn than to Mozart, and, going further back, to Emmanuel Bach than to the school of Mannheim which is the source of the Mozartean style, technically speaking. Even the mature Beethoven of the middle period is often strikingly anticipated in the music of Haydn, many of whose works, such as the overture to *L'Isola disabitata*, to mention only one characteristic example, reveals a depth and intensity of expression that we can only call Beethovenian, and we have already had occasion to draw attention to equally remarkable foreshadowings of the later style of the Bonn master in the work of the younger Bach. In any case the art of Beethoven, whatever its qualities, entirely lacks from the very outset the poise, serenity, grace, and sheer perfection of utterance of the inimitable and unapproachable Mozart.

Again, Beethoven is, like Haydn only even more so, essentially an instrumental composer ; as he himself said, " I always hear my music on instruments, never on voices ". His opera, oratorio, and vocal works generally, are markedly inferior to his orchestral and chamber music. Even the great *Missa Solemnis* is a magnificent failure—infinitely transcending the successes of almost every other composer perhaps, but nevertheless a failure—and the last movement of the *Ninth*

Symphony, for all its sublimity of conception and superb moments, cannot altogether be accounted a success. Mozart, on the other hand, as we have already observed, was primarily a composer of operas ; even in his orchestral music his melodic style is vocal rather than instrumental.

Beethoven's treatment of symphonic form, moreover, is diametrically opposed to that of Mozart. The latter treats his themes in much the same way that he treats the characters in his operas ; they come into existence apart from and antecedent to the scheme of the movement as a whole, whereas with Beethoven the general conception of the movement as a whole would seem to have taken shape in his mind first, and the thematic material then gradually and painfully evolved in compliance with the preconceived formal exigencies. In fact the difference between their respective methods is much the same as that between two types of novelist, the one of which conceives his characters first and then brings them into contact with each other, while the other conceives his plot first and then constructs his characters in accordance with it. With the first the plot is evolved as a natural consequence of the interaction of completely formed and sharply defined characters or themes, as the case may be, upon each other ; with the second the actual protagonists, whether characters or themes, are frequently insignificant in themselves, and only become significant by virtue of the dramatic situations in which they are placed, or in consequence of the developments to which they are subjected in the course of the movement. And so we generally find that the centre of interest in Mozart's symphonies lies in the conflict or reconciliation of themes, while with Beethoven it lies rather in the conflict or reconciliation of keys or tonalities.

Now it is surely obvious that the method of Mozart is infinitely better adapted than that of Beethoven to the triune principle of exposition, development, and recapitulation, which constitutes the essential feature of the classical symphonic forms and demands a certain conventionality of plot, analogous to that of the love story in which the two main characters come together in the end and live happily ever after. In fact the parallel is a very exact one, for after the adventures gone through in the development section, the two main themes are brought together into the same key and the whole is rounded off by a *coda* which is the precise equivalent of the conventional epilogue in classical novels.   With Beethoven, on the contrary, to whom the interest of the plot was paramount, the recapitulation of the opening section consisted a stumbling-block and a formal problem of considerable magnitude.   It was precisely the same difficulty, under another guise, as that encountered by the operatic composers of the eighteenth century in attempting to reconcile dramatic exigencies with the symmetrical *da capo* aria.   In order to palliate and modify the momentary slackening of interest inevitably entailed by the conventional repetition of the exposition, Beethoven was obliged to lengthen his development section, to curtail as much as possible the recapitulation, and frequently to introduce a *coda* of such large dimensions as to displace the centre of gravity altogether.   The " happy marriage " of the two main themes in the same key is no longer the main interest and logical climax of the movement, but only a mere incident of comparatively slight importance.

In fact it cannot be too strongly insisted on that the symphonic form as Beethoven found it was fundamentally unsuited to his purposes, and was only induced to conform to them by the introduction into it of elements which largely impaired and sometimes even destroyed its original character. In the latter symphonies, and in the *Ninth* particularly, the form is strained up to and beyond its possible limits ; and in the posthumous quartets and later piano sonatas the old form is virtually abandoned, and an attempt made to arrive at the creation of a new formal principle altogether, largely based upon fugue.   It is a mistake, therefore, to regard Beethoven as the perfecter of symphonic form, in the strict sense of the word.   In reality he was, abstractly considered, first its corruptor and then its destroyer.   So far from continuing in the footsteps of Mozart he decisively turned his back upon them in his last and most important works.

It is as well that this should be clearly recognized, for up to the present time Beethoven's achievement has been to a great extent misunderstood, and its true value and significance ignored.   This may perhaps seem to be a somewhat curious statement to make concerning a composer who has for more than a century occupied one of the most eminent places in musical history and in both popular and enlightened favour,

N

but it is a fact none the less. It is certainly true that he was at once recognized by his contemporaries as one of the greatest musicians of their age, but when we come to look closely into the matter we discover that their appreciation was largely based upon his early prowess as an executant and an *improvisatore*, and that his only really great successes as a composer were earned by his feeblest productions such as the unspeakably bad *Battle of Vittoria*, the dull and undistinguished *Mount of Olives*, the quite pleasant but essentially unimportant *Septet*, and by his earliest and least characteristic works generally. His later music was received for the most part with respectful bewilderment, and only very rarely enjoyed anything more than a *succès d'estime*. In fact we may safely say that so far as his contemporaries were concerned, Beethoven's greatness was realized in a sense, but hardly appreciated, certainly not understood.

Similarly, the Beethoven who was the idol of both the Romanticists and their neo-classical antagonists, of Berlioz and Liszt on the one hand, of Mendelssohn and Brahms on the other, was the Beethoven of the second or middle period, exemplified by such works as the *Fifth Symphony*, the *Emperor Concerto*, the *Appassionata Sonata* ; and this is also the Beethoven against whom the recent generation of musicians has reacted so violently. By all alike, whether contemporaries, Romanticists, Classicists, or Impressionists and the rest, the works of the last period, with the exception perhaps of the *Ninth Symphony*, have been practically ignored : regarded as insoluble enigmas by the first, contemptuously rejected without scrutiny by the last, and only accorded a qualified esteem by the others on account of their veneration for the composer rather than for the intrinsic qualities of the works themselves.

That they were not really understood or appreciated during the last century, even by Beethoven's greatest admirers, is clearly shown by the fact that certain peculiarities which differentiated them from all his other work—and indeed, from all other music whatsoever—were, and often still are, customarily apologized for as if they were defects, and excused on the alleged grounds that the composer's deafness must have deprived him of the power of calculating their precise effect in performance. Wagner is a notable exception to the general rule, but his appreciation of the last quartets, though certainly genuine enough, was of a somewhat passive and negative order ; they did not exercise any influence at all on his work, or on that of any other composers of the last century who may have similarly admired them.   The enormous influence which Beethoven has exerted on music up to the present time has been almost wholly derived from the works of his middle period.

It is the growing recognition of the supreme importance of Beethoven's last works, and of the posthumous string quartets in particular, and the realization that they, and not the middle-period symphonies, should be regarded as not only his finest works but also as the culminating point and logical conclusion of his artistic development, that constitutes the most striking and significant feature of the modern attitude towards Beethoven. And the very qualities in them that seemed strange and inexplicable to the musicians of the last century appear to us to-day to be not merely perfectly intelligible and æsthetically necessary, but intrinsically beautiful as well ; not imperfections resulting from the loss of the composer's hearing, but the final flowering and consummation of his whole art, bearing the same relation to his earlier music that the later plays of Shakespeare, such as *The Tempest*, bear to the earlier poems and plays, or that the second part of *Faust* bears to the rest of Goethe's work.

The fact of the matter is that Beethoven's deafness and its influence on his art have always been greatly exaggerated by sentimental biographers understanding nothing of a great composer's method of work. It is absurd to suppose that such a consummately gifted musician as Beethoven was in the slightest degree dependent on external aids to composition, or that he was unable to reproduce in his mind's ear the exact equivalent of the notes which he wrote down. Practically none of the touching complaints that he makes about his affliction in correspondence and conversation has any reference to his art ; they are almost entirely concerned with the disabilities that it involved on the human and social side of his existence. No doubt he would have liked to hear music occasionally, but inability to do so is not necessarily a great deprivation ; many composers in full possession of their faculties never enter a concert-hall from one year's end to the other.

In short, the direct influence of Beethoven's infirmity on his art was precisely nil, and the indirect influence, so far from being harmful, was probably, from a purely impersonal and inhuman point of view, more beneficial than otherwise, involving as it did the virtual abandonment of his career as a virtuoso. The immediate consequence of this was the progressive disappearance from his art of the improvisatory elements that play such a large part in the music of his earlier period, during which his output consisted for the most part of works for the piano which were often undoubtedly little more than the notation and development of ideas that he had thrown off in the course of extemporizations. This is clearly shown by the ease and rapidity with which they were composed, in such striking contrast to the painful and laborious process of gestation through which his later and greater works were compelled to pass ; and the extent to which this gestation was necessary to the achievement of his highest flights can be gauged by a reference to his sketch-books, where the ideas, in the form in which they first appear—which would probably have satisfied him in earlier years—are frequently so lacking in distinction as to be almost commonplace.

It would not, therefore, be going too far to say that many of the finest characteristics of Beethoven's mature art are indirectly traceable to the affliction from which he suffered, but it would certainly be wrong to suppose that it was directly, or even indirectly, responsible for the steadily growing inclination towards abstraction and for the disdain of merely sensuous beauty which constitutes his artistic development and culminates in the posthumous quartets, for it is a development which is to be observed in the late work of many, and perhaps most, great artists, and certainly in that of the very greatest, as we have already seen. One might even go further and say that the history of every expressive art, viewed as a whole, and of every artistic medium, exemplifies a definite tendency to evolve from the concrete and immediately sensuous to the more abstract and what, for lack of a better word, we must call metaphysical conceptions ; and if one grants music the right to a place among the expressive arts and accepts Combarieu's definition of it as " the art of thinking in sounds ", one must perforce accept the inevitability and inherent rightness of this development in Beethoven's art, and recognize in his later work, and in the posthumous quartets in particular, the highest point to which music, considered as an artistic language, has yet attained.   To deny this is to deny that music is an expressive art at all, and to relegate it to the rank of a mere decorative art or a pleasant physical sensation : which is, of course, to a great extent, the modern æsthetic, or more accurately the æsthetic of yesterday, for there is abundant and increasing evidence to show that this conception of musical art no longer reflects contemporary opinion.   Professor Dent, for example, in his " Terpander ; or Music and the Future", questions whether Beethoven's music " is still convincing to modern ears ".   If by this the writer means the Beethoven of the middle period, the composer of the *Emperor Concerto*, the *Waldstein* and *Appassionata Sonatas*, the *Rasoumoffsky Quartets*, and the *Fifth* and *Sixth Symphonies*, he is unquestionably right.   It is music that, with all its great qualities, is unmistakably dated.   It belongs to a period, and speaks the same language and utters dogmatically in music the same order of ideas and emotions that Rousseau, Shelley and other literary men of his time expressed in words—the brotherhood and equality of man, the perfectibility of human nature, and all the rest of the outworn shibboleths of that age which have no longer any meaning for us, or when they have, repel us with their inadequacy and seeming falsity.   But if Professor Dent means to include the music of the last period in his implied stricture, we must emphatically dissent.   Indeed, it is probably true that, contrary to his supposition, the later music of Beethoven is about the only music that *is* still convincing to modern ears.   All the *Sturm und Drang* of the music of the last century, all the restlessness and conflict of the music of our own time, seems to fade away into nothingness and silence before the unearthly beauty and serenity of such music as the slow movement of the A minor quartet, called in the score a *Song of thanksgiving offered up to the Divinity by a convalescent*.   There is a symbolic significance for us in the inscription.   We too to-day are convalescents ; the world is only just emerging from a paroxysm of madness, hatred, strife and disillusion, and it is this music, more than any other, that corresponds with our innermost experiences, expresses our most intimate thoughts, and satisfies our deepest and most heart felt desires.

The conception of musical history as a single line of evolution, in which the work of each artist is resumed in that of his successor, is so far misleading that we are able, on the contrary, to note a definite distribution or allotment of, seemingly, almost pre-ordained fields of activity to each great composer, in such a way that none of them achieves his greatest work in the same form or category as his most eminent contemporaries or immediate predecessors and successors. We have already seen, for instance, how Josquin, Palestrina, Lassus, Victoria, Gabrieli, Byrd, all excelled in different ways, and how each gave something that none of the others could have given ; similarly we have seen how Bach and Handel shared the world of music between them in such a way that they never trespassed on each other's domains. So with the Viennese masters. Despite the admirable achievements of Haydn in symphony, sonata, and quartet, it is probably *The Creation* which, of all his works, exhibits him at the summit of his powers ; despite the bewildering versatility of Mozart, and his capacity of writing exquisite music for every conceivable medium and in every possible form, it is undoubtedly his operas that constitute his chief title to immortality ; despite the grandeur and sublimity of the *Missa Solemnis* and the great moments of *Fidelio*, Beethoven's enduring achievement lies in the larger instrumental forms ; and the one form or category which Haydn and Mozart conspicuously neglected, in which Beethoven failed to give of his best, namely the instrumentally accompanied solo song, was the one in which the fourth and last of the great line of masters belonging to the Viennese school accomplished his finest work.

Schubert is first and foremost a song composer. This is shown in the first place by the fact that, while he only attained to maturity and individuality in his very last instrumental compositions, and even then only incompletely, he was already in his seventeenth and eighteenth years writing songs, such as *Gretchen am Spinnrade* and the *Erlkönig*, as fine as any he subsequently wrote. Indeed Schubert presents an even more remarkable instance of precocity than Mozart, for there is certainly nothing in the latter's early work to compare with the ripe maturity of such specimens of Schubert's art as those mentioned—and they are far from being isolated examples. This contrast between his absolute mastery in song and his comparative immaturity in other directions is so striking that it is impossible to resist the conclusion that he was to a great extent dependent, in his highest flights at least, on the extraneous fecundating suggestions and *stimuli* afforded by poetry, and it is probably this fact that occasioned Liszt's celebrated and often-quoted dictum to the effect that Schubert was " le musicien le plus poète que jamais ". It is probably true of Schubert at his best, but if we are speaking of his work as a whole it would probably be nearer the truth to say, in a somewhat depreciatory sense, that he was the most musicianly of all musicians who have ever lived : the least in contact with the outside world or with anything apart from music, the most completely lacking of all great composers in the purely cerebral power which is the necessary concomitant of the highest artistic achievements, and the most dependent on the common-place formulas and *clichés* which are the stock-in-trade of the professional hack musician. He, indeed, and not Mozart, is the very type of the conventional music-machine, contentedly turning out work after work, day after day, without any expenditure of mental effort, and unrestrained by any faculty of self-criticism. He was, moreover, entirely devoid of literary taste, and would often set to music the most trivial and tasteless poems with no less enthusiasm than he devoted to the lyrics of a Goethe or a Schiller—a trait which could hardly be said to be characteristic of " the most poetic musician that has ever lived ".

It is also an interesting fact that the most striking and successful as well as the most numerous examples of the imitations of natural phenomena that are largely responsible for the attribution of the term " poetic " to him, are those of sounds—aural rather than visual sensations, in fact—such as the rustling leaves in the *Lindenbaum*, the evening bell in the *Abendbilder* and in the *Zugenglöckchen*, the post-horn in *Die Post*, the hurdy-gurdy in *Der Leiermann*, the spinning wheel in Gretchen's song, the creaking of the tree-branches and the galloping of the horse's hoofs in the *Erlkönig*, the murmur of the brook in *Liebesbotschaft*, and bird-songs innumerable throughout his entire output. He had actually little of Bach's or Berlioz's faculty for graphic pictorial depiction, none of Mozart's power of psychological characterization, and very little of the literary understanding and appreciation of a Wagner or a Strauss—

only the ability to seize upon and realize in music the general emotional atmosphere of a poem, and to find for the words the most felicitous vocal phrase possible. He was not even particularly scrupulous in matters of declamation ; indeed, in such matters his poetic conscience was often singularly deficient, and he seldom hesitated to sacrifice the precise accentuation of the text to the greater beauty of his melodic line and rhythmic flow. This is no doubt largely why he is such a great song writer, but it certainly does not earn for him a right to the title of "most poetic of musicians".

Schubert's greatest strength as a song-writer lies in his astonishing and uncanny power of hitting upon a melodic phrase so suited to the poem that it is henceforth impossible for us to imagine any other conceivable setting of it, or to think of the one without thinking of the other. Poetry and music are one and indissoluble. One does not even feel that the words have been " set to music " at all ; it is as if they had always been together from the very beginning, from the moment the words entered the poet's mind—as if all Schubert had done was to recapture by means of some faculty of clair-audience, the melodies which the poet had imagined, but had been unable to set down. Such a feat was perhaps only possible in dealing with the German lyric poetry of his time, which always seems to have been expressly written with a view to a musical setting, without which it is incomplete.

In this one is strongly reminded of Robert Burns, who had a similar faculty of fitting words to a folk-tune or popular melody so faultlessly that it is difficult to believe that they ever existed apart from each other. There are many other points of resemblance between them ; indeed, their respective careers, personalities, and artistic achievements were strikingly analogous in almost every way. Both musician and poet lived their days in abject poverty, both were given to dissipation, and both died young in consequence. Both excelled in the lyric *genre*, the poet inspired to his best efforts by music, and the musician by poetry. Both failed equally in ambitious works on a large scale and cast in the traditional forms and moulds of their time. The work of Burns other than that written in the vernacular, and under the influence of Young, Goldsmith, Fergusson, and other minor poets of the eighteenth century, is almost invariably tame, conventional, and uninspired ; the works of Schubert in symphonic and operatic form, modelled on Mozart and Beethoven, are with few exceptions, similarly lacking in vitality and originality. Finally, both in their respective spheres occupy precisely the same historical position, for both are precursors of the Romantic movement and yet belong to the classical period at the same time.

As a general rule the artist who reveals a similar duality, and stands with one foot in one age and another in another, achieves his best work from a purely æsthetic point of view in the traditional paths, while as an innovator his work is of merely historical interest and significance. The contrary is true of Schubert, as of Burns. Their finest work is that which is absolutely new and unlike anything else in their age ; their least successful work that which continues the tradition in which they were born. It is certainly true that some of Schubert's later and larger instrumental works contain much fine music, such as the great C *major Symphony*, the two movements of the *Unfinished, the Octet*, the *Quintet in A*, and a few other works, but they are all in varying degrees diffuse in form, slipshod in craftsmanship, and unequal in content ; side by side with the most exquisite moments we find whole stretches of listless and flaccid music-making and sterile repetition. It is just possible that if he had lived long enough to submit himself, as Mozart did and as he himself had the intention of doing in the last years of his life, to a course of rigorous contrapuntal discipline, he might in time have come to achieve as much in the larger forms as he had achieved in the smaller. But all the probabilities are against any such development. There was a lack of intellectual fibre and grit about his whole personality—a flabbiness and superfluity of adipose tissue in his mind as in his body, together with a complete lack of self-criticism which must almost infallibly have prevented him from achieving great works on a large scale, despite his possession of natural gifts to an extent denied even to the very greatest masters of all time, except only Mozart.

CHAPTER XIII

While the great Viennese masters excelled alike in opera and oratorio, in symphony and song, there remains one important field of activity in which the school must be conceded to have failed to equal its achievement in other directions, namely, in church music. The masses and other sacred compositions of Haydn and Mozart undoubtedly contain a great deal of beautiful music, considered simply *quâ* music, but they are utterly unsuited to the purposes of the ritual. Indeed, they strike one as being distinctly pagan, both in style and sentiment. Those of Haydn, one feels, would be a more appropriate accompaniment to the bucolic rites of Ceres and Demeter than to those of the Catholic church, while those of Mozart, not even excepting the famous *Requiem*—a fine but nevertheless somewhat overrated work—with their subtle, sensuous charm, suggest pagan divinities in disguise, like the Saint John and Saint Anne of Leonardo da Vinci, whose characteristic *sfumato* style, incidentally, is strikingly analogous to the chromatically inflected style of Mozart. As for the great *Missa Solemnis* of Beethoven, it is pantheistic rather than Christian, mystical rather than religious, besides being quite unsuited to church performance both on account of its vast dimensions and its frequently dramatic, secular style ; and much the same may be said of the masses of Schubert, despite their many pages of undeniably fine music. The highest achievements in church composition during this period are to be found in the work of Luigi Cherubini, whose masses in general, and his magnificent *Requiem* in particular, by virtue of their superb contrapuntal workmanship in the best traditional style coupled with their profoundly devotional feeling, are among the most conspicuous landmarks in the history of sacred music since the time of Palestrina.

Cherubini is one of the most difficult of all composers to place, and one to whom complete justice has not yet been done by musical criticism. His place in history is perhaps better explained by his dates than by any words, for he was born in 1760—i.e., only four years later than Mozart, and died in 1842, in the full flood-tide of the Romantic movement. Consequently he partakes to a great extent of the characteristics of both periods, classic and romantic, eighteenth and nineteenth centuries, and yet at the same time stands slightly aloof from both. In his orchestral and chamber music he is a mere epigone, the servile follower and imitator of Haydn, Mozart, and Boccherini, but with an added dryness that they do not possess ; in his operas written for the French stage, on the other hand, he played a most important rôle in the formation of the musico-dramatic idioms of the nineteenth century. At the same time, in his sacred music, he is the last great representative of the long line of Italian church composers, with a distinct affinity to Durante in particular.

It is quite true, therefore, that from one point of view he is, in the words of Sir Hubert Parry (" Studies of Great Composers "), " the representative of all that was old-fashioned and conventional in art ", but it would be a mistake to dismiss thus lightly, as a curmudgeonly old pedant, the composer whom Haydn described as " the greatest of all living composers ", whom Beethoven called " the greatest dramatic composer of his time ", whom Weber warmly admired and enthusiastically praised in similar terms, and of whom Brahms said that his *Medea* was "the opera which we musicians between ourselves regard as the highest point in dramatic music ". His operas have not held the stage, partly because they contain few purple patches or detachable lyric sections which linger in the memory, and partly because, in the words of Fétis, " trop enclin à développer ses idées par le mérite d'une admirable facture, il oublie les exigences de l'action ; le cadre s'étend sous sa main, la musique seule préoccupe le musicien, et les situations deviennent froides ". But if his operas seem to-day dead beyond recall—although they are still occasionally performed in Germany—their influence on his contemporaries and successors was immense and lasting. Beethoven's *Fidelio* is not by any means the only work that shows unmistakable traces of it. In the overture to *Les deux Journées*, for example, one finds the germ, if not more than that, of many important innovations, mainly orchestral, for which the credit is generally given to Weber, and the descending figure in the basses at the beginning of it is clearly the direct ancestor of one of the most important themes in Wagner's Ring, associated with Wotan.

On the whole, then, or rather so far as his secular compositions are concerned, Cherubini would seem to occupy much the same kind of position in musical history as Emanuel Bach—that of a link between two distinct styles or epochs, concluding one and beginning another—and consequently to be a figure of historical rather than of æsthetic importance. On the other hand, his sacred music is the last fruit of a great tradition stretching back through the centuries to Palestrina and the Flemish masters, uninfluenced by any changes of taste and environment, and of intrinsic and enduring significance even to-day.

Another composer of Italian extraction who played an equally decisive part in the history of French opera was Gasparo Spontini, whose music may be said to bear much the same relation to that of Gluck that Roman sculpture and architecture do to those of Greece. As in the triumphal arches of Constantine and Severus in Rome, the workmanship is coarse, clumsy, and somewhat lacking in distinction ; at the same time his work undoubtedly possesses a grandeur and monumentality which are entirely its own, and are at once convincing and impressive. In its strange mixture of vulgar ostentation and true sublimity, it is a typical product of the Napoleonic age and the dreams of world-empire ; it is essentially a *Soldatenkunst*, of a piece with the heroic, pseudo-Roman art of the painter David and other artists and writers of the period in France. The influence of Spontini, moreover, is clearly in evidence in the music of many of his greatest successors, such as Meyerbeer, Wagner, and Berlioz, and particularly in the latter's *Les Troyens*, the last, and in the opinion of many, the greatest of all his works.

If Cherubini is the last of the great line of Italian church composers of the eighteenth century, so Spontini can be fitly regarded as the last great master of the old Neapolitan tradition of the *opera seria* ; similarly Gioacchino Rossini is the last outstanding figure in the field of *opera buffa*. His achievement in tragic opera is no longer of any value or significance to-day ; even his most ambitious essay in this direction, *Guillaume Tell*, despite its great merits, must nevertheless be reluctantly accounted a failure. His *Barbiere di Siviglia*, on the other hand, is perhaps the greatest of all comic operas without exception, and is as fresh and living at the present time as the day when it was written ; and other scarcely less admirable works of his in this *genre* which are undeservedly neglected are the *Italiana in Algeri, Cenerentola,* and *Le Comte Ory*. The characteristics of his art, as exemplified in these works, are well summed up by Stendhal in his " Vie de Rossini " : " Surpassé de bien loin par Mozart dans le genre tendre et mélancolique. . . . il est le premier pour la vivacité, la rapidité, le piquant, et tous les effets qui en dérivent . . . le style de Rossini est un peu comme le Français de Paris, vain et vif plutôt que gai, jamais passionné, toujours spirituel, rarement ennuyeux, plus rarement sublime ". It should be added, however, that although his serious operas, apart from a few of their brilliant and scintillating overtures, are no longer to be heard to-day, their historical significance is by no means entirely negligible. He would seem to be the first Italian composer, in his *Elisabetta,* to do away entirely with the old *recitativo secco* with harpsichord accompaniment in favour of recitative with orchestral accompaniment throughout the work, and he also put an end once and for all to the age-long tyranny of the singers by writing out his *fioriture* in full instead of leaving them to be improvised. The resourcefulness of his orchestral writing, too, particularly for the wind instruments, together with his frequent harmonic piquancies, constitute a notable advance in musicianship on the work of his immediate predecessors in Italy.

It would be difficult to imagine a more complete contrast than that between Rossini and Vincenzo Bellini, the most highly gifted of his successors in the field of Italian music. While the former excelled in comic opera by virtue of the incomparable verve and exuberance of his style, the latter's greatest strength lay rather in serious opera, and in the musical realization of situations of a melancholy and tragic order. While Rossini is the last of a long line and the inheritor of a great tradition which practically died with him, Bellini, in his mature work, is one of the most original composers in the whole history of music : owing little, if anything, to any predecessor, and exercising a most decisive and dominating influence on all who were to come after him. It is only necessary to compare a typical melody, such as the celebrated *Casta diva* from

Norma, or *D'un pensiero* from *La Sonnambula*, with any melodies written before them to realize the enormous historic significance of the rôle played by Bellini in the idiomatic evolution of modern music. Indeed, it would probably not be going too far to say that Bellini is to a great extent the father of modern melody. The particular vein of passionate ecstasy and elegiac melancholy which suddenly comes into music in the first half of the nineteenth century, and sharply distinguishes it from that of all preceding centuries, has its source in the operas of Bellini and nowhere else. In this respect there is a distinct analogy between him and Keats, whose rich, imaginative imagery has exercised a similarly decisive influence, both for good and bad, on English poetry. The work of both, moreover, exhibits precisely the same uncertain critical sense and lack of taste, the same frequently over-luscious sentimentality, the same cloying and slightly morbid effeminacy—defects which are largely attributable in both cases to rapid and precocious development, and would probably have eventually disappeared had death not prematurely intervened before either of them had attained to complete maturity. The close parallel between them is all the more striking since both suffered and eventually died from the same complaint, consumption, and later we shall have occasion to allude again to this highly significant fact in another connection.

The most distinguished among Bellini's compatriots and contemporaries was Gaetano Donizetti, probably the most prolific of all modern operatic composers, seeing that in the course of his comparatively short career he wrote no fewer than sixty-six operas. As might be expected, this gigantic output is exceedingly unequal in quality, and only very little of it can be said to repay our attention. The fact remains that when he chose to take enough trouble he was capable of attaining to remarkable heights, as in *Lucia di Lammermoor*—undoubtedly his best work as a whole—and particularly in the justly celebrated *Sextet* which is one of the very finest examples of concerted vocal writing in the whole range of opera. On the whole, however, it must be admitted that the prestige of his serious operas has considerably waned of recent years, and that they are unlikely ever to regain their lost position in popular favour. In opera as in the boxing-ring there is no " come-back "; once a work has dropped out of the permanent repertoire it seldom, if ever, returns to it. His delightful comic operas, on the other hand, such as *Don Pasquale* and *L'Elisir d'Amore*, which reveal an entirely different aspect of his talents, have recently begun to receive the attention they richly deserve. In sparkle, brilliance, and comic verve, they are scarcely, if at all, inferior to the *Barbiere* of Rossini, on which they are obviously modelled, though they perhaps lack the superabundant vitality and sheer animal exuberance of that immortal masterpiece.

Before these more recent developments had taken place in Italy, however, Carl Maria von Weber had revolutionized German opera and initiated a new era in the history of dramatic music. One might even say that if Bellini is the father of modern melody, Weber is the father of modern orchestration. With him for the first time purely colouristic considerations assume an independent existence and a significance of their own apart from the melodic and harmonic content of the music ; many passages in his scores, indeed, show clearly that sometimes the instrumental conception definitely took precedence of all other elements of composition in his mind, and was of much greater importance than the actual notes in which it was embodied. He is also the first composer to exploit systematically the immense and hitherto almost untouched field of resources afforded by the more unusual or abnormal registers of the wind instruments, and the new effects to be obtained by the employment of mutes or by the sub-division of the string units into several parts for special purposes. And while the rôle of the orchestra in opera had hitherto been the essentially subordinate one of providing a background or accompaniment, however elaborate, to the voices, with Weber the instrumental element becomes increasingly important and self-sufficient, and sometimes even plays the leading part in the action as, for example, in the famous scene in *Der Freischütz* of the casting of the silver bullets.

His innovations in operatic form, too, are of great and far-reaching importance. As early as 1817 he had conceived the idea of creating " a complete work of art in which all the constituent parts unite harmoniously to form a perfect whole ", thus anticipating Wagner in theory ; and although in practice he never wholly attained the ideal set forth in this and other similar declarations, we find in *Euryanthe* for the first time a tentative attempt to break down the hitherto universal convention of fixed and separate numbers, to link together to a certain extent the various sections of the work, and to wield them into a more definitely homogeneous and coherent organism. Weber is also the first to make extensive use of what is called local colour ; in his *Preciosa* he creates a specifically Spanish atmosphere, in *Turandot* and *Oberon* respectively he employs Chinese and Turkish folk-songs, in his *Polonaises* for piano he largely anticipates Chopin in his employment of Polish dance rhythms, and in *Freischütz* and *Euryanthe* the element of the supernatural plays a prominent part.

In all these directions Weber was the pioneer, and has consequently exerted a greater influence on music, both for good and evil, than almost any other composer who has ever lived. All the qualities and defects of the music of the nineteenth century, considered generally, are contained in embryo in his music. The elements which were secondary and largely fortuitous in the work of his predecessors, such as Schubert, who most closely resembles him in this respect, become with Weber primary and essential. Colour takes precedence of logic and design, and formal considerations are sacrificed to the attainment of dramatic force and emotional expressiveness. In a word, Weber is the first of the Romantic composers, and the musical representative of the tendencies exemplified in the writings of Tieck, Novalis, and other German writers of the time.

It will generally be found that the artist who breaks fresh ground and suggests new possibilities is remembered for his influence on those who come after him rather than for his actual works, and Weber is no exception to this general rule. Apart from one or two of his overtures, *Der Freischütz* is the only one of his operas which has succeeded in maintaining itself in the modern repertoire, and even it is seldom to be heard outside Germany. Yet there is no doubt that, despite the remarkable boldness and originality of that work, *Euryanthe* is by a long way, not only his most ambitious attempt, but his greatest achievement, and the most important landmark in the history of German opera between Mozart and the later Wagner whose *Flying Dutchman*, *Tannhäuser*, and even *Lohengrin*, are as manifestly inferior to Weber's masterpiece as they are profoundly indebted to it. The reason why it is no longer to be heard on the stage to-day, whereas the latter works are, is to be found in a quite unwarranted prejudice against the libretto which, if admittedly somewhat weak and incoherent, is much less so than that of many an opera which nevertheless survives—certainly much less so than the preposterous farragos of nonsense which are the texts of *Gotterdämmerung* and *Parsifal*, to name only two examples.   It is sincerely to be hoped that this prejudice—for it is nothing else—will some day be overcome, and that this truly magnificent work will be restored to the honoured place which it deserves in the permanent operatic repertoire, along with the finest examples of musico-dramatic art.

Heinrich Marschner, the most important of Weber's followers in the field of German romantic opera, is generally dismissed as being a mere imitator of the latter, but this is distinctly unfair.   He is not only a composer of considerable originality, but is in some respects even Weber's superior.   He may not possess the same fiery and brilliant imagination, the same grace and refinement of style, but his craftsmanship is much more solid and assured, and his work possesses a sombre grandeur and power which that of Weber generally lacks. Marschner particularly excels in the domain of the grisly and the *macabre*, in the depiction of " the passion of supernatural fear " which is the chief ingredient of the German *Schauer-romantik* and the Gothic Romance or Tale of Terror in England. The difference between the romanticism of Weber and Marschner in fact, is much the same as the difference between Tieck and Hoffmann, between Scott and Maturin, whose *Melmoth the Wanderer*, incidentally, bears a striking resemblance in con-ception to the *Hans Heiling* of Marschner which is his best work.   With Weber the element of the supernatural is only incidental, and always subsidiary to the human interest ; with Marschner, on the other hand, it plays the principal rôle, and the impression of gloom and terror which he admirably evokes is strengthened, not relieved as it is with Weber, by the *volkstümlich* numbers cunningly interspersed here and there, which effectively prevent the darkness of the surrounding picture from becoming tedious and monotonously oppressive.

In his *Vie de Rossini*, written in 1823, Stendhal compares the German and Italian operatic traditions to two great rivers which, taking their rise in different and widely separated

o

regions, like the Rhone and Saône, might similarly come together. " Ces deux grands courants d'opinions et de plaisirs différents, representés aujourd'hui par Rossini et Weber, vont probablement se confondre pour ne former qu'une seule école ; et leur réunion, à jamais mémorable, doit peut-être avoir lieu sous nos yeux, dans ce Paris qui est plus que jamais la capitale d'Europe ". It speaks highly for Stendhal's prescience that his prophecy should have been realized within a few years of its being made, by Meyerbeer, in whose operas, written for the Paris stage, the characteristically Italian melodic idioms of Rossini and Bellini are to be found side by side with the elaborately colouristic orchestral style of writing introduced by Weber.

It has long been the fashion to decry Meyerbeer even to the extent of denying him the possession of any redeeming features whatsoever, apart from a remarkable orchestral virtuosity and an unerring sense of theatrical effect, but this is altogether too harsh and sweeping a verdict, and one which is not warranted by an impartial and dispassionate examination of his works. It is true that in order to do him justice we must to a certain extent discard purely æsthetic standards of judgment and take into consideration the time at which he wrote and the enormous influence which he exercised. The fact of the matter is that we are apt to debit Meyerbeer with the undoubted weaknesses and faults of his music, and to credit others with many admirable conceptions which are originally to be found in his work. Passages which everyone admires in the art of Wagner and of Verdi, for example, are often nothing more than thinly disguised variations, adaptations, and elaborations of suggestions embodied in the scores of their much maligned predecessor. In a word, all that was fruitful and enduring in Meyerbeer's art has been assimilated by others and has become public property, while only its by-products and detritus are recognized as his own. Even so, much of his music, judged by the more exacting standards, is by no means as contemptible as it is generally supposed to be by those who are content to receive their opinions ready-made, or pre-digested, from musical primers and elementary text-books. How many people, one would like to know, have ever looked at the score of *Struensee*, which contains some of his best music ? By far the greater part of *Les Huguenots*, too, despite the cheap sneers it elicited from the critical confraternity at its recent revival at Covent Garden—when the unfortunate work was first cut about and disfigured until it was entirely unrecognizable and then atrociously performed—and a great deal of *L'Africaine* as well, will sustain favourable comparison with any dramatic music of its time. The chief reproach made against Meyerbeer consists in his alleged insincerity, but whether it is justified or not, it is at least certain that the insincerity of a man of talent like Meyerbeer is preferable to the sincerity of a mediocrity. Sincerity, indeed, is too often only the consolation prize that we award to the " also-rans " of art, of whom it is impossible to say any more than that they possess it ; the fact that we do not say so of Meyerbeer is a proof that, although he may not be one of the first in the race, he is certainly not among the last.

In one respect the prophecy of Stendhal was not fulfilled. Meyerbeer did not actually found a school. The Italian and German traditions which came together for a moment in his work eventually separated again, although they both continued to bear evident traces of their momentary confluence for some time, and attained two of their highest points in the art of Verdi and of Wagner respectively.

The artistic careers of these two great masters present a similar combination of analogies and differences to that which we have already had occasion to note with regard to Bach and Handel, Haydn and Mozart, or other similarly assorted pairs of contemporary figures in musical history. They were both of them born in the same year, and both of them developed slowly and painfully from the most unpromising beginnings to the attainment of absolute mastery. There is as little to be said for *Oberto* and *Il Finto Stanislao* as for *Die Feen* or *Liebesverbot*. While Wagner's sway eventually extended over practically the whole of Western Europe to the Alps, Verdi remained unchallenged in his supremacy beyond them ; in the words addressed to Attila in his early opera of that name— " Avrai tu l'universo, resti l'Italia a me "—there would almost seem to be a prophetic allusion to the rôles which the two great masters, one the accredited representative of Latinity and the other the all-conquering Teutonic barbarian, were subsequently fated to play on the stage of musical history. Both composers too, apart from their artistic significance, are figures of great cultural importance. Wagner was a

symbol of German unity and expansion ; in his *Meistersinger,*
which is primarily a glorification of German civilization and a
hymn in celebration of its triumphs in the fields of both art and
war, he quite consciously speaks as such through the mouth-
piece of Hans Sachs.   In the personality of Verdi, on the other
hand, is strikingly prefigured the aspirations of Italy, her
struggle to attain independence, and the eventual triumph of
the Risorgimento.   It was not merely because the letters of
his name, by an astonishing coincidence, stood for " Vittorio
Emmanuele, Rè d'Italia ", that the cry Viva Verdi was the
rallying cry and watchword of the Italian people during the
critical years ; but also because at a time when the written and
even the spoken word was so closely scrutinized and censured
that the public expression of political sentiments was virtually
impossible, Verdi made the most innocent and unexceptional
passages in his librettos, which escaped even the alert eyes of
the Austrian officials, implicit with ardent revolutionary
sentiments by virtue of the sheer force and point of his music,
thus helping to sustain the spirit of the common people—like
Tyrtæus in ancient times—which alone, in the end, made
victory possible.   Examples of this kind of thing are to be
found throughout the works written during the critical period :
the chorus in *I Lombardi*, " O Signore dal tetto natio ", "Io ho
la lingua, egli ha il pugnale " in *Rigoletto*, " A Carlo Quinto (by
whom was implied Carlo Alberto, king of Sardinia, and father
of Vittorio Emmanuele) " sia gloria ed honor " in *Ernani*—all
illustrations of the truth that, to adapt the words of Beau-
marchais, what is too dangerous to say in words can be sung to
music.   In this way it is probably not going too far to say that
Verdi played a more important and decisive part in the
liberation of Italy than even Mazzini, Garibaldi, or Cavour
themselves, individually, although the fact has yet to be
recognized by historians.

In his own artistic development, too, Verdi is a symbol of
the Risorgimento and the achievement of Italian independence,
for in his two last and best works, *Otello* and *Falstaff*, he finally
succeeds in purging his art of the last remaining traces of foreign
influences, and arrives at the creation of a wholly personal and
essentially Latin style.   It is important that this should be
recognized, for these two master-works are generally represented
as having been written under the influence of Wagner—a truly

fantastic suggestion, and one for which there is not the slightest justification.   Anything less Wagnerian either in spirit or in style it would be impossible to imagine.   Verdi was never in the slightest degree indebted to his great German contemporary. It is true that there are traces of foreign influences in the works which precede his two masterpieces, in *Aïda* particularly, and also in the *Vêpres Siciliennes* and *Don Carlos*, both of which were written for the French stage, but it is not the influence of Wagner, but of Meyerbeer.   In other words, any superficial resemblances that may be detected here and there between the later Verdi and Wagner are simply the outcome of an influence to which both were subjected.   This Meyerbeerian element is even to be found in such a comparatively early work as *Il Trovatore*, written long before Wagner became a dominating force in music.   As Dannreuther rightly says in the " Oxford History of Music ", " the rôle of Azucena is but that of Fidès in *Le Prophète* of Meyerbeer, translated into Romany ", and *Aïda* is musically little more than a grandiose pendant or sequel to *L'Africaine.*

Verdi's occasional use of the *leit-motiv*, moreover, is strikingly different from that of Wagner ; it is associated, not so much with individuals or definite objects as in the *Ring*, but rather with ideas and emotional situations, as in *Otello* for example, where a theme from the love music of the first act recurs at the close of the work.   The continuous texture of *Falstaff*, again, so far from being Wagnerian, is of identically the same kind as is to be found in the old Venetian opera of Cavalli or in the *Incoronazione di Poppœa* of Monteverdi, in which aria and recitativo are so interpenetrated with each other and interfused as to form a homogeneous *arioso* style which is neither one or the other.   This fact lends additional force and significance to Verdi's often-quoted dictum " Tornate all'antico e sara un progresso ".   In short, the legend—for it is nothing more— that Verdi was influenced by Wagner in his last works, and that their excellence is due to this cause, is simply a palpable piece of propaganda on the part of the Wagnerians, to whom the idea that excellence could be achieved in any other way than by the wholehearted acceptance of the principles and methods of their idol, is anathema.   So far from it being true, the greatness of *Falstaff* is largely the consequence of its diametrical opposition to and independence of the art of Bayreuth.   When Nietzsche, in his vitriolic attack on Wagner, sought for a form of operatic art which he could oppose to that of the latter, he was compelled for lack of anything better, to fall back upon Bizet's *Carmen*, and thereby greatly weakened his case ; for *Carmen*, though certainly a charming little work, is far too slight and unimportant a thing to stand comparison for a moment with the majestic and monumental creations of the great German master. *Falstaff* was then, unfortunately, still unwritten ; otherwise Nietzsche could hardly have failed to recognize in it the living embodiment of his artistic ideals, for which he had hitherto sought in vain—" a mocking, nimble, volatile, divinely undisturbed, divinely artificial art, which blazes up like pure flame into a cloudless sky—a music which, unlike other music, would not die away, nor pale, nor grow dull beside the blue and wanton sea and the clear Mediterranean sky ".

It is by virtue of this work, and *Otello* also, that Verdi lives for us to-day, and, it is fairly safe to say, will continue to live as long as music itself.   *Aïda*, despite its great reputation and popularity, is a very much overrated and somewhat disagreeable production, impure in style, grandiose and pretentious in conception.   It is essentially a transition work, and like so many works of which this can be said, less perfect and less satisfying than others which are comparatively immature. It belongs to a stage of development similar to that of adolescence, possessing neither the charm and innocence of youth, nor the wisdom and dignity of complete maturity. Infinitely preferable to it are some of the earlier works, such as *Rigoletto*, *La Traviata*, and even *Il Trovatore*, with their immortal, sublimely vulgar barrel-organ tunes, which will continue to haunt the ears of men for centuries to come, despite the horror and disapproval of all the pedants, past, present and future.

While Verdi's artistic development consists in a gradual elimination of foreign impurities and in the final attainment of complete individuality through a process of refinement and concentration, Wagner's steady advance towards mastership is, on the contrary, a process of triumphant assimilation and expansion.   He seems almost to suck the strength and vitality from the art of all his predecessors and contemporaries, one by one, like a vampire, leaving them pale and lifeless ; he does not so much sum up the work of others, as Bach does, but rather robs them—in *Rienzi* Meyerbeer and Spontini, in the *Flying Dutchman* Marschner, in *Tannhäuser* and *Lohengrin* Weber, in *Tristan* and the *Ring* Liszt, in *Die Meistersinger* Bach even, in all of them, of course, Beethoven—these are only a few of the more obvious sources from which he derives his artistic substance.   But there is hardly a single composer of note that he does not forcibly lay under contribution, including even the most unlikely people.   The *Liebestod* in *Tristan* is unmistakably a gigantic expansion of the final scene from Bellini's *Norma*, the Rhine music in the *Ring* is the working out and elaboration of a motive in the *Melusine Overture* of Mendelssohn, and the influence of Chopin's irridescent chromatic harmonies is in evidence throughout the entire work of his maturity.   Few composers have actually invented less than Wagner ; not even Handel has ever turned to better use the inventions and discoveries of others, and in this miraculous power of assimilation and reproduction, combined with a lack of original creative power, he typifies the Teutonic spirit, of the nineteenth century at least.

Yet this gigantic musical synthesis was not even an end in itself, but only one single element in an even greater art-synthesis.   Wagner might justly be called the Napoleon of music, for in the same way that the latter sought to establish a world-empire and used France merely as a means to the accomplishment of his purpose, so Wagner aimed at the creation of the *Gesamtkunstwerk*, embracing all the arts, in which music was only to be one among many means, though possibly the most important of them all, to this end.   In order to attain his ambition he was as willing to sacrifice the interests of music as ruthlessly as Napoleon sacrificed the lives of his French subjects.   When Wagner declared that music should only be the means to the end of drama, we are reminded of Napoleon's contemptuous exclamation made in the course of negotiations with Metternich—" what are the lives of a million French soldiers to me " !   No ruler with the interests of his subjects at heart, no composer with the interests of music at heart, could possibly speak thus ; and the explanation of it is to be found in the simple fact that Wagner was no more a true musician at heart than Napoleon was a Frenchman.   As Wagner himself admitted in one of the expansive moods of cynical and disarming frankness which he occasionally allowed himself in conversation with his intimates, and which again strongly remind one of the great historical figure to whom we are comparing him, he learnt to compose music as one learns a foreign language. He gradually mastered the medium completely, and was eventually able to express himself with perfect ease in it, but, like Napoleon, he never lost his foreign accent.

We find here the explanation of the peculiar qualities of Wagner's art, so different from those of any other composer who has ever lived, and the secret of his popularity with the masses and with the average, semi-cultured man who is interested in the arts in a vague way only, and of his un-popularity with musicians. There is nothing specifically musical in his thought. He was one of these men of universal potentialities who could probably have expressed himself just as well in any other artistic medium, or at least in some other. Bad though his poetry and prose may appear, critically considered, they are certainly no worse than his early music ; and it is more than probable that if he had chosen to take the trouble of perfecting himself in this direction rather than in music, he would have been as great a writer as he became a composer.

The reason why Wagner adopted music as the principal vehicle for the expression of his ideas is simply to be found in the fact that music was, more than any other art, the dominant art of the nineteenth century, and the one best fitted to his purposes. As I sought to show in " A Survey of Contemporary Music ", we shall generally find that at any given period there is one art in particular which best expresses and embodies the values of that period. " In the Middle Ages, for example, the predominance of architectural conceptions and methods is immediately noticeable. . . . the characteristic art-expression of the succeeding era, to which all the others continually tend, is painting—the eighteenth century is primarily that of literature . . . and similarly neither the consummate literary achievements of the century, nor the splendid hierarchy of the French painters from Delacroix to Cézanne, can alter the fact that, collectively speaking, music is the art of the nineteenth century—the medium which, better than any other, realizes and embodies the characteristic aims and ideals of the time, and which alone could adequately express them." This is only a bald summary of the argument which is there developed and illustrated at length. The seeming paradox that during this period literary conceptions are perhaps commoner in music than ever before, so far from militating against the truth of this statement, tends rather to confirm it ; for as a result of this aptitude of music for expressing the romantic values, the medium attracted to it many artists such as Wagner, who as we have already suggested, would probably in other times have expressed himself in some other way. The idea and conceptions underlying Wagner's art are of that vague, indeterminate, universal order which is not bound up with any specific artistic medium, and might just as well be expressed in any of them. Wagner, in fact, was a *condottiere* of the arts, whose sword was at the disposal of whichever of them could offer the most advantageous terms for his services or the best opportunities for distinguishing himself ; and, as it happened, it was music at that particular period that was best able to do so, in the same way that France served as the instrument of Napoleon's ambitions.

For a time the impossible seemed to have come true. Bayreuth became the artistic capital of the world, to which all the emperors, kings, and petty princes of the arts flocked to do homage to their conqueror; and the *Revue Wagnérienne*, whose contributors represented the intellectual *élite* of every form of artistic or philosophic activity, was founded at Paris. Wagner's reign, however, was as short-lived and as insecurely based as that of Napoleon. The subject arts arose in revolt and, shaking off his yoke, regained autonomy ; poets, painters, dramatists, and philosophers, " crept out again to feel the sun ". The Wagnerian Empire of the *Gesamtkunstwerk* crumbled into dust. Even the kingdom of music itself, which was the instrument he employed to subjugate the other arts, renounced its allegiance , and restored again the true principles of the art and the great masters of the past to the throne from which they had been banished by the great usurper. Left weak and exhausted, however, by the fierce Wagnerian domination, music to-day is hag-ridden by the alien and equally pernicious influences of literature and the plastic arts.

It is exceedingly difficult for us of the present generation to do justice to Wagner, or to arrive at any final and impartial conclusions concerning the permanent value of his gigantic achievement. As after a great war, we can only see the destruction, the damage, the irreparable loss it has entailed, the irretrievable harm that his reign has done to the art of music, from which we are only now beginning to recover. Its benefits can only be apprised by a later generation which has ceased to suffer from its effects.

It is true, of course, that many, perhaps even most, great artists produce a similar effect on the minds of their successors, and that it is only the figures of lesser rank and smaller stature who, probably because they suggest more than they actually achieve, exercise a benign, fruitful, and stimulating influence on those who come after them. It is even possible that the greater an artist is, the more devastating his influence ; and it is conceivable that the successors of Palestrina, Bach, or Beethoven, felt a despondency and hopelessness similar to that which modern musicians feel to-day after Wagner. One feels that there is a difference, none the less, between him and them, a definitely pernicious quality in his work, quite apart from its shortcomings—indeed, one feels it even more in his best work than in his worst—which has poisoned music for a generation, and from the effects of which we are only now beginning slowly to recuperate.

However that may be, there can be no two opinions concerning the gigantic stature and demoniac vitality of the creator of this vast world-empire of art. Whatever of his actual tangible achievement survives, whatever the nature of the influence that remains, he is, abstractly considered, unquestionably one of the most significant and arresting figures not merely in all music, but in all art ; and of all his works the one which is most likely to be accounted his masterpiece, despite its manifest faults and intolerable *longueurs*, is surely the *Ring*—one of the grandest and most ambitious artistic projects ever conceived and carried to completion by a single human brain, and comparable in its immensity only to such gigantic creations as the Gothic cathedrals of the Middle Ages or the temples of Boro Budur, at which whole generations have laboured.

CHAPTER XIV

The French School of the Nineteenth Century

The masters of the nineteenth century with whom we have been dealing in the foregoing chapter were all primarily, and most of them exclusively, operatic composers, of German and Italian nationality. We now have to consider those of their contemporaries whose activities were wholly or mainly confined to the concert-room, and whose general artistic tendencies may best be described as French ; for in the same way that Weber, Marschner, and Wagner were the musical exponents of German romanticism, and Bellini, Donizetti, and Verdi those of Italian romanticism, so in the work of Hector Berlioz, Franz Liszt, and Frédéric Chopin we find the musical expression of the ideals and tendencies exemplified in the poetry of Hugo, de Musset, and Lamartine, and in the painting of Delacroix, although actually only the first-named of the three can properly be said to be a Frenchman.

The position of Berlioz is probably unique in the history of music. Throughout his lifetime, from the very outset of his career even, his work never ceased to provoke the wildest enthusiasm on the one hand, and the most violent hostility on the other. Even to-day, although fifty years and more have elapsed since his death, the musical world is still as sharply divided into two camps concerning him as it was a century ago. To his admirers he is simply one of the very greatest of all composers who have ever lived ; to his adversaries he is a less than second-rate figure, a mere scene-painter in sounds, with nothing save a gift for orchestration to commend him. If the latter have so far probably been in the majority, the former have made up for their numerical inferiority by a fanaticism which opposition has only served to strengthen and confirm.

But although Berlioz is the object of a cult, it is one which, unlike most other cults, is entirely devoid of preciosity. Further, his worshippers make no propaganda on his behalf. Like the Druses, they are a race apart ; they do not seek to make converts, because they do not want them. You are either one of them or you are not.   Either you receive at once, from the very first work of his that you hear, a thrill akin to an electric shock, or else you are completely insulated and rendered for ever immune by a pachydermatous rubber hide of indifference or distaste.

The reasons why his music does not, and never can, appeal to the majority, are readily explicable.   The original conceptions and daring experiments in it, which repel the pedants and academicians, are equally uncongenial to those who go to music mainly for its physical and emotional appeal, for they are primarily addressed to the intellectual and imaginative faculties of the listener—his alleged sensationalism, for example, is always entirely free from the hot, animal sensuality of Wagner and other modern composers.   His strength and virility likewise disconcert the aesthetes and those who appreciate only the caviare and high game of music.   Finally, he never does the expected, and this is for most people the virtue that cannot be forgiven.   Consequently the mere mention of his name has always been sufficient to cause Wagnerians and Brahmsians, and classicists and modernists of every description, to desist momentarily from their internecine feuds and vendettas, and to close their ranks against the common enemy, chanting in unison, with joined hands, the time-honoured anathemas and objurgations handed down unaltered from the days of Hanslick and Fétis.   The general verdict may be best summed up by saying that, while he is admitted, somewhat grudgingly, to have been an incontestable master of orchestration and rhythmical device, he has been declared to be completely devoid alike of melodic invention, harmonic instinct, and contrapuntal resource.   To such an extent has this opinion crystallized into an irrefragable dogma of musical criticism that until quite recently it was very rare to encounter a musician who had ever dreamt of questioning it, or who had ever thought of looking at the music for himself with a mind unclouded by prejudice and preconceived notions concerning it. Weingartner, for example, has described his surprise and pleasure on looking for the first time at the score of the Overture to *Benvenuto Cellini*—a comparatively unimportant work—which he had come across by chance.   " I began to laugh, both with delight at having discovered such a treasure, and with annoyance at finding how narrow human judgment is.   From that day on there has been for me another great citizen in the republic of art."

That Berlioz should, in particular, be reproached with a lack of melodic invention is one of the most astounding ineptitudes of musical criticism. He is a melodist first, foremost, and all the time : perhaps the greatest since Mozart, certainly the greatest since Beethoven. As a French critic has pointed out, his phrases most frequently consist of twelve, sixteen, eighteen, or twenty bars, while with Wagner, for example, phrases of eight bars are rare, those of four most common, those of two still more so, and those of one bar are most frequent of all ; and what is true of Wagner may be said of practically every composer of the nineteenth century. In fact, in Berlioz's own words, his melodies are often on such a large scale that " an immature or short-sighted musical vision may not clearly distinguish their form—shallow musicians may find them so unlike the funny little things that they call melodies that they cannot bring themselves to give the same name to both ".

Again, in the matter of harmony there is considerable misunderstanding. It is true that Berlioz's harmonic writing may often sound crude and awkward when played on the pianoforte or read in score ; the fact remains that in orchestral performance it sounds perfectly logical and coherent. It is not generally recognized that harmonic subtleties often disappear entirely when transferred to the orchestra, or serve merely to obscure the issue, especially when written for the wind, and for the heavy brass in particular. The simpler and more primitive harmonic combinations are invariably the most successful, and the glitter and brilliance of Berlioz's scoring is largely the direct outcome of his appreciation of this fact.

The reproach of poverty of contrapuntal resource, though possibly more justifiable than either of the others, hardly carries so much weight at the present day, when this particular weapon in the composer's armoury is conspicuously neglected by the vast majority of representative music-makers. Berlioz, like them, had no particular use for it, but that is not to say that he was incapable of making use of it when it happened to suit his purpose. For example, there is as fine contrapuntal writing in parts of the *Te Deum* as in any music of the post-Beethoven period.

No, the underlying cause of the organized opposition with

which the music of Berlioz has hitherto had to contend does not reside in any of the fallacious objections that we have been examining, but in his astonishing originality—a quality he possessed to a greater extent than any composer who has ever lived.   Let anyone who questions this consider the fact that the *Symphonie Fantastique*, in which a whole new world of musical possibilities is revealed, dates from 1830, only three years after the death of Beethoven, when the composer was only twenty-seven years old ; and that the *Francs Juges* Overture and a considerable amount of the *Faust* music had already been written before that, at a time when the music of Weber and Beethoven was almost wholly unknown to him.   He owes nothing to any predecessors and, apart from his orchestral innovations, his art has exercised little or no influence on his successors.   It is often said that a great musical work is always the outcome of a definite tradition and a long period of development.   It may be true as a generalization, but it certainly does not apply to Berlioz, which is largely the reason why he is frowned on by conventional criticism.   Almost alone among innovators and experimenters, he was able to turn his back on the past, to be entirely independent of his contemporaries, and yet to achieve work of lasting power and beauty.   In that unknown land of boundless extent which girds about the narrow beaten path of musical tradition—a Sahara desert littered by the bones of so many visionaries and adventurous spirits who have wandered there, lost themselves, and perished—Berlioz has reared up gigantic pyramids of sound which will endure as long as music itself.

Of all those who have written about the art of Berlioz, it is probably the poet Heine who has best defined the paradoxical duality of his genius when he called him a " gigantic nightingale, a lark the size of an eagle, such as they say existed in the primitive world ".   And of all the works of his the one which best exemplifies this titanic sweetness, this sublimity so strangely blent with tenderness—the work of which Berlioz himself said that if he were faced with the prospect of the total destruction of all his compositions with one single exception, it was the one for which he would ask grace—this work is surely the great *Messe des Morts*, or *Requiem*.

In his *Mémoires* Berlioz tells us that the whole work was written with almost inconceivable rapidity.   "Ma tête semblait prête à crever sous l'effort de ma pensée bouillonante. Le plan d'un morceau n'était pas esquissé que celui d'un autre se presentait ; dans l'impossibilité d'écrire assez vite, j'avais adopté des signes sténographiques ". Even without this knowledge the impression which the work makes in performance is that it has been conceived and executed in one single, unflagging, volcanic burst of creative inspiration.   At the same time, one of its most remarkable features consists in the degree of restraint which the composer displays in employing the enormous material resources at his disposal, including four brass bands stationed one at each corner of the *ensemble*, and no fewer than sixteen kettledrums. With the exception of the *Tuba Mirum*, *Lacrimosa*, and *Rex tremendæ majestatis*, the level of dynamic intensity in the other eight movements is comparatively low throughout.   Here we touch on one of the main reasons of Berlioz's unpopularity with the multitude. Most of them feel that they are not getting their money's worth if the whole orchestra, and the organ as well, are not kept blaring away most of the time, as in the " 1812 " Overture of Tschaikovsky. But the quite overwhelming effect of the *Tuba Mirum* and the *Lacrimosa* depends precisely on the contrast which they present with the other movements.

The *Requiem* stands alone in music : there is nothing with which we can fitly compare it.   Another choral and orchestral work which contains some of the finest music of his middle period is the *Roméo et Juliette*, and the early *Symphonie Fantastique*, one of the most astonishing achievements in all music, probably represents his highest point in purely instrumental music. *Les Troyens*, on the other hand, a gigantic music-drama in two parts, is the masterpiece of his last period, and reveals hitherto unsuspected aspects of his genius.   In his earlier works he is the typical representative of the French Romantic movement, here he is a classical master in the pure Latin tradition ; the volcanic, tempestuous energy of the early works gives place to a majestic dignity and restraint worthy of Sophocles himself, and to a serenity and sweetness that can only be called Virgilian. In sheer grandeur and vastness of conception there is nothing in the whole range of opera to be compared to it with the exception of the very different *Ring*. In the one the whole world of Teutonic mythology and folk-lore, with its gods, giants, dwarfs, monsters,

Rhine-maidens, Valkyries, comes to life in music ; in the other, the Greek and Latin legend of the fall of Troy and the foundation of the city of Rome. The two works are complementary, and equally great in their different ways, but the work of Berlioz has yet to receive the appreciation that is its due. It is quite safe to say that in time it will, for signs of change in the critical attitude towards it have already appeared.

While Berlioz excelled in works conceived and executed on a heroic scale, and only failed in the few instances in which he confined himself to a small canvas, as in his feeble and undistinguished songs with piano accompaniment, Chopin was essentially a miniaturist, and invariably failed when he attempted the larger forms, as in his piano concertos. The former was primarily an orchestral composer, possessing an intimate knowledge and understanding of the characters and capabilities of all the instruments and of every conceivable combination of them ; the latter's feeling for *timbre* or colour was entirely restricted to the narrow range of possibilities afforded by a single instrument—the only one, by the way, for which Berlioz seems to have had no liking—namely, the pianoforte. While Berlioz was always greatly influenced by literary and pictorial conceptions, both in his life and in his work, neither literature nor any other art played any part in Chopin's mental development or in his music. Not merely had he an instinctive and profound aversion from anything in the nature of " programme music ", but he was never known even to read a book. In short, nothing in the outside world, neither human relations, feeling for nature, nor appreciation of any art save his own, exercised the slightest influence upon his work either for good or evil. From purely musical influences too, he was singularly free. He would seem to have actively disliked almost all music except his own, and particularly that of his greatest contemporaries. Berlioz, Liszt, and Meyerbeer, he particularly detested, not, one suspects, on account of their faults, but for their very virtues ; even to Schumann, strangely enough, he remained entirely unsympathetic, and in Beethoven he cared only for *cantabile* passages bearing a certain similarity to his own. He seems always to have entertained a morbid and deeply rooted antipathy for anything robust, virile, or heroic.

Altogether, in fact, Chopin is the most one-sided, the most spiritually isolated composer who has ever lived, and his work reveals all the characteristic qualities and defects that spring from this condition.   Possessing as he did a keen critical sense, he would seem to have accepted his limitations rather than attempted to disguise or overcome them.   Practically all his attempts in larger forms and in *media* other than the solo piano, belong to his early period ; as if acutely aware of their short-comings, he resolutely turned his back on them and concentrated his entire energies on developing and perfecting that side of his talents in which he felt his greatest strength lay.   In this way he was able to transform his faults into something very like virtues, and he certainly reaped a magnificent reward for his voluntary renunciation of the larger forms.   Alone among all the romantics he has so far triumphantly defied all the changes in taste and fashion which have taken place since his time. With other and even greater masters we tend to forgive their defects on account of their great qualities, but there will always be many amongst us for whom the former outweigh the latter The art of Chopin, on the other hand, slight and limited though it may be, is, humanly speaking, perfect ; and for that reason it has continued to command the admiration and respect of musicians of all schools, tendencies and sympathies.   All unite in praise of Chopin as they unite in condemning Berlioz.   There are and probably always will be Wagnerians and anti-Wagnerians, Brahmsians and anti-Brahmsians, people who like and dislike, both with equal reason, the work of almost every composer ; Chopin alone among them all it is impossible to do otherwise than admire, even if we happen to be tempera-mentally unsympathetic to him.   In the same way, it may be noted, the equally perfect and limited art of de Musset has worn better in the course of time than the incomparably bigger and more robust work of the great Romantics such as Victor Hugo. In fact, quite apart from their relations with George Sand, there are many close resemblances between Chopin and de Musset

The favour and esteem enjoyed by Chopin, however, are by no means confined to musicians and the cultured few.   On the contrary, there is no composer whose popularity exceeds his with the general public, and even with the otherwise unmusical ; indeed it is by no means exceptional to encounter people who care for no music but his.   It is probably also true to say that a larger number of people owe their first authentic

P

musical thrill in early years to him than to any other composer. Question anyone as to the first piece of music which he remembers to have stirred him deeply in childhood or adolescence, and the chances are as much as ten to one that it will turn out to be some piece by Chopin.   To no composer, in fact, has the power been given to such a large extent of pleasing both the connoisseur and the man in the street, the musician and the general public ; and this universality of appeal, strangely enough, is in direct ratio and probably largely attributable to the narrow limits within which he deliberately chose to confine his talents, resulting in a directness and lucidity of utterance, a concentrated intensity of expression almost without parallel in music.

The main reason for Chopin's immense and enduring popularity, however, is perhaps to be found in the fact that he is incontestably the favourite composer of women, who after all constitute by far the larger part of musical audiences, at piano recitals in particular.   There is very little music in existence which is predominantly feminine in its appeal, largely because no female composers of eminence have yet appeared, or are ever likely to appear.   Such as there are would seem to make it a point of honour almost to be *plus royalistes que le roi*, and to attempt to outdo mere man in exhibitions of strenuous masculinity.   In the sensitive, capricious, and volatile art of Chopin, on the other hand, women find the expression of their most intimate thoughts and sensations, their most secret and unspoken desires ; he is the Rudolph Valentino of music, the musical personification of ideal love, of love as women would have it—chaste yet passionate, ardent yet tender, innocent yet understanding—hermaphroditic, sexless almost.   This is the lap-dog Chopin, as Wagner, perhaps too contemptuously, called him, the Chopin of the *Valses* and *Nocturnes* in particular.

Second in order of popularity comes the Chopin of the *Polonaises*, and *Mazurkas*, the national composer, the tone-poet of Poland in native costume—the cap adorned with a heron-feather, a brilliant sash around the waist, and bright scarlet hose—music full of sumptuous, glowing colour and heroic attitudinizings.   But the greatest Chopin of all is the Chopin of the *Études*, *Préludes*, and *Scherzos*, owing nothing to either nationality or environment, French or Polish, but expressing only the varying moods and aspects of his own solitary, unique and enigmatic personality.

The art of Chopin was, on the whole, too exclusively individual, too limited in scope, to exercise any decisive and dominating influence on subsequent composers.   One aspect of it, however, namely, his harmonic style of writing and his chromaticism in particular, is of considerable historical significance, and has undoubtedly played an important part in the idiomatic evolution of modern music, similar and equal to that played by Weber and Bellini in the direction of instrumental and melodic writing respectively.   Indeed, we may say that if Weber is the father of modern orchestration and Bellini the father of modern melody, Chopin is the father of modern harmony.

It is a very remarkable fact which is surely something more than a coincidence, that all these three masters, representing in their different ways the main formative elements in modern, or at least in nineteenth-century music, were consumptives : and it would consequently be fascinating to speculate to what extent, if any, this disease is to be held responsible for the appearance in the work of all three of similar characteristics, both stylistic and psychological, and for the fact that Weber and Bellini are the only two composers who exercised any influence on Chopin's art, or for whose music he cherished an active sympathy.   That the poetry of Keats, who also suffered from the same complaint, should also reveal unmistakably the same peculiar features and should exercise precisely the same important influence on the poetry of the nineteenth century, lends striking and additional confirmation to the suspicion that there is probably a definite connection between the two phenomena, and that the specifically Romantic element in art was to a great extent conditioned by pathological circumstances.   It is at least undeniable that the Romantic movement was largely the creation of pulmonary consumptives in all the arts, and in music almost entirely so ; and this fact would seem to account satisfactorily for the strain of morbidity and feverish exaltation which is one of the most prominent characteristics of the art of the period, and at the same time one of the most familiar symptoms of the disease.

The history of Italian music in the eighteenth century is mainly confined to that of opera, in the nineteenth century entirely so, with the exception of one strange and solitary figure, Niccolo Paganini, whose almost legendary prowess as a virtuoso of the violin has been allowed to eclipse his by no means negligible gifts as a composer.   From one point of view he may be regarded as the last great representative of the long line of Italian violin composers which can be traced back without a break to Corelli ; from another and probably more important standpoint he is one of the most vital inspirational forces of the Romantic movement—not merely by virtue of his uncanny and impressive personality, which served as a model for Hoffmann's Kreisler, nor even simply on account of his astonishing virtuosity as an executant and his skill in inventing new effects, which undoubtedly inspired Liszt to emulate him in the sphere of piano-playing—but as a composer.   In the first place the elaborate arabesques and ornamental figurations that are such a prominent feature of his music, constitute one of the most important influences in the formation of the style of piano-writing of both Chopin and Liszt ; and the intrinsic merits of his *Capricci*, which are his most significant contribution to musical literature, are so great that no fewer than three of the most eminent composers of the century—Liszt, Schumann and Brahms—transcribed and adapted them for the piano. Other lesser known but equally important aspects of his creative talent are to be found in his violin concertos, which are by no means mere idle displays of virtuosity, but highly original, admirably constructed, and finely scored works ; and in certain quartets for the unusual combination of two violins, one 'cello, and guitar, chiefly remarkable for a peculiarly individual and daring use of chromatic harmony and abrupt modulation which undoubtedly exercised a considerable influence on many of his contemporaries and successors, and on Liszt in particular.

The considered verdict passed by musical critics of the most antagonistic tendencies on the music of Liszt, as on that of Berlioz, has hitherto been singularly unanimous.   But whereas the latter has at least always had his devoted circle of admirers and adherents, Liszt never has ; apart from a few solitary individuals, all unite in decrying him still as they did during his lifetime—the classicists on account of his daring innovations and experiments, the "modernists" on account of his Romanticism and frequent sentimentality. The general consensus of authoritative and conventional opinion is perhaps best summed up in the words of Sir Henry Hadow ("Music", Home University Library) : "Most of his composition is glitter and tinsel, fragments of weak or trivial melody decked out in elaborate and incongruous ornaments, covered with paste jewels and tawdry embroideries, . . . shallow displays of brilliance, which still retain some power to astonish, but very little to delight ", and " his place in musical history is determined not so much by his own work as by the help and encouragement which he gave to that of Richard Wagner ". Tinsel, paste, tawdry, shallow—these are the epithets which perpetually recur, *ad nauseam*, in almost all descriptions or critical estimates of Liszt's work to be found in musical histories.

Now it is certainly true that in Liszt's vast output there are many thoroughly bad works, and a great deal that is at best second-rate ; he was admittedly a somewhat unequal composer. There is nothing exceptional in that, however ; the same could be said of many great masters. Schubert, Schumann, Mendelssohn, Franck, to mention only a few names at random, all wrote very much more bad music than good ; even Mozart, Beethoven, and Handel, wrote a vast amount which is better forgotten. Rightly or wrongly, however, we ignore these numerous lapses in our critical estimates of their achievements and are content to judge them on the strength of their best work, but we persist in judging Liszt on the weaknesses of his worst work. His best music, which is almost totally unknown and hardly ever performed, is no more tawdry or shallow than the work of any other composer, and could only seem to be so to those for whom brilliance and glitter are necessarily suspect and pernicious qualities in themselves, and who are unable to distinguish real diamonds from paste. And in Liszt's huge and unequal output there are assuredly, for those who care to look for them, enough gems of the first water to build him a crown of imperishable glory equal to that of any composer of his age, but they lie hidden from sight and contemptuously ignored by all save a few, in the midst of a heap of second-rate and even worthless rubble.

The main reason for the neglect of his best music, and for the lack of appreciation which has hitherto been accorded it, is to be found in the fact that all his most fruitful innovations and discoveries have been adopted by his contemporaries and successors, who have in many instances received the credit for them. Like Meyerbeer, in fact, but to an even greater extent, Liszt is commonly credited—or rather discredited—

only with what is least admirable in his work : with the dross and slag which are the inevitable concomitants of any great creative effort. It is not only Strauss and other modern composers of symphonic poems who are directly and profoundly indebted to him, to such an extent that they could not possibly have existed without him, but also the great Russian composers of the last century, particularly Balakirev their leader, and Borodin, and through them a great part of modern music. Most of the procedures of the French Impressionists are already to be found in such pieces as the *Jeux d'eau de la Villa d'Este*, or *Au bord d'une source*, and even Scriabine is markedly under the influence of Liszt. He is, moreover, after Weber, the founder of modern orchestration to a far greater degree than Wagner, whose intricate polyphonic texture is not for everyone, or Berlioz, whose methods of scoring are altogether too personal and inimitable to be of great practical service to anyone but himself ; and the harmonic audacities to be found in the *Années de Pélérinage*, some of which date back as far as the " eighteen-thirties ", anticipate many modern experiments by close on a century. But above all, the extent to which Wagner was indebted to Liszt in the matter of both melody and harmony is seldom sufficiently emphasized. A work such as the great *Faust Symphony*, for example, fairly teems with melodic phrases which undoubtedly suggested to Wagner some of the finest pages in his later works. It is to the latter's credit that he quite frankly avowed the fact, and it is certainly not going too far to say that the phenomenal stride forward which the latter made between *Lohengrin* and *Rheingold* is almost entirely due to the fruitful stimulus he received from the music of Liszt, who had already by that time attained to complete maturity.

No one, then, it is safe to say, invented more than Liszt, no one has exercised a profounder influence on music. In fact the generosity and practical assistance, financial and otherwise, which he lavished on all who came to him with their work is only paralleled by the artistic benefit which they and subsequent composers derived from his music. His purse and princely hospitality were at the disposal of all, and his works served as a quarry of ideas to generations of composers ; he died penniless and neglected by those who owed most to him, and posterity has treated his artistic achievement with the same shameless ingratitude.

So much for Liszt's influence and his consequent historical importance. His absolute value as a creative artist is more difficult to determine. His whole output, in its immensity, variety, and inequality remind one involuntarily of the description of the antique shop in Balzac's *Peau de Chagrin*— an " océan de meubles, d'inventions, de modes, d'œuvres, de ruines ", in which " rien de complet ne s'offrait à l'âme ". Where and what, is one tempted to ask, is the personality, if any, behind all this vast accumulation of treasures and tinsel, of riches and rubble ? It is a personality strikingly similar to that of the old man to whom the shop belonged, in the novel of Balzac. "Un peintre aurait, avec deux expressions différentes et en deux coups de pinceau, fait de cette figure une belle image du Père Éternel ou le masque ricaneur de Mephistophelès, car il se trouvait tout ensemble une supreme puissance dans le front et de sinistres railleries sur la bouche ".

This reads exactly like a description of Liszt. Compare it, for example, with that made of him by a young pupil of his (Miss Amy Fay, " Music Study in Germany ") : " One moment his face will look dreamy, shadowy, tragic, the next he will be insinuating, ironical, sardonic, but always with the same captivating grace of manner. . . . He is all spirit, but half the time at least, a mocking spirit ". His work exhibits precisely the same curious mixture of the saintly and the satanic, and it is this duality which so peculiarly fitted him to be the musical interpreter of Goethe's *Faust*. In the symphony which bears the title of Goethe's masterpiece, Liszt for once expressed himself completely ; in the first movement the restless experiment and the search after knowledge, in the second the idealism and love of beauty, in the third the spirit which steadfastly denies—the three different aspects of his strange and enigmatic personality. In spite of many excellent songs and piano pieces, in spite of the truly great things to be found in his oratorios and symphonic poems, there can be little doubt that this symphony is by a long way his best work. There is in it nothing of the formal slackness which characterizes so much of his music ; it is throughout logical, coherent, and well-knit. It is safe to say that the day is not far distant when this magnificent work will be recognized for what it is, namely, one of the greatest landmarks in the orchestral music of the nineteenth century.

If the *Faust Symphony* represents his most perfect and enduring artistic achievement, it is nevertheless his symphonic poems that have exercised the greatest influence on modern music on account of the important formal innovations embodied in them.   In a foregoing chapter we compared the symphony to the novel, and pointed out how in the hands of Mozart the main interest consisted in the creation and presentation of clearly defined thematic personalities, so to speak, in the exposition, their subsequent relations with and interactions upon each other in the development section, and their reconciliation and symbolic marriage in the recapitulation ; how with Beethoven, on the other hand, the interest lay rather in the plot and in the conflict of opposing principles, represented by tonalities rather than by themes, ending as a rule in the triumph of one over the other rather than in their reconciliation, and how the modifications of the form which he introduced were the necessary and inevitable consequences of his conceptions.   Now, the inner essence of the romantic ideal, in whatever form of art it may be embodied, consists in soliloquy and contemplation rather than in drama and action, in introspection and self-expression rather than in the objective presentation of thematic personalities and their interaction on each other.   This characteristic propensity is to be observed in the work of all the great literary romantics—in the poetry of Lamartine, Byron, de Musset, and in the prose of Chateaubriand, to name only a few typical examples—and it is also to be found in the music of the great romantic composers.   It is surely obvious that neither the pure classic symphonic form of Mozart, nor the modified form of Beethoven's middle period, was suitable to the expression of this type of conception ; and to Liszt is due the credit for the invention of a new form more fitted to it, in which a single theme takes the place of the former duality or multiplicity, and serves as the material out of which the whole work is constructed. It should however be mentioned that in this he was to a certain extent anticipated by Berlioz's employment of an *idée fixe* or representative theme, dominating the entire work, in his *Symphonie Fantastique* and *Harold en Italie*, and by Schubert in his *Wanderer Fantasia*, to say nothing of the method of thematic transformation occasionally to be met with in the work of Sweelinck, Frescobaldi, and Frohberger a century and a half earlier.

Liszt's choice of name, i.e., symphonic poem, for this new form was somewhat unfortunate, for it inevitably suggests the intrusion into music of alien principles derived from literature—a suggestion which the poetic programmes attached to his experiments in this direction would seem to confirm. It has even been generally supposed that his incentive in making this formal innovation was his desire to illustrate literary conceptions in music, and that this desire is in itself the cause of the undeniable formal weaknesses in his music. But this is quite a mistaken idea. There is actually very little illustration in Liszt's symphonic poems, and if some of them are formally somewhat incoherent it is the fault of the composer, not of the form, and certainly not the outcome of the employment of a literary programme. The main defect of almost all Liszt's music is that he is apt to rely too much upon his amazing improvisatory virtuosity and fertility of invention to the neglect or exclusion of purely formal considerations, and the same weaknesses of construction are to be found in a work such as his piano sonata which has no programme at all attached to it.

In short, the symphonic poem is in essence as purely musical a form as the fugue, which similarly consists in the development of one single main theme, and Liszt was led to it for purely musical reasons and because it was better suited to the expression of the romantic ideals than was the ordinary symphonic form. His programmes were almost invariably chosen for their suitability to his musical conceptions, which are for the most part mere variants on that of his *Tasso*, consisting practically in the simple formula of " Lamento e trionfo ". The programme, in fact, should be regarded as an elucidatory commentary on the music rather than the music as an illustration of the programme.

Similarly the programmatic elements in the music of Berlioz have been greatly misunderstood. His intention was not, like that of Wagner, to use music as a means to a literary or dramatic end, but, on the contrary, to compel literary ideas to subserve a musical end, which is a very different thing ; and so far from allowing foreign elements belonging to the other arts to intrude into the domain of music, he rather extended the boundaries of music in such a way and to such an extent that it was able to express, free and unaided, many conceptions which had hitherto been considered exclusively literary or pictorial, but were, as he conclusively showed, equally suited to musical realization.   In a word, the art of Berlioz represents an extension of the frontiers of music, a victorious invasion of the territory of the other arts by music : not, as is generally supposed, an invasion of musical territory by literature and painting.   His aim was not the subjection of music to alien conceptions, but rather the liberation of music from any dependence on extraneous assistance in expressing any conception whatsoever.   This is shown not only by the works themselves, but also by many passages in his writings and correspondence, for example : " I want music to be proudly free, to be victorious, to be supreme.   I want her to take all she can, so that there may be no more Alps or Pyrenees for her. .   .   .   She has the right to say with Medea : I myself am enough ".   That he sometimes pursued his ideas too far into hostile territory and occasionally failed through losing touch with his musical base may be readily admitted, but such failures are the exception, not the rule.

It is extremely important that this should be recognized, for a great deal of the prejudice against Berlioz and Liszt is founded on the mistaken notion of their dependence on literary or pictorial suggestions, and their inability to achieve anything without them.   Curiously enough, as we shall see in the following chapter, some of their contemporaries, commonly regarded as composers of absolute music, are far more subject to the influence of the other arts, and far less able to dispense with them.

CHAPTER XV

Miscellaneous Schools of the Nineteenth Century

It is related of Weber that " as he sat in his travelling carriage
the scenery through which he passed would present itself to
his inner ear as a piece of music . . . with him any
external impression at once clothed itself in musical form ",
and Felix Mendelssohn would seem to have possessed a similar
faculty of transmuting visual into aural sensations. All his
best music, in fact, is the outcome of some pictorial stimulus or
other, and, it is not altogether irrelevant to observe, he was an
amateur painter of considerable ability. He remarks somewhere in his correspondence that he took particular pleasure
" in composing the memory of things seen ", and that " in
front of the pictures of the great Venetian masters, and Titian
in particular, I feel music rising up inside me. It is in pictures,
ruins, and in natural surroundings, that I find the most music ".
Both the Italian and Scotch symphonies are pictures in sound,
and the main themes of each sprang spontaneously from direct
visual impressions. The beginning of the latter work, for
example, was actually sketched from nature, as he sat among
the ruins of the chapel at Holyrood in Edinburgh, and the
fantasies or caprices of Op. 16 are avowedly depictions in sound
of flowers—still-life compositions of carnations and roses.
The music of the *Midsummer Night's Dream*, *Hebrides*, *Melusine*,
and *Calm Sea and Prosperous Voyage* Overtures, is all suggested
by, and in its turn suggests to the listener, pictorial impressions.
His dependence on such sources of inspiration may be gauged by
the fact that all his best work is based upon them, and that his
progressive emancipation from them in his later work coincided
with a definite decline in the quality of his art. As a landscape
painter in sounds, as Wagner said, Mendelssohn was a composer
of the first rank ; as a musician pure and simple, however
he is comparatively undistinguished, derivative, and even
second-rate, with the exception, perhaps, of his admirable
violin concerto.

In the same way that Mendelssohn was an amateur painter so Robert Schumann was in the habit of expressing himself in verse, and his music is as full of literary conceptions as that of Mendelssohn is of pictorial ones. As Mr. Herbert Bedford justly remarks in his biography of Schumann, " there probably never was a composer   .   .   .   who in his music was influenced by literature and by ideas derived from literature, to a greater extent than was Schumann ". Indeed, if Mendelssohn was primarily a landscape painter in sounds, Schumann is the musical poet *par excellence*—" le musicien le plus poète que jamais ", to adopt the words mistakenly applied by Liszt to Schubert. He himself half seriously declared that he had learnt all his counterpoint from the writer Jean Paul, to whom he had the same affinity that Weber had to Tieck and Novalis, and Marschner to Hoffmann. It is at least certain that his early piano pieces, which are possibly his best and undoubtedly his most wholly personal and original works, are so full of obscure poetic allusions and mystifications as to be barely intelligible without reference to their literary prototypes. And again like Mendelssohn, as he gradually weaned himself from these literary influences, so his work progressively lost all its savour and originality.

And so we see that, so far from Berlioz and Liszt being the culprits who brought music into subjection to literary and pictorial conceptions, and Mendelssohn and Schumann being the champions of music pure and undefiled, as they are generally represented to be in musical histories (see for example Dannreuther in his volume on the Romantic Period in the " Oxford History of Music "), the contrary is nearer the truth : namely, that the two former extended the expressive scope of music so as to include territory which had formerly been the undisputed possession of the other arts, and planted the banner of music in their very citadels, while the two latter, on the contrary, were dominated by pictorial and literary conceptions respectively and were unable to achieve anything of lasting value or importance without having recourse to the external assistance provided by them.

Mendelssohn and Schumann, again, were pre-eminently lyricists. As M. Bellaigue observes in his book on the former " les deux motifs de l'allegro " in his symphonies, " sont des *lieder* qui se répondent plutôt qu'ils ne se développent ou se combinent " ; and the same is true of all Schumann's essays in symphonic form, which consist mainly of successions of short episodes, like songs or piano pieces, loosely strung together, reminding one of the gigantic lyrics of Swinburne in which each stanza is complete and self-contained, and might easily be left out or inserted elsewhere without making the slightest difference to the general sense or structure of the whole. The main themes in the symphonies of both, in fact, are never sufficiently differentiated from each other to engender the action, as in those of Mozart ; the development or plot is not of sufficient interest or dramatic power to bring out any latent potentialities that they might possess, as in those of Beethoven ; and at the same time neither composer achieves the unity of mood and atmosphere which is the *cachet* of Romantic art, on account of their acceptance of the formal convention of the dual thematic generation. In short, the symphonies of both Mendelssohn and Schumann consist of romantic, lyrical impulses, embodied in classical and epic forms which are fundamentally unsuited to them. Consequently, if only because of the inner correspondence between idea and form, Berlioz and Liszt must be conceded to have excelled both Mendelssohn and Schumann in the larger forms, and it would even seem that this is pretty generally recognized to-day. The symphonic works of the former, despite the abuse to which they are continually subjected, are performed far more frequently—and increasingly so as time goes on—than those of either of the latter, despite the eulogies of them which are to be found in most musical histories.

The fact of the matter is that both Mendelssohn and Schumann are essentially miniaturists, like Chopin, and would have been well advised if they had similarly renounced their more grandiose ambitions and had chosen to concentrate their energies on tasks more suited to the modest nature of their talents. It can hardly be doubted that the gradual but steady falling-off that is such a striking feature of the artistic development of both is largely, if not entirely, due to this conflict between the intimate, lyrical, romantic, miniaturist, nature of their respective talents, and the crippling obsession of the classic, epic, and large-scale forms. Mendelssohn never achieved anything better than the *Midsummer Night's Dream Overture*, written at the age of seventeen—one of the most remarkable instances of precocity in all art—and Schumann's finest work similarly consists of his early piano pieces and songs written in and before his thirtieth year. All their best work is Romantic in feeling and tendency ; as their neo-classical aspirations gradually. assumed the upper hand, however, their respective talents correspondingly dwindled and finally became virtually extinct.

The most admirable quality in Mendelssohn's art undoubtedly resides in his keen and sensitive feeling for instrumental values. His scoring is invariably clear, transparent, brilliant, and sonorous, and he particularly excels in his imaginative handling of the more subtle and delicate orchestral tints. In fact one might say that if Berlioz, Liszt, and Wagner are painters in oil, Mendelssohn is essentially a painter in water-colours. Schumann, on the other hand, like Chopin, is singularly deficient in his understanding of instrumental values other than those of the piano. Apart from his shorter pieces for that instrument his chief importance lies in the part which he played in the development of the modern song, similar to that played by Weber in the development of opera. In the songs of his predecessors the accompaniment, however elaborate or subtle, remained nevertheless a mere background to the vocal part ; with him the piano part begins to play as important a rôle as the voice, and even in many cases actually takes precedence of it. In many of his later songs, for example, the voice part consists of more or less recitative-like phrases, while the main weight of the musical discourse is confided to the piano.

On the whole, however, it must be admitted that the music of Schumann has aged more rapidly and irremediably than that of any other composer of the nineteenth century, mainly on account of his excessively romantic *Schwärmerei*, his flabbiness and lack of intellectual fibre, the mawkishness and sentimentality of his emotion, and the turgidity and thickness of his style of writing. It belongs to a period which is particularly remote from and antipathetic to us at the present time, but even making all due allowances for this it is extremely unlikely, to say the least, that he will ever be restored to the exaggeratedly prominent place which he formerly held in both critical and popular esteem. On the other hand, there is little doubt that Mendelssohn has been unduly depreciated in recent years, as a natural and altogether healthy reaction from the excessive adulation of him which prevailed in Victorian days, and it is probable that the near future will witness a reawakening of interest in his music, if only on account of the clarity, delicacy and refinement of his instrumental style.

The artistic development of Johannes Brahms is in many ways strikingly analogous to that of both Mendelssohn and Schumann, and reveals a similar conflict between the fundamentally romantic character of his thought and his neo-classical aspirations. But while with them the latter element gradually assumed the upper hand and eventually stifled their talents completely, the conflict is more equally balanced with Brahms, first one and then the other obtaining the mastery. His early work, like theirs, is essentially romantic, not only in thought and feeling, but in form as well. In his early piano sonatas, for example, we find him flirting with the Lisztian device of thematic transformation ; in the first the theme of the *finale* is demonstrably derived from that of the initial movement, and in the second the same theme serves as a basis for the two middle movements. Literary allusions, too, in the manner of Schumann, are also to be found in the third sonata and in the *Ballads* of Op. 10. His sudden metamorphosis into a neo-classicist was not so much due to any decisive psychological development or change as to outward circumstances, and to the famous article written by Schumann in 1853 in particular, in which Brahms was hailed as " he who was to come ", i.e., the long-awaited successor of Beethoven and the heir to the classic tradition.

Schumann has often been praised for his remarkable prescience in thus divining immediately the future greatness of Brahms, but it is difficult not to be somewhat sceptical about the whole affair. In the first place there was nothing so very noteworthy in the early works of Brahms on which the article was wholly based ; even looking at them now in full knowledge of, and consequently somewhat prejudiced in their favour by, his subsequent eminence, it is still very difficult to understand what Schumann could see in them to justify such extravagant eulogies. The prosaic explanation of the matter is that Schumann was rather given to writing wildly enthusiastic notices concerning the music of all kinds of unimportant mediocrities. Who, for example, has ever heard of Hermann Hirschbach ? Yet Schumann describes his works in glowing terms that which would be appropriate only to the works of the greatest masters : " His string quartets are the most colossal to be met with to-day. A passionate tragic writer, original both as to form and treatment, an overwhelming imagination ". and so forth ; and similar panegyrics devoted to complete nonentities are to be found scattered in profusion throughout his entire critical work. Far too much stress, then, has been laid on this one only among many such utterances in which he happened to " spot a winner ", as the saying is. The more than usually solemn and apocalyptic manner of its pronouncement, however justified it may seem to us by Brahms's subsequent achievements, was nevertheless out of all proportion to the merits of the music on which it was based, and must undoubtedly be ascribed to the mental malady from which Schumann was then beginning to suffer, and in particular to the obsession with the idea of the " successor to Beethoven " which was one of its primary symptoms.

No one at the time seems to have taken the utterance very seriously—indeed no one could be expected to, seeing that Schumann was in the habit of shouting " wolf, wolf ", on the slightest provocation—except, unfortunately, Brahms himself, on whom the effect of it, together with that of the coincidence of the fact that his name happened to begin with the same letter as the names of Bach and Beethoven, was immediate and decisive. From being " un jeune audacieux qui s'avise de faire de la musique nouvelle ", as he appeared to Berlioz when he met him, he became a timid, uneasy, self-conscious imitator of the classical masters.   His *Serenade* in D, Op. 11, for instance, is nothing but a feeble and laboured *pastiche* of Haydn, Schubert and early Beethoven.   It is true that, by dint of sheer tenacity of purpose and unremitting industry, he eventually succeeded in acquiring to a great extent the grand manner, the classical gesture and intonation, but they never came naturally to him. It is this that is responsible for the impression that his essays in the larger forms invariably give the listener—the sense of strain and effort, as of a man who is engaged on a task not so much beyond his powers as fundamentally unsuited to them. This preoccupation with the classical ideal dominates his entire middle period, and culminates in the morose and ascetic *Fourth Symphony*, after which, in the last years of his life, a return to the Romantic ideals of his early period is to a certain extent to be observed. Even during his middle period the real Brahms is never entirely in abeyance, but finds expression in various beautiful works, such as the violin sonatas and concerto, and in the songs especially.

The real Brahms, in fact, the great Brahms, is not the composer of the symphonies, but of the songs. The reason why his symphonies, despite many admirable pages, must on the whole be accounted failures, is to be found in the fact that, like both Mendelssohn and Schumann, he was by nature a lyricist and a miniaturist, and unable consequently to conceive either vital and strongly contrasted themes which between them could engender the course of the movement, or a dramatic musical action which could impart significance to his material. A clue to this inability is to be found in the confession he made to a friend that whenever he wished to compose he thought of some folk-song, and then a melody presented itself to him. This explains the essentially lyrical and contemplative nature of his most characteristic melodies, and it is his attempt to make them perform heroic and epic tasks for which they are manifestly unfitted, that the greatest weakness of his symphonic writing resides. The few occasions on which Brahms attempted to create virile and heroic themes fitted to perform the exploits for which he had destined them, as in the first and third symphonies, he failed entirely to imbue them with the warm breath of life. This deficiency is further accentuated by his painfully noticeable inability to write a *scherzo* or fast movement of any kind. He entirely lacks *tempo* and energy ; his *allegro* movements are only slow movements in disguise, andantes played fast. On the other hand, probably no composer with the exception of Schubert has written such a large number of first-rate songs, and it is by virtue of them that he will assuredly live.

For Brahms, as for Schubert, a song is primarily a piece of music with a logic of its own which should be immediately intelligible as such without any reference to the words. Hugo Wolf, on the other hand, the greatest of Brahms's contemporaries in the field of song, is an exponent of precisely the opposite æsthetic principles. In the words of his admirer, Mr. Ernest Newman, " he allowed the poet to prescribe for him the whole colour and shape of a song, down even to the smallest details—he set his face sternly against the suspicion of mere

Q

music-making ".   While Brahms, confronted with the problem that so frequently arises in song-writing, of choosing between the sacrifice of poetic propriety and that of musical beauty, would invariably prefer to sacrifice the first, Hugo Wolf would sacrifice the second.   Like Wagner, he would have said that in song music was not the end, but only a means to the enhancement of poetry ; and his whole method of composition is not only strictly in conformity with this theory, but also to a great extent directly influenced by the art of Wagner. While Brahms's first concern was for the voice part and then for the movement of the bass, the rest being of secondary importance in his eyes, Wolf would appear to have started at the other end, evolving the general texture of the piano part first, elaborating a figure of accompaniment which is generally developed sequentially in the Wagnerian manner throughout the song, and then adding a voice part, the melodic line of which was of less moment than its declamatory accuracy and veracity of expression.

Such a conception of song naturally commended itself to the generation immediately succeeding Wagner, and under his dominating influence ; to-day, however, there is a distinct reaction against it, even to the extent of questioning whether it does not rest on an aesthetic fallacy as great as that of Wagner's theory of music-drama, from which it is obviously derived.   Some would even go so far as to dispute the capacity of music to enhance poetic beauty.   As Mr. W. J. Turner, who is a poet of distinction as well as a musical critic, and therefore qualified to speak with authority on the subject, says in an essay in his " Music and Life ", " a poem is a completed thing : it is a finished creation to which nothing can be added and from which nothing can be taken away. . . . the value of the song is entirely musical.   The composer can do nothing, absolutely nothing for the poet.   To imagine that he can is to imagine that you can interpret a sculptor's nude figure by dressing it in an appropriate costume ".   Those who are inclined to agree with this—and they are to-day in an increasing number—find the songs of Wolf unsatisfactory, for their purely musical interest is often of a comparatively low order. Dissociated from the words they generally fail to evoke our interest or to retain our attention.

In the same way that Wolf sought to apply Wagnerian

procedures to the art of song, so Anton Bruckner sought to apply them to symphonic music. His harmonic idiom and his manner of scoring are alike Wagnerian ; his melodic vein, on the other hand, is more personal, revealing, however, a certain affinity to that of Schubert, especially in the trios of his scherzos with their characteristically Viennese *melismata* and waltz-like rhythms. He also possesses in common with Schubert a remarkable fluency and spontaneity of invention, and the same unconscious and uncritical faculty for sheer music-making, which constitutes the greatest strength and charm as well as the greatest weakness of his gifted predecessor. His form is likewise somewhat loosely knit and diffuse, as we should naturally expect from his other qualities, but nevertheless reveals certain remarkable peculiarities. Whereas the main point of interest in the classical symphony of Haydn, Mozart, and Beethoven is centred in the first movement, in the symphonies of Bruckner a distinct tendency is observable to throw it back on to the later movements. The *finale* is no longer a kind of *envoi* in the form of a rondo—a sort of perfunctory " Ite, missa est "—but often the most important of all the movements, drawing together and clinching the arguments of the foregoing ones. With Bruckner, in short, the form is more definitely progressive and cumulative than with any of his predecessors, and the various movements are more closely co-ordinated with each other. Within each movement, too, the same tendency is to be observed ; the centre of interest no longer resides in the working-out section, or even in the recapitulation which he practically omits in his eighth and ninth symphonies, but in the peroration at the close. In this he is, formally speaking, the successor of Beethoven to a much greater extent than Brahms is, though it is still the Beethoven of the middle period, not of the last. Speaking generally, however, it must be admitted that, despite many attractive qualities, his works have not succeeded in establishing themselves in the concert repertoire of any countries save Austria and Germany. Like so many *vins du pays*, they do not travel well.

Probably no composer makes such an immediate appeal, such a favourable impression when we first become acquainted with his music, as César Franck. His lofty sincerity and nobility of purpose, his careful and distinguished craftsmanship, his strong sense of design, and the highly personal cast of his melodic and harmonic idioms, all seem to justify us in regarding him as one of the greatest masters of music belonging to the second half of the nineteenth century. As time goes on, however, and we become increasingly familiar with his works, doubts begin to insinuate themselves into our minds ; we find that our admiration, so far from increasing with the years, or even remaining unaltered and unimpaired, tends rather to diminish in intensity. We never succeed in recapturing the thrill which his music first induced in us, but begin to experience instead a distinct disillusionment which grows steadily with each successive hearing until in the end we find ourselves almost positively disliking it, and wondering what we could ever have seen in it. What is the explanation of this complete change in our attitude towards Franck ? For it is not as if one were alone in experiencing it ; practically every intelligent musician or listener whom one comes across seems to have passed through a precisely similar progression from initial admiration to subsequent indifference, and even aversion.

In the first place, it is no doubt due in large part to Franck's stylistic mannerisms which, though they may at first attract, do not stand the test of familiarity, and soon begin to pall on one ; to the narrow circle of ideas and conceptions within which he moves, and to the restricted technical vocabulary that he employs. His themes, with their curious tendency to hover round one note, are nearly all variations on one another ; progressions built up by means of semitonally sliding chromaticisms in the inner parts represent practically the whole of his harmonic equipment ; and his perpetually recurring two-part canons, reminding one of two small children repeating the same story, one of them always half a sentence behind the other, are almost his sole contrapuntal resource. It must also be admitted that he has little or no feeling for instrumental *timbres*, and that all his works give one the impression of having been originally written for the organ, or conceived in terms of it, like the works of Bruckner also. Still, serious though these defects undoubtedly are, they are hardly sufficient in themselves to account for our dissatisfaction ; equally glaring faults may be discerned in the music of many composers whom we continue to admire. The source of the trouble lies deeper down than that.

A clue to the problem is afforded by the description of Franck's method of composition which is given by his pupil and biographer, M. Vincent d'Indy. "How often we used to see him pounding away on his piano in a jerky and continually increasing fortissimo the overture to the *Meistersinger*, or something by Bach, Beethoven, or Schumann ! After a time the deafening noise sank to a murmur, then silence—the master had found his idea." The mere fact in itself, of course, is not of the slightest importance. Berlioz and Liszt frequently had recourse to literature, and Gluck to copious libations of champagne, in order to invoke the coy muse ; Wagner was unable to compose well unless he was wearing a satin dressing-gown, or Sacchini unless he was surrounded by a number of cats and mistresses. What matters is the work, and not the way in which it was written. Nevertheless, Franck's habit of stimulating and exciting his imagination with music is symbolically significant, and points unerringly to the contral defect and fatal weakness of all his work, which is, that it is essentially music derived from other music, and divorced from all contact with life and reality.

It is always exceedingly difficult to perceive or define the exact relation that a work of art bears to the personal experience of its creator, and to trace the extent to which the one is the outcome of the other. It is probably more difficult to do so in music than in any other art because it is the most self-contained and seemingly the least in contact with anything outside itself. Few, however, will be disposed to deny that the work of art which has no such relation to life, but is derived from aesthetic experience only, is incapable of holding our attention once the seductive glamour of the first encounter has given place to familiarity. A good literary example of this is to be found in Swinburne, with whom we pass through precisely the same stages of enthusiasm and disenchantment as with Franck. Though it would certainly be difficult to imagine two artists more completely unlike in other ways, the spirituality of Franck, nevertheless, like the sensuality of Swinburne, is factitious and sterile, and equally fails to convince because it has not been fertilized by reality and experience. The spiritual ardour and intensity which we imagined ourselves to have perceived in his music are merely the result of his habit of intoxicating himself with the music of Bach, Beethoven and Wagner, in the same way that the eroticism of Swinburne is only the outcome of an over-indulgence in the poetry of Gautier and Baudelaire. And like all people in a state of intoxication, Franck frequently traverses the fine line that separates sentiment from sentimentality, eloquence from rhetoric, sublimity from bombast, and achieves only a blatant nobility and a saintly vulgarity which are unique in music. As a characteristic example of this one need only cite the well-known passage in the first movement of his symphony, where the second subject—called by devout Franckians the theme of Faith—is blared out *fortissimo con espressione* by the trumpets, first and second violins, flutes, oboes, clarinets, and *cor anglais* in unison, accompanied by chords in the horns and trombones.

This excessive fervour and exaltation bordering on hysteria are to be found in all Franck's larger works, which consequently pall on one very soon. A more enduring satisfaction, however, is afforded by the fine piano works —the *Prelude, Chorale, and Fugue*, and the *Prelude, Aria, and Finale*—the three *Chorales* for organ, and the *Variations symphoniques*, in all of which his fine craftsmanship and sure sense of design are able to control and hold in check his grandiose aspirations.

CHAPTER XVI

The Russian School

ONE of the most important differences between the music of the nineteenth century and that of all its predecessors consists in the emergence for the first time of specifically national idioms, hitherto confined to popular or folk-music. Racial differences of outlook and mentality had, of course, always existed to as great an extent in music as in any other sphere of activity. In spirit Morley is as English, Jannequin as French, Schütz as German, as any subsequent composers, but the fact remains that they were content for the most part to express their racially coloured thoughts in a universal, cosmopolitan idiom which, like Latin in the Middle Ages, was regarded as the only possible vehicle of expression for the highest order of musical conceptions. Up to the end of the eighteenth century, from Lisbon to St. Petersburg, from London to Palermo, one uniform musical speech prevailed, and the same composers were appreciated throughout the civilized world without national distinctions or reservations. Even when folk-songs or dances were deliberately employed as the thematic basis of compositions, as in the symphonies of Haydn or in the Rasoumoffsky quartets of Beethoven, no attempt was made to present them in such a way as to draw attention to their origin or to emphasize their idiomatic peculiarities in any way ; they were, on the contrary, translated, as it were, into the current international idioms, and treated in exactly the same way as any other subjects.

With the passing of the eighteenth century, however, and with the successive collapse of the ideal of the brotherhood of man and the Napoleonic dream of world-empire, this European solidarity gave way to a more specifically national mode of thought, and this new political orientation was faithfully mirrored in the arts, and more particularly in music. No longer does the composer consciously address his message to the whole human race, as did Beethoven, Mozart, or Haydn, but primarily to his compatriots ; the uniform musical speech of the eighteenth century gives way to a great extent to idioms or dialects which, if not actually unintelligible to other races, can only be fully appreciated by those who share the same cultural traditions, or else possess a temperamental affinity to them. For example, the music of Schumann can never be completely understood by the average Italian, that of Ravel by a typical German, or that of Vaughan Williams by the ordinary Frenchman. The subtle psychological associations, the intimate suggestions and hidden allusions, so to speak, which largely constitute their various appeals, will inevitably escape the alien listener.

It is necessary to distinguish carefully between this kind of nationalism and that to which we have already referred in connection with Weber, and probably first tentatively employed by Marcello, in which exotic idioms are only made use of in order to obtain local colour. This latter type is merely a part of the romantic equipment and the cult of the picturesque, the bizarre, and the fantastic, which prevailed throughout the nineteenth century ; it is concerned solely with externals, and consists for the most part in a few simple *clichés*, melodic, harmonic, rhythmic, or colouristic, which can easily be acquired and handled by composers of any nationality whatsoever. Familiar examples of this sort of thing are to be found in the *New World Symphony* of Dvořák, the Spanish *Fantasias*, *Rhapsodies* and *Capriccios* of Debussy, Ravel, Glinka, Rimsky-Korsakov, and others, and the countless similar productions which aim at giving an impression of the East. Although the artistic merits of such works naturally vary considerably in accordance with the degree of talent possessed by their respective composers, it is at least safe to say that no other form of composition can show such a high proportion of thoroughly bad works or such a low proportion of good ones, and probably the only examples of it which might conceivably be regarded as masterpieces in the strict sense of the word are a few semi-oriental works of the Russian school. But here we are already on slightly different ground. Russia is both geographically and ethnographically as much Asiatic as European, and such works may therefore quite legitimately be regarded as appertaining to the category of genuinely national music which seeks to express racial ideas and emotions felt and experienced, not merely to exploit the picturesque possibilities of exotic and unfamiliar idioms.

However that may be, it is certainly no coincidence that the country which took the lead in the process of the nationalization of music to which we have been referring, and succeeded in producing a school of specifically national composers, should be the one which had hitherto played no part whatever in the history of music prior to 1800. As late as the seventeenth century even there was no other form of secular music in Russia than folk-song ; in the eighteenth we still find nothing else except the imported art of the Italian operatic composers which, however, was only a court diversion, and played no part whatsoever in the lives of the people. No native imitators, even, of the foreign style appeared until the end of the century, and the influence of western music remained entirely sterile and unproductive. Only the emancipation of Russia from the dominance of the pseudo-European culture forcibly and artificially imposed on the country by Peter the Great, together with the breakdown of European solidarity and the rise of distinctively national modes of expression, made it possible for Russia to produce a great school of music ; the main reason being that only those nations at the centre of the European comity, and already largely assimilated to each other, can with impunity, and even actual advantage, submit themselves to the inoculations of foreign cultures. It is at least certain that when the Russian in particular denies or abjures his own culture and strives to emulate Europe and her ways, he tends to lose all his positive qualities without acquiring those of the models he would fain imitate. Like the giant Antaeus in ancient mythology, the Russian artist derives his main strength from contact with the soil ; the exclusive influence of western art and civilization saps him of all vitality.

The first composer to perceive this and to realize that only after Russian music had been firmly established on a genuinely national basis was it possible to assimilate with advantage the rich traditional heritage of western music, was Mikhail Ivanovitch Glinka ; and in acting upon this intuition he played the same part in music as that almost contemporaneously played by Puskhin in literature. Dostoevsky, in his famous speech on Pushkin said that " not in so-called European culture (which by the way never existed with us), not in the monstrosities of European ideals and forms only outwardly assimilated, did Pushkin discover beauty, but he found it in the spirit of the people alone ", and precisely the same may be said of Glinka. For in the same way that Pushkin started by imitating European poets such as Byron and Chénier, and only found himself after saturating himself in the *builinas* and other forms of native poetry, so Glinka similarly began by imitating current European, and particularly Italian models, and only found himself after an intensive study of Russian folk-songs and popular dances. His importance, however, does not so much consist in the fact that he occasionally made use of folk-songs as the thematic material of his compositions—some of his predecessors such as Cavos and Wertowsky had already done so before him without any fruitful results—as in his successful cultivation of a melodic style based upon them, and a harmonic and orchestral manner of treatment not only admirably suited to them and unmistakably Russian, but also highly original at the same time.

The first work in which these qualities appear is his opera *A Life for the Czar*—his best-known and most popular work, though by no means his best. It is still largely permeated by the Italian influences from which, incidentally, Glinka never entirely succeeded in freeing himself, and the passages in which they are most in evidence often afford a striking and slightly disagreeable contrast to the pure national style encountered elsewhere, such as in the wedding chorus in 5/4 time, for example, which is the germ from which so much subsequent Russian national music is unmistakably derived. The work, moreover, is not only unequal in style, but in content as well ; comparatively trivial and uninteresting numbers alternate with others of a very high order of musical interest.

His second opera, *Russlan and Ludmilla*, marks a great advance on the earlier work as regards cohesion of style, musical interest, and craftsmanship in general ; the orchestration particularly is very much more brilliant and assured. Indeed in this respect Glinka is responsible for some remarkable innovations which he arrived at simultaneously with and independently of Berlioz, as, for instance, his employment of the *cor anglais*, harp, and piano, as integral factors in the orchestral *ensemble*. The work is further noteworthy from the historical point of view in that it contains the first successful attempt to exploit the semi-oriental vein which plays such an important part in the music of many of his successors ; the Persian chorus in particular remains the model and prototype of all subsequent efforts in this direction, and yields to none of them in respect of intrinsic merit. So far as form is concerned, however, *Russlan and Ludmilla* is decidedly weak. It is, in fact, little more than a succession of loosely knit episodes bearing little or no organic relation to each other. This has generally been attributed to, and consequently to a great extent condoned on account of, the undoubted weakness and incoherence of the libretto ; but since it cannot honestly be said that his other works are very much superior in this respect, the composer can hardly be thus acquitted of all responsibility. Besides, the complete absence of any formal sense or constructive ability that all his work exhibits save in miniature, constitutes the characteristic and cardinal defect, not only of almost all Russian music generally speaking, but of almost all Russian art of any kind. As Tchadaiev says in his *Philosophic Letters*, concerning his countrymen, " there is a profound lacuna in our intellectual organization—the capacity for logical thinking, the spirit of method, and the feeling for continuity, are entirely lacking in us ". In literature, to take a few examples, the *Boris Godounov* of Pushkin, the *Dead Souls* of Gogol, the *Steppe* of Tchehov, the *War and Peace* of Tolstoi, the trilogy of Meredjkowsky—the masterpieces, in fact, of their respective writers—and all the novels of Dostoevsky without exception, lack formal organization in the proper sense of the word, and generally achieve their effect by means of an accumulation of small and insignificant details. Indeed, Turgenev would seem to be the only example of a great Russian writer who possesses a true inborn sense of formal design, balance, and structure, and in this he is certainly the exception that proves the rule, for he is often regarded, rightly or wrongly, as un-Russian, by his countrymen. And in music we find precisely the same thing. Almost without exception the composers of the Russian school are entirely devoid of any constructive ability, and are unable to develop their ideas logically and coherently. As a general rule they only achieve a semblance of continuity by means of the integral repetition of the same theme over and over again, with varying harmonic and orchestral decorations superimposed upon it. This characteristically Russian method of construction is already to be found fully developed in the music of Glinka, who is thus, both in his virtues and in his defects, the fountain-head from which the whole national Russian impulse is derived, in the same way that the entire course of the German Romantic movement is prefigured in the music of Weber.

It would appear, however, that in the last years of his life Glinka became acutely conscious of the formal deficiencies of his work, and increasingly dissatisfied with its onesidedness. He seems eventually to have come to the conclusion that it was virtually impossible to achieve a national art which could be fitly compared to the greatest European art without, to a certain extent at least, evolving along similar lines : and that, once a genuinely national form of art had been firmly established, the next step should be the adoption and adaptation to Russian requirements of the traditional methods and forms of western art.   With this end in view he left Russia for Germany in the last years of his life in order to study music anew from the very beginning—an act which as clearly shows him to possess the modesty and humility that distinguish a great man as it speaks highly for his keen and unerring artistic intuition.   It is certainly no mere coincidence that Glinka should have arrived at identically the same conclusion as that arrived at by Mozart, Beethoven, Schubert, Wagner, and indeed, practically all the great composers in their later years, and realized that the very highest achievements in musical art could only be attained along the lines of the great contrapuntal traditions of the past. With Glinka, however, as with Schubert, this realization unfortunately came too late to affect his art, for he died before he had been able to put his newly acquired knowledge and experience into practice.   Whether his musical powers would have proved equal to the task of reconciling Russian ideas and conceptions with European forms and structural principles may legitimately be questioned—Glinka was no giant—but it is probable that if he had been able to carry out his intentions the ultimate course of development of Russian music might have been a very different one from what it was.

On the death of Glinka the leadership of the school devolved on his younger contemporary and rival, Alexander Sergeivitch Dargomijsky.   To a much greater extent than the former he was primarily a dramatic composer, for although Glinka's most ambitious efforts were in operatic form, his musical gifts were not really suited to the requirements of the stage, and probably his best music is to be found on the whole in his orchestral fantasias, such as the *Kamarinskaya, Une nuit d'été à Madrid*, and the *Jota Aragonese*, rather than in his operas. His greatest strength, in fact, lay in his purely musical invention, and in the handling of clear-cut, straightforward lyrical forms. He had little capacity for musical characterization, and the weakest parts of his operas are undoubtedly those in which a dramatic situation arises. Dargomijsky, on the contrary, wrote little music of any consequence apart from his operas, and particularly excelled in realizing dramatic situations, and in psychological characterization ; he failed precisely where Glinka succeeds, namely, in those parts in which the purely musical interest should be paramount, as in the overture and dances in his *Russalka* which are by far the weakest parts of the work. Again, Glinka is most at home in the region of the fantastic and the imaginative, Dargomijsky least so, as in the final scene of the said work, which is distinctly feeble. On the other hand the latter is particularly successful in the depiction of actuality, whether of types or situations ; the miller in *Russalka* is the first living figure in Russian opera, and the scene in the second act between the marriage-broker and the young women is a masterpiece of graphic delineation and comic veracity. Dargomijsky, in short, is more concerned with the attainment of dramatic felicity and truth to life than with musical beauty abstractly considered. As he himself said, " it is my wish that the music should interpret the words—I have not the slightest intention of reducing music to a mere pastime for *dilettanti* ". He belongs, in fact, to the race of operatic " reformers " who believe that the ideal music-drama is that in which the musical interest is most completely subordinated to that of the drama, and in which the music is only a kind of elaboration of the words similar to the illumination of mediæval manuscripts.

The most striking feature of Dargomijsky's style consists in his invention and consistent employment of a species of melodic recitative which must not, however, be confused with that of Wagner, or regarded as being in any way an imitation of it. In the first place, not only was the music of the German master totally unknown in Russia at the time when Dargomijsky wrote his *Russalka*, but his mature and most characteristic work was then as yet unwritten ; in the second place Dargomijsky's whole method is entirely different from, and indeed fundamentally opposed to, that of Wagner. With the latter the elaborate orchestral tissue which is undoubtedly the main consideration in his work, is generally conceived first, and a vocal part subsequently fitted to it ; with the former the principal interest is always to be found in the preconceived and carefully moulded voice parts to which the orchestra provides a mere background. His last and, at his death, unfinished opera, *The Stone Guest*, a word for word setting of Pushkin's version of Don Juan, represents the logical conclusion and best exemplification of his dramatic ideals, and a more striking contrast to Wagnerian music-drama could hardly be found. With the exception of two interpolated short songs, intended to be such by the poet, the whole work consists entirely of recitative with a strictly subordinated orchestral accompaniment possessing no independent existence or musical interest of its own. Both in this respect and in the extensive employment throughout the latter half of the work of the whole-tone scale, Dargomijsky's opera constitutes a remarkable anticipation of the *Pelléas et Mélisande* of Debussy, who must undoubtedly have been acquainted with and greatly influenced by it. The work, however, is of more value as an experiment than as an achievement, and it is said by those who have heard it to be infinitely more impressive on paper than in actual performance.

In the last years of Dargomijsky's life his house became the meeting-place of a group of young musicians who eventually, in their various ways, brought the largely unfulfilled aspirations and incompletely realized achievements of both Glinka and himself to a triumphant consummation. With Mily Alexeivitch Balakirev, their leader, the nationalism and particularly the semi-orientalism of the former attains its fullest and most convincing expression in the superb symphonic poem *Thamar*, the fantasia for pianoforte *Islamey*, and other works ; in the symphonies and quartets of Alexander Porphyrievitch Borodin, his conception of the union between characteristically Russian thematic material and European forms and methods of treatment was finally realized ; and the operas of Modeste

Petrovitch Moussorgsky are not only the most perfect embodiments of the national ideal in opera, both in subject-matter and in musical style, but also the successful realization of the dramatic ideal formulated by Dargomijsky and imperfectly exemplified in his *Stone Guest* and *Russalka*. The work of the other two members of the *cenâcle* is of infinitely less importance. The large output of Nicholas Andreievitch Rimsky-Korsakov consists merely of so many attempts in different directions to achieve what had been better achieved by one or other of his colleagues. His *Scheherazade* and *Antar* are greatly inferior to *Thamar*, *Ivan the Terrible* to *Boris Godounov*, *Mozart and Salieri* to the *Stone Guest*, and his later works, in which European influences are perceptible, to the symphonies and quartets of Borodin. His chief claim to remembrance rests less on his original work than on the service, and in the case of Moussorgsky the lamentable disservice, he rendered in completing and scoring the unfinished works of other members of the school. César Cui is of even less importance ; he is, indeed, completely negligible as a composer, and would certainly never have been heard of had it not been for his intimate association with the foregoing men and his lip-service to the common ideals which, however, he never made the slightest attempt to put into execution. His work is uniformly feeble, and is moreover written in a colourless pseudo-European style.

Balakirev is one of the most remarkable figures in the history of the second part of the nineteenth century in music. Although entirely self-taught, he possessed such great natural gifts and such a keen and unerring critical sense that his best work, though small in quantity, is as solid and technically accomplished as that of any school-trained musician. Like Liszt, however, whom he resembles in many ways, he is chiefly remembered for the important part he played in directing and inspiring the activities of those whom he gathered around him, and the great value of his creative achievement, both intrinsic and influential, has in consequence been undeservedly underestimated. His *Thamar* is not only a consummate masterpiece, but also the source of a great deal for which the credit is generally given to others whose works are more familiar and more frequently performed than his. Dostoevsky once said that all Russian novelists had come out from under *The Overcoat* of Gogol, and it is equally true that most subsequent Russian composers have at some time or another lain in the couch of the voluptuous and terrible Queen Thamar, and fallen victims to her witchery and fatal fascination.

One of the very few to do so and to escape to tell the tale was Borodin—himself, incidentally, an Asiatic Russian, and like the legendary Thamar, of Georgian ancestry—a fact which possibly explains why the sensuous glamour of such things as the dances from *Prince Igor* is so convincing and impressive.   If he escaped the fate which generally overtakes those who succumb to the seductive charms of oriental local colour, however, it is not only because he was inoculated, so to speak, against its more pernicious effects by his Asiatic blood, but also because he was at the same time, strangely enough, more closely in sympathy with European ideals than any of his colleagues.   It is this duality that is responsible for the peculiar quality and appeal of Borodin's music which is barbaric and oriental in its intrinsic substance, and westernized in its form and method of treatment.   In some of his work this duality leads to a certain stylistic inequality, as in parts of *Igor* in which elegant and facile Italianisms are to be found embedded in authentically primitive and Russian surroundings ; but more often the two elements are reconciled and welded into an indissoluble stylistic whole.   He is a consummate master of form, the only member of the group who was capable of thematic development, as his superb symphonies and string quartets testify, and his part-writing is generally as limpid, fluent, and correct as that of Mozart.   It is important that this should be recognized, for insensitive critics, addicted to the habit of making hasty generalizations, often include Borodin in their strictures concerning the formal deficiencies of Russian music. He is on the contrary the one great exception to the general rule, and in this respect resembles Turgenev in literature whose novels reveal a similar duality of Russian content and western form, faultlessly combined.

As an opera composer his ideal was the precise opposite of that promulgated by Dargomijsky.   To quote Borodin's own words, " recitative does not enter into my nature or disposition —I am more drawn to definite and concrete forms.   In opera as in decorative art, details and *minutiæ* are out of place.   Bold outlines only are necessary ; all should be clear and straight-forward ".   In fact it would be difficult to find two works more fundamentally dissimilar than *Prince Igor* and *The Stone Guest*. The latter is almost entirely composed of " details and *minutiæ* ", and carefully studied recitative ; the former consists mainly of set lyrical numbers of symmetrical cut and design, such as arias, dances and choruses.

Moussorgsky, on the other hand, was, to a very much greater extent than Borodin, a follower of Dargomijsky, aiming less at musical beauty primarily than at realism and veracity of action and character. " Music ", he says in a letter to a friend., " is a means of communication between men, and not an end in itself —the pursuit of beauty alone, in the literal acceptation of the word, is a childish stupidity, a rudimentary form of art ". Above all he desired to express in music the life of the common Russian people, their joys and sorrows, hopes and fears, loves and hates, agonies and aspirations, and to depict in music all the strange individual types of which its vast anonymity is composed. The extent to which he succeeded in carrying out this project in his operas and songs is one of the most astonishing achievements in all music. No composer who has ever lived, not even Mozart himself, possessed to a higher degree the power of vividly delineating men and women, not merely their acts, characters, and inner thoughts, but even their very physical appearance and living presence ; the peasant woman in the *Hopak*, the poor mother in the *Berceuse of Eremouchka*, the philosophic moujik in *Kallikrat*, the mushroom-picker, the orphan, the seminarist, the street urchin, and countless others, all rise up before us in the flesh by virtue of the sheer magical, evocative power of the music. His capacity for creating individuals is only equalled by his uncanny insight into the psychology of crowds and masses, and his power of realizing it musically. Some of the choral writing in *Boris* is in this respect unique. There is nothing in music to which one can fitly compare the way in which he builds up a host of small individual traits and impulses into one great unified organism, and creates a mass psychology without depriving its constituent members of their separate living personalities.

Not only is Moussorgsky the greatest musical psychologist of all time, both in the treatment of individuals and masses, but no one can surpass him in his ability to realize in music the inner meaning and all the latent implications of a dramatic situation. There is nothing in opera more poignant, more gripping in its pathos and emotional intensity than the scene in *Khovantschina* in which the old prince, the representative and symbolical embodiment of the perishing order, goes forth to meet his end to the chanting by his maid-servants of a hymn in praise of him and his house : " Swim on, glide on, thou snow-white swan, Ladou, Ladou ; oh, swim to meet thy noble mate, Ladou, Ladou "—one of the loveliest little fragments of melody ever penned. Or again, take the scene in the monastery cell in *Boris*, with the old monk Pimen engaged in writing his chronicle in the silence of the night, pregnant with historic fate. For not only is Moussorgsky a supreme musical dramatist, but a great historian as well. There are no more vivid reconstructions of past events in the pages of Carlyle and Michelet than in the scores of *Boris* or *Khovantschina* ; there is more of Russian history condensed in them than is to be found in the folios of Karamzin or any other chronicler. He even seems to have been able to divine the future, for in the final scene of *Boris* the recent revolution and the events of 1917 are set to music fifty years before the event ; and in the song of the idiot with which the work closes there would almost seem to be a prophetic cry of despair at the impending fate of his unhappy country. The very soul of Russia is in this scene ; no one with the slightest sensitivity or imagination can avoid being stirred to the depths of his being by it.

It might be perhaps asked by some purist what all this has to do with music. The reply is that it has everything to do with it, for, although practically all Moussorgsky's music is set to words, it would be a mistake to imagine that they are in any way responsible for the intrinsic quality of the emotion which his operas and songs arouse in the listener. It is latent in the music itself, and repeated experience conclusively shows that it can be as powerfully, though naturally more vaguely, experienced by those who have not any knowledge of the text as by those who have. It is the supreme merit of Moussorgsky that he clearly demonstrated the fact that music need not be only a pleasant combination of sounds signifying nothing outside of itself, but is capable, in the hands of a great genius, of embodying ideas and conceptions the expression of which was formerly regarded as the unalienable privilege of literature alone.

In so far as it is possible to speak of the music of Moussorgsky apart from the ideas and conceptions which it expresses, its

most remarkable feature consists in the extreme simplicity—
one might almost say the extreme poverty—of the means
employed, and the bareness and seeming crudity of its texture.
This characteristic was at first regarded, and still is by many,
as the consequence of insufficient technical training on the part
of the composer, and until quite recently it was believed that
his music had necessarily to be subjected to drastic revision and
alteration before it could be performed with success ; even
to-day the only versions of his operas that are to be heard on
the stage are still those made by Rimsky-Korsakov, which are
in many important particulars the merest travesties of the
originals. We are only now beginning to realize that this
starkness and uncouthness are æsthetically necessary, and the
inevitable outcome of his artistic conceptions, which can only
be impaired or destroyed by the unintelligent editing his works
have received. Elaborately woven counterpoints, subtle and
refined harmonies, glowing and irridescent orchestration,
decorative but meaningless figurations, are all as unsuited to
his art as brocaded shirts, silk underclothing, and lace
embroideries would be to a peasant or worker. Such things
are best left to the *grands seigneurs* of the academies and
conservatoires, and to the lions of the drawing-rooms and
salons ; they have no place in the art of the proletariat, of
which Moussorgsky is the first and still the sole representative.

Moussorgsky, in fact, knew very well what he was about, and
the time has certainly come when his works should be performed
as they were originally written, without the alteration of a
single note. The only possible excuse that can be offered in
extenuation of Rimsky-Korsakov's bowdlerized versions is that
they have kept the works of Moussorgsky alive in some shape
or form during half a century when the original versions would
never have been tolerated at all. His music was, indeed, so
far in advance of its time, and has been so universally misunderstood up till the present day, that it would probably
never have had the chance of becoming known to us at all if it
had not been for Rimsky-Korsakov's equivocal assistance.

The reproach of technical incompetence which has been cast
up unceasingly against Moussorgsky by academic critics is not
by any means confined to him alone, but is often extended,
with as little real justification, to the entire Russian school,
with the solitary exception of Rimsky-Korsakov. This is of

course largely due to the well-known fact that none of them were professional musicians in the strict sense of the word. Glinka and Dargomijsky were both members of the leisured classes, and were consequently not obliged to earn their livings at all ; Borodin was a professor of chemistry and only wrote music in his spare time ; Moussorgsky was, during the greater part of his active career, a minor government official, and therefore unable to devote his entire time and energy to composition ; and Balakirev, though a whole-time musician, was self-taught and occupied an official post as director of the St. Petersburg Conservatoire, which left him little time or opportunity for writing music. Hence they have all been patronizingly and contemptuously dismissed as mere amateurs and *dilettanti* ; certain qualities in their work which differentiated it from that of other composers have been accounted for on the ground of the alleged insufficiency of their musical training and technical equipment, and it has been suggested that they would have written very differently if they had known better. This is a complete and pernicious fallacy. Not merely is the work of Moussorgsky insusceptible of any improvement, but the technical ability of Balakirev or Borodin is, in the works they wrote, beyond reproach, whatever deficiencies they may have possessed from the point of view of scholasticism which, however, has about as much to do with creative art to-day as the Holy Roman Empire has to do with practical politics. It is true that the members of the Russian school, with the exception of Rimsky-Korsakov, wrote only a comparatively small handful of works each, and this may to a certain extent have been the result of their inability to devote sufficient time to creative work. A small output, however, is by no means necessarily an unmixed misfortune. Most professional composers write far too much, either from habit, in self-justification, or in order to make money, and are consequently prone to repeat themselves ; those, on the contrary, whose means of subsistence are derived from other sources than composition, only take up their pens when they are irresistibly impelled to do so, and only write the works they wish to write, without *arrière pensée* ; in consequence of which their work, though smaller in bulk than that of their professional colleagues, is generally on a very much higher level of inspiration. The output of Borodin, to take an example, may only consist of an unfinished opera, two complete and one incomplete symphonies, one symphonic poem, two string quartets, and a small handful of songs, but they are all without exception first-rate works ; that of César Franck, to take a good example of the " professional " musician, consists of about a hundred works of different kinds, but only an exceedingly small proportion of them, amounting in all to less than the total output of Borodin, is of the finest quality. In other words, what will eventually survive of the amateur Borodin will probably come to more than what will survive of the professional Franck.

Another important point in this connection which is frequently overlooked is that the professional musician, in actual practice, often, and even generally, has less time to devote to composition than the amateur. Unless he is fortunate enough to possess private means or a wealthy patron, he is obliged to spend the greater part of his time and energy in giving lessons in pianoforte playing or elementary harmony—an occupation which has not merely nothing to do with creative work, but is even positively harmful to it. Take the case of Franck again, whose life in this respect is typical of the vast majority of professional musicians. His biographers tell us that he was seldom able to give more than two hours a day to composition; the rest of the time, from morning to nightfall, was spent in journeying about Paris giving lessons. It is surely obvious therefore, that not only did Glinka and Dargomijsky enjoy infinitely greater opportunities than Franck for composition and for perfecting themselves in their art, but that even men such as Borodin or Moussorgsky, quite apart from the question of leisure—of which they almost certainly possessed more than Franck—must have come to their creative work with a very much fresher mind and a more independent outlook. It is precisely the stuffy professionalism that exudes from all Franck's music—the inevitable outcome of his circumstances— that constitutes his prevailing fault ; it is the absence of this quality which, so far from being the failing of the Russians, is rather their chief virtue, and the redeeming feature of their least successful achievements. And apart from the intrinsic power and beauty of the major part of their work, the greatest service performed by the Russian school was to show conclusively for the first time that music was not necessarily a mere craft which should be acquired as one acquires any other craft, such as carpentry or shoe-making, the trade secrets of which are accessible only to initiates and members of a kind of musical guild or trade-union, but an expressive art like any other, which could be not only successfully but superlatively well practised by anyone possessing the requisite æsthetic sensibility and creative imagination, however lacking in theoretic training and knowledge ; and that the technique necessary for the expression of one's ideas was to be acquired in the actual process of composition rather than in learning to handle the outworn or obsolescent formulas of the schools. It is not necessary for us to go to an academy to learn how to write poetry, neither should it be necessary for us to do so in order to learn how to write music.

There are so many remarkable parallels, both in outline and in detail, between the Russian school of music and the Russian literary movement which was more or less contemporaneous with it, that it is impossible not to recognize that they are each a part of one single impulse and can hardly be completely understood without reference to one another. Not only is the morphology or course of development the same in each case, but one also finds that the rôles played by individual members in the one are frequently strikingly analogous to those played by individual members in the other. For example, we have already noted the close functional resemblance between Puskhin and Glinka, and shown how Borodin, in his union of Slavonic thought and western form may be regarded as the Turgenev of music, although of course temperamentally they have little or nothing in common. An even closer parallel could be drawn between Moussorgsky and Dostoevsky, for not only are they in their respective spheres the most completely uncompromising representatives of the Russian spirit, pure and undiluted, the most consistently hostile to the influences of western art and ideology, but as individual artists they also strikingly resemble each other in many important respects ; for example, we find in the work of both the same uncouth, rough-hewn style, the same apparent formlessness combined with a mysterious inner logic and necessity, the same deep, mystical quality of emotion springing in both cases from the intimate and loving contact with the people and the soil of Russia ; and such creations as the innocent in *Boris* and Savichna in the song of that name are only variations, like Alyosha in *The Brothers Karamazov* and Myshkin in *The Idiot*, on the most characteristically Russian of all artistic themes—the Christ-like innocent through whom all the evil and suffering in the world is redeemed. Similarly there is a distinct analogy between Peter Ilyitch Tschaikovsky and Tolstoi, not so much in temperament—although they both possess the same habit of morbid introspection and self-laceration—as in the nature of the parts which both played in their respective schools, considered abstractly. Both are cosmopolitan and eclectic to a greater extent than any of their colleagues, and belong more to European than to Russian art; both similarly became known to the west a long time sooner, largely owing to this reason, and for a long time their purely personal qualities were erroneously regarded as typical and representative of all Russian art; finally, both are suffering to-day from the subsequent revelation brought about by our knowledge and appreciation of the work of their rival compatriots, and from the natural tendency to depreciate and underestimate them as much as it was formerly the fashion to overpraise them. The reaction, however, has been allowed to go too far. When critical stability has been attained, it will have to be admitted that, with all his detestable qualities, many of which he shares in common with Tolstoi, Tschaikovsky possessed musical gifts of a high order; and that his craftsmanship in general and his orchestration in particular often go a long way towards reconciling us to the undeniable vulgarity and unwholesome sentimentality of his ideas.

The great achievement of the Russian school is undoubtedly the most important collective manifestation in music, as it was in literature, during the second part of the nineteenth century; indeed there is nothing else to be compared to it. Here and there attempts were made with varying success to found national schools on the same lines in different parts of Europe, such as the Bohemian or Czech school represented by Smetana and Dvořák, the Norwegian school represented by Grieg, and so forth; but none of them produced figures of anything like the same stature and eminence as the Russian school. Apart from these a few isolated figures appear here and there in the larger or more central European countries, but none of them are sufficiently important to merit more than a passing mention in a book such as this which, if only for reasons of space, must be strictly confined to a consideration of the broader aspects and most outstanding personalities only. As for the present century and living composers, it may be fairly contended that they do not yet form part of the history but only of the politics, so to speak, of music, and as such have no place here. Those readers, however who desire to pursue the story further in the company of the same writer are referred to his "Survey of Contemporary Music", in which the most salient personalities and tendencies in music at the present time are exhaustively treated.

CHAPTER XVII

An Outline of Musical Æsthetic

It is commonly believed that the more we learn of any aspect of life or of any artistic activity, the less satisfaction we are capable of deriving from it ; that increase of knowledge inevitably and, as it were, automatically, tends to impair our emotional pleasure, and that, in the words of Hegel, " Reality, anywhere and everywhere, whether the life of Nature or of mind, is defaced and slain by its comprehension ". This belief receives, of course, the warm and enthusiastic support of all those who are incapable of thinking consecutively for more than two seconds, and of the equally numerous body who are too lazy even to attempt such a hazardous experiment. But even if we might legitimately question either the practical or the hedonistic utility of intellectual curiosity, and even if we were to admit its dangers, especially to the creative artist, we cannot deny the irresistible nature of the fascination that it exercises over us. It is, after all, a deeply rooted instinct that impels us to seek a more intimate knowledge and understanding of the thing we love, even if, like Psyche in the exquisite allegory of Apuleius in the *Golden Ass*, we run the risk of awakening the sleeping Amor with our burning drop of midnight oil, and losing him for ever. And everyone who is in any way occupied with music or with any other art, whether as creator or only as appreciator, must surely at some time or another have experienced the desire to learn more concerning its essential nature and its relation, if any, to life and to other human activities. One might even go so far as to say that the artist or art-lover who has never experienced it is incomplete, almost a monstrosity. But while they are at least free to dispense with the obligation of inquiring closely into such problems, for the critic or historian there is no choice ; certainly no survey over the entire field of musical art such as the present work, however sketchy and inadequate, could possibly claim validity or even expect any measure of serious consideration unless an attempt were made to arrive at some more or less definite conclusions concerning the nature of the art with which it purports to deal. For in the first place our entire critical apparatus and standard of values are inextricably bound up with fundamental issues. It is surely obvious, for example, that our judgments on different composers and different works must inevitably depend to a great extent on whether we consider absolute music to be necessarily superior or inferior, as the case may be, to what is called programme music ; or on whether we believe music to be an expressive art or merely, according to Dr. Charles Burney, " an innocent luxury, unnecessary, indeed, to our existence, but a great improvement and gratification of the sense of hearing "—in a word, a mere pleasant physical sensation.

In the second place, philosophic and æsthetic conceptions play a very much larger and more important part in the history of music than we are at first apt to imagine or willing to admit. For while it is a commonplace that the artist is entirely uninfluenced by theories, he is in reality extremely susceptible to them, and musicians in particular, despite all their emphatic protestations to the contrary, entertain a respect for them almost amounting to veneration. There have even been periods in musical history, as we have seen, when the whole course of direction was entirely altered by æsthetic theorizings and which cannot, therefore, be properly understood without reference to them. The experiments of the Florentines, the reforms of Gluck and later of Wagner, are only three well-known examples of this ; and, as we have repeatedly shown in the course of the present work, there has always been in every period a definite and sometimes a very close relation between music and other forms of artistic and literary activity.

In view of these facts, no apology would seem to be necessary for an attempt to arrive at some solution of the eternal problems by which music is hedged in and surrounded. Yet it is an undeniable fact that anyone who is thus impelled to seek an answer to the inevitable and natural questions which we all ask ourselves—What is the function of art ?—What is music ? —What is or should be the nature of the pleasure we derive from it ?—and so forth, are generally met with replies couched in some wholly unintelligible metaphysical jargon concerning beauty in the abstract, emanating from philosophers either actuated by a profound enmity and hostility towards art and artists, or else possessing little or no knowledge or understanding of them. Apart from these, there remain only the effusions of æsthetes with a certain appreciative faculty, but wholly devoid of the intellectual grasp and reasoning power which might lend substance to their conclusions. The creative artist, who alone might conceivably combine the requisite qualities, is quite evidently better employed in making works of art than in writing about them. Music, at any rate, has never produced creative artists who were at the same time thinkers of the calibre of, say, Goethe or Leonardo da Vinci. Musicians have always been content to have their thinking done for them, sometimes with disastrous results, as we have had occasion to observe in the course of our narrative. They have, indeed, been so long reproached with being inarticulate and unable to express themselves in language that others could understand, that they have even begun to take a secret pride in it, as if it were a virtue, and not, as it actually is, a serious defect. They like to feel that, in the words of Browning, " The rest may reason, and welcome ; 'tis we musicians know ".

Consequently we find that utterances on the subject of music emanate almost entirely from writers without the slightest understanding of the nature or knowledge of the history of the art, and who are frequently unable to distinguish one tune from another. It certainly could not for a moment be denied even by their most fervent admirers, that the vast majority of those who are by universal consent regarded as the greatest thinkers of all time cut a very sorry figure indeed when they attempt to explain or define the nature and *raison d'être* of art. Æsthetic, indeed, is perhaps of all possible fields of philosophic enquiry the one in which most nonsense has been talked and written. There must, one feels, be something about art which completely upsets philosophic equilibrium. However much at his ease the sage may feel in the company of these plain and homely sisters, the Good and the True, he is completely *bouleversé* when he is suddenly confronted with that fascinating and enigmatic third sister, the Beautiful. In fact he seems to lose his head, and to behave in much the same way as when he encounters her in real life, in concrete female form. It is almost pathetic to see the way in which he becomes either fatuously ecstatic or puritanically disapproving, according to his temperament ; he either falls at her feet in adoration, like Schelling or Bergson, or, more often, calls her a slut and turns her out of the house, like Plato or Tolstoi.

And as art is the *pons asinorum* of philosophers, so is music that of æstheticians. From the very outset music has been a problem and an enigma to thinkers—the dark horse among the arts, a changeling differing from the rest seemingly in every way. Its very origin and existence are wrapped up in impenetrable mystery, and have never been satisfactorily accounted for by thinkers. Unlike the other arts, music seemingly neither represents nor imitates anything. While the study of life or of natural forms is in some way or another essential to literature, painting, or sculpture, music need neither rely upon nor employ any subject-matter outside of itself and its prescribed forms. Music, in short, appears at first sight to have no direct contact with life or reality, and no direct relation to any of its sister arts. What is the essential nature of this strange art, at once the most sensuous and physical in its appeal, yet at the same time the most disembodied and intangible ; the most abstract and intellectual in some of its aspects, and the most profoundly emotional in others ; the most formal, yet the most elusive and unsubstantial ; sounding air, yet a spiritual reality ? Let us first examine the answers submitted by former enquirers into these questions to see if they can help us at all.

Although, properly speaking, the history of musical æsthetic begins with Plato, it is necessary first to say a few words concerning the Pythagorean conception of music, not merely for the sake of completeness, but because it has exercised a considerable influence on some of its successors. To a great extent the Pythagorean philosophy of nature was based upon the theory of the laws of sound, which constituted one of the most important discoveries of Pythagoras himself. Indeed, the fundamental doctrine taught by his followers—that everything is in its essence number—was most strikingly borne out by, and in all probability owed its inception to, the mathematical basis and the numerical relations of musical intervals. Similarly, the recognition of a prevailing system and order regulating the movements of and distances between the planets, gave rise to the belief that " what the eye sees in observing the stars, the ear perceives in concord of tones ".

Plato, indeed, tells us that the Pythagoreans regarded Harmony and Astronomy as two sister sciences. ("Republic", VII, 530, D.) To say that all things are number—which is the cardinal tenet of Pythagorean philosophy—was equivalent to saying that all things are a harmony, that the universe is a harmony. The final stage in this identification was the curious cosmogonical theory of the "Harmony of the Spheres", which rested on the notion that, as every body in rapid motion produces a musical tone, this must also be the case with the heavenly bodies. And so Pythagorean philosophy arrived in the end at the conception of the seven planets, corresponding with the seven strings of the lyre, revolving in space and sounding the seven notes of the musical scale, the heavenly heptachord.

All this, of course, has nothing to do with music as an art, strictly speaking, but is only a fanciful interpretation, in which science and mysticism are curiously blent, of the physical laws of sound. Nevertheless its influence can be traced in Leibnitz's definition of music as "Arithmetica nescientis se numerare animi",—i.e., music is an unconscious counting, or a felt relation of numbers ; also in Sir Thomas Browne's description of it as "a shadowed and hieroglyphical image of the whole world", and, *mutatis mutandis*, in Schopenhauer's conception of the world as "embodied music".

Plato starts his enquiry from the assumption that all art is the imitation of reality, and that the work of art must be judged to possess the same qualities and defects as the objects imitated. Consequently the representation of what is contrary to morality or religion will necessarily have an evil influence on its contemplator. A peculiarity of his theory consists in the fact that not only does he regard a work of art as a mere reduplication of something already in existence without anything else being added to it, but a mere "copy of a copy", since the natural world itself, according to Platonic doctrine, is only a copy of ideas in the mind of God.

Now, as Plato clearly saw, the artist is more attracted towards what he calls the rebellious principle, "which furnishes a greater variety of material than the wise, calm temperament, which is always equable", and consequently offers fewer opportunities for artistic treatment. For these reasons the artist is excluded from the ideal Republic as a dangerous fellow, a conspirator against the safety and well-being of the State.

It is interesting to note that Plato attributes to music an even greater subversive power than to any of the other arts. For while they are imitations of actual phenomena, according to him, music is the imitation of mental and spiritual states ; " Any musical innovation is dangerous to the State and ought to be prevented . . . when modes of music change the fundamental laws of the State change with them ", and it is interesting to note that the ancient Chinese philosophers held identically the same views concerning music.

This is not by any means as absurd as it appears at first sight. It has always seemed peculiarly anomalous that once we grant, as most people do, that art has to some extent at least a moral effect, music, beyond question the most powerful of all in its direct physical and emotional appeal, should be permitted every latitude, while the other arts must conduct themselves with the utmost circumspection ; that Wilde's *Salome* should be considered immoral while Strauss's music, which goes very much further, can be listened to any day ; that while the lovers in the second act of *Tristan* are ostensibly engaged in talking *Schop*, the orchestra is unmistakably depicting the final and most intense stages of sexual intercourse. It must be admitted that Plato is at least logical in his attitude.

It is easy to see from the very earnestness and persistence of his investigation, from his constant obsession with the problem of art and beauty, that Plato, himself an artist in prose it must be remembered, was profoundly dissatisfied with his conclusions. And in the later dialogues we still find him reverting to it, and searching for a way out—some point of view in which could be reconciled the Good and the Beautiful. But this no philosophy can hope to do which bases itself firmly and uncompromisingly on the one, and seeks to make the other conform to it.

Plato's attitude, indeed, is a *resumé* of all ethical philosophy on the subject of art, and the best illustration of the hostility and antagonism which have always prevailed between the artist and the moralist from the earliest times. The same point of view is expressed in the *Pensées* of Pascal, and Tolstoi's " What is Art ? " is little more than a restatement and amplification of the principles enunciated over two thousand years before by Plato. Tolstoi starts from the contention that by means of words man transmits his thoughts, by means of art

his feelings, with exactly the same implications and consequences. Like Plato, he dismisses the artist from decent
society, or, what amounts to the same thing, he declares
Bach, Beethoven, Michael Angelo, Titian, Velasquez, Shakespeare, and many others, to be bad artists. And so we find
both ancient and modern ascetics and moralists united in
common cause against the artist.

Aristotle's outlook on art, as one might expect, stands in
strong contrast to that of Plato. He is not, like the latter, a
philosopher with a rigid *a priori* system to which everything
must be made to conform ; he has no moralistic axe to grind,
and consequently approaches the subject in a spirit of dispassionate curiosity. Indeed, in method he is less a philosopher
than a scientist, possessing both the characteristic virtues and
defects of the scientist—i.e., he is strong in observation, weak
in deduction. This is only natural. If one starts examining
an object with some preconceived idea one will have no difficulty
in making facts conform to it, or even illustrate it. Objectivity
under these conditions is virtually impossible ; facts are
susceptible of so many diverse interpretations that one is
apt unconsciously to pervert them to one's own ends. The
empirical and impartial observer, on the other hand, seeks to
determine the essential nature of the object of enquiry, and
sooner or later becomes involved in perplexities and contra-
dictions for the same reasons. He is frequently compelled to
fall back upon some previous conclusion even if it should seem
to impeach the validity of his observations. And this is what
happens to Aristotle ; he makes brilliant, illuminating, and
often profound observations, but for the most part fails to
follow them up, or to deduce satisfactory conclusions from
them.

No one is more liable to misinterpretation than Aristotle. His
statements are sometimes obscure and contradictory, and do
not always mean what they seem to mean. For example, when
he declares that art imitates nature he does not use the words
in the same sense as Plato. In the first place the word he
employs—$\phi\acute{v}\sigma\iota\varsigma$—does not signify so much the visual world
as the creative principle of the universe—Nature spelt with a
capital letter ; secondly, that he does not use the word
" imitate " in its present-day signification can be readily seen
from the following statement in the *Poetics* : " The poet being

an imitator, must of necessity imitate one of three things : things as they are or were, things as they are said or thought to be, or things as they ought to be ".   This last category shows that the word is not to be understood in our strict and limited sense.   Again, he makes the following remark, which indicates a great advance on Plato's somewhat crude and elementary conception of the relation existing between the work of art and the object imitated : " In general the impossible must be justified by reference to artistic requirements or to the higher reality—a probable impossibility is to be preferred to a thing improbable yet possible.   It may be that there should be no men such as Zeuxis painted, but the impossible is the higher thing, for the ideal type must surpass the reality ".

In fact we may logically infer that for Aristotle, art in general, so far from being the imitation is rather the idealization of reality, the revelation of its essential and significant aspect, the completion of and improvement upon nature.   In this he has been followed by many modern thinkers, Taine for example: " Le propre d'une œuvre d'art est de rendre le caractère essentiel de l'objet, et pour celà l'artiste élague les traits qui les cachait, choisit ceux qui le manifestent, corrige ceux dans lesquels il est altéré, refait ceux dans lesquels il est annulé ".

So far as music is concerned, Aristotle represents a certain advance on Plato.   While the latter would appear to imply that music, apart from the words to which it is set, is almost meaningless and wholly contemptible (see, for example, "Laws", book II), Aristotle questions whether perhaps musical sounds themselves may not " possess emotional import ", and " contain likenesses of moral moods " ; but he seems unable to follow up this suggestion or to base any workable hypothesis concerning the function of the art upon it, preferring to fall back on the characteristically Greek conception of music as a means to education and moral improvement.   At the same time he is not a rigid moralist like Plato, and readily conceded to music a recreative function and a pleasurable value apart from the " message " to be conveyed.   This is the direction in which later pagan thinkers incline.   Philodemus, for example, an Epicurean philosopher contemporary with Cicero, categorically refuses to admit that music can be anything else but a mere physical sensation ; " music is irrational and cannot appeal to the soul or the emotions, and is no more an expressive art than cookery ".

And so we find that all Greek and Roman æsthetic before the Christian era unites in regarding music as a mere empty sensual pleasure by itself, but useful, perhaps, as a means to moral improvement and for the inculcation of ethical virtues, like the spoonful of jam concealing the unpalatable medicine. That it could conceivably express anything at all apart from words is an idea that was never seriously entertained by Greek or Roman thinkers, except speculatively and hesitatingly by Aristotle, but finally rejected by him, or at least not pursued any further. Even the much later Plotinus, whose attitude towards art in general represents a notable advance on that of Plato, does not take us any further, so far as music is concerned. When he claims in the *Enneads*, that " the arts do not simply imitate the visible, but go back to the reasons from which Nature itself comes, and further that they create much out of themselves and add to that which is defective, as being themselves in possession of beauty ", he is only speaking of literature and the visual arts.   Music, for him as for all his predecessors, is an inferior art compared with the others, and the ear a less noble organ than the eye.

It is not until we come to Christian thinkers that music is not merely regarded as an expressive art, but singled out from among all the others for special favour and commendation. In the words of St. Isadore, " sine musica nulla disciplina potest esse perfecta ; nihil enim est sine illa " ; Rhabanus Maurus claimed music to be the key to divine wisdom, and declared that without a knowledge of it no one could become a cleric or a teacher of philosophy ; Boethius said that without the aid of music it was impossible to attain to truth ; and St. Thomas Aquinas called it " the first among the seven arts, and the noblest of all the sciences ".   This pre-eminence of music among the arts lasted throughout the Middle Ages.   It was the only one that formed part of the mediæval educational curriculum called the *quadrivium*, together with arithmetic, geometry, and astronomy ; and without some acquaintance with its principles and practice it was considered impossible to become a master of grammar, dialectic, or rhetoric.   Music, in short, from the beginning of the Christian ascendancy up to the time of the Renaissance, was regarded, not merely as the first of all

s

the arts, but as the key to all wisdom and all knowledge, no less of earthly than of heavenly things.   It was now the visual arts that were considered to be mere sensual pleasures.

With the Renaissance, however, all this changed.   As we have already seen, even the musicians themselves reverted to the Greek conception of their art as a mere embellishment of literature ; and in the eighteenth century men such as Diderot, d'Alembert, and even Rousseau, regarded it wholly from the same standpoint, and only granted to music the possession of meaning and significance in association with words—pure instrumental music being, in their eyes, merely a pleasant physical sensation.   Kant completely sums up the attitude of the eighteenth century when he says, in his *Critique of Judgment*, " if we estimate the worth of the arts by the culture they supply to the mind, music will have the lowest place among them (as it has perhaps the highest among those arts which are valued for their pleasantness) because it merely plays with sensations ".

When we get to the nineteenth century, however, music is again put forward as the first of the arts.   Schelling speaks rapturously of " the archetypal rhythm of nature which, by means of this art, breaks through into the world of secondary existence ", whatever that may mean ; and Hegel says that "we find operative in music not merely the profoundest ideality and soul, but the most rigorous rationality . . . if we are in a general way permitted to regard human activity in the realm of the beautiful as a liberation, as a release from constraint and restriction—it is the art of music which conducts us to the final summit of that ascent to freedom ".   But it was left to Schopenhauer to proclaim the absolute supremacy of music among the arts.   " Music ", he says, " is by no means like the other arts, the copies of Ideas, but the copy of the Will itself . . . that is why the effect of music is so much more powerful and penetrating than that of the other arts, for they speak only of shadows, but it speaks of the thing in itself ". Music is " the metaphysical to everything physical in the world, and the thing-in-itself to every phenomenon ; it expresses in a perfectly universal language, in a homogeneous material, mere tones, and with the greatest determinateness and truth, the inner nature, the in-itself of the world.   We might just as well call the world embodied music as embodied will ".   Meanwhile,

" regarded apart from its æsthetic or inner significance, and looked at merely externally and purely empirically, music is the means of comprehending directly and in the .concrete, complex relations of numbers. By the union of these two very different but correct views of music we may arrive at a conception of the possibility of a philosophy of number such as that of Pythagoras ". And so we find the completest and most elaborate modern conception of music linked up with the oldest and most primitive of which we have any record.

At different periods, then, and in different circumstances and environments, music has been variously regarded by philosophers as a key to the understanding of the nature of the universe, as a form of mathematics, as an imitation of reality, as an idealization of reality, as a means of improving or corrupting morals, as a means to the attainment of a literary end, as an expression of emotion, as a vehicle for the conveyance of religious truths—always, in short, as the embodiment of every conceivable kind of " content ", or alternatively, nothing but a mere sensual pleasure.

If we turn from philosophy to æsthetic, and to particularized writings dealing directly and solely with the problems of music, our plight is little better, if not actually worse. The æsthetic critic, starting from the concrete work of art instead of from an *a priori* conception of what it ought to be, lacks as a rule the synthetic and co-ordinating faculty which alone would enable him to deduce general principles from his frequently accurate observations. He invariably tends, moreover, to base his conclusions upon the particular aspect of art which happens to prevail at his own particular time, with the result that his values fluctuate in accordance with the ideals and fashions of his period. Hanslick, for example, whose essay *Vom Musikalisch Schönen* represents perhaps the only tolerably complete system of musical æsthetics in existence, takes up his position on the field of purely instrumental composition as exemplified in the work of the great Viennese school and their successors ; with the inevitable result that his conclusions are hopelessly biased and one sided. In striking contrast to those we have so far been examining, they amount to a categorical denial of the capacity of music to convey or express anything outside of itself, and to an emphatic condemnation of any attempt to make it do so ; for him it cannot even express emotion, for " the emotional effect of music cannot be ascribed so much to the artistic forms created by and appealing to the mind, as to the material with which music works ". Consequently, according to him the music that sets out to express anything whatsoever is an inferior order of art compared to pure music, possessing only formal beauty.

Now, however satisfactory this attitude may be in theory—and it must be admitted that Hanslick makes out quite a strong case for it—in practice it cannot be maintained. The whole history of music shows us clearly that there is no composer of eminence—except perhaps Chopin—whose best music does not largely consist of works which, to some extent at least, either through association with a literary text, as in song, opera, cantata, oratorio, motet, madrigal, and mass, or in a less direct way, as in what is called programme music, make use of or suggest ideas belonging, strictly, to the domain of some other art. Indeed, it is probably not an exaggeration to say that at least three-quarters of the world's greatest music has a connection with something outside of itself, some extraneous implication, whether literary, pictorial, illustrative, psychological, or anything else you like to call it. Everyone will admit, of course, that, in the words of Professor Dent, one of the most consistent and distinguished latter-day followers of Hanslick, " unless the work is intelligible simply as music alone, constructed on its own purely musical principles, apart from all external considerations, it must fall short of perfection as a work of art ", but that is quite a different matter. The point is that this intrinsically musical perfection can gain an added significance and appeal through association with or, more accurately, through embodying or expressing, an idea which we loosely call literary or illustrative—loosely, for it does not necessarily follow that because a conception can be realized in words, or in line and colour, it is, therefore, proper only to that particular medium and unfitted for musical expression also. The boundaries of the arts overlap to a great extent, and many of the greatest artistic themes are capable of realization in any medium whatsoever.

To take a concrete example, could anyone seriously suggest that Victoria's profoundly moving motet, generally sung in Easter Week, on the words " O vos omnes qui transitis per viam, attendite et videte, si est dolor similis sicut dolor meus ", etc., is merely a beautiful pattern of four interwoven voices ? Victoria himself, it is certain, would have been the very first to repudiate such a suggestion with indignation.   For it is not as if the music was merely associated with the words ; rather is their tremendous significance indissolubly embodied in the music, and anyone who would, simply on that account, maintain that the work was necessarily inferior to a piece of pure music such as a movement from a string quartet or symphony, is simply talking nonsense, for considered simply as music it is as perfect as anything that has ever been written.   And if there are any for whom this added significance over and above the purely musical beauty does not exist or has no appeal, we can only say that we are very sorry for them, because they miss a great deal.

This must not be construed into a plea on behalf of programme music, or regarded as a suggestion that it is superior any more than that it is inferior to what is called pure music—if, indeed, such a thing exists outside the realm of theory and abstraction. It is possible to derive just as much æsthetic pleasure from a fugue or symphony as from a song or opera ; it is a different order of pleasure, that is all, but both are equally legitimate. But to attempt to limit the scope of music to a single restricted field of activity, or to suggest that pure music is *per se* preferable to programme music, as so many musical æstheticians seek to do, is the merest preciosity.   To maintain such an attitude in its uncompromising integrity virtually amounts to a rejection of at least three-quarters of the world's greatest music, or to the implication that it is *a priori* inferior to the other quarter ; since only for a comparatively short period, i.e., from about 1750 till 1830 at the most, can it possibly be said that the greatest achievements in musical art are entirely devoid of extraneous implications of some kind or another, and it would be a bold man who would say even that.   For quite apart from the extent to which the words enter into our appreciation of vocal music, or the programme into our appreciation of programme music, it is unquestionably true that all kinds of, strictly speaking, foreign elements, are to be found in the music of every period.   In the admirable words of M. Romain Rolland " musique est architecture des sons en certaines siècles d'architecture et chez les peuples architectes elle est dessin, ligne, beauté plastique chez les peuples qui ont le sens et le culte de la forme, chez les peuples peintres et sculpteurs comme les Italiens—elle est poésie intime, effusions lyriques, méditation philosophique, chez les peuples poétiques et philosophiques comme les Allemands—elle est un art de cour galante et poétique sous François I et Charles IX—de foi et de combat avec la Réforme, d'orgueil princier sous Louis XIV, de salon pendant le XVIII siècle—expression lyrique de personnalités revolutionnaires pendant le XIX siècle ".

The conclusion, then, to which we inevitably come, whether we approach the question from the philosophic angle or from that of a purely æsthetic consideration of the history of music, is, that sounds constitute an artistic language which can no more be limited in its scope than words can ; capable of expressing the most diverse ideas and conceptions, including even those that we regard as properly belonging to the spheres of the other arts.   And what is true of music is true of them all. Each of the arts tends in precisely the same way to extend itself in every direction heliotropically, and to enlarge its confines and sphere of influence in an everwidening circle so as ultimately to include within its circumference as much of the formerly undisputed territory of the other arts as possible, and to enable it to express, singlehanded, the whole of life, reality, human experience—call it what you will.   When Pater uttered his celebrated dictum to the effect that all the arts aspire towards the condition of music, he was uttering a dangerous and misleading half-truth, for music herself is continually aspiring towards the condition of other arts.   There is, indeed, nothing that music cannot be made to do in the hands of genius.   It can be pure tonal arabesque and formal beauty, as in the sonatas of Domenico Scarlatti ; it can be Gothic architectonics, as in the masses and motets of Okeghem and Josquin des Prés ; it can be a means to moral improvement, as in the works of Beethoven's middle period, and a metaphysical language in those of his last ; it can be an instrument of psychological and even physiological delineation, as in the operas of Mozart and in the songs of Moussorgsky ; it can be the expression of emotion, as in the music of Liszt and Wagner ; it can be a purely physical sensation, as in the work of Stravinsky ; and Bach, in his setting of the *Credo* in his *B minor Mass*, has clearly shown, to quote the words of Schweitzer, that the dogma of the Trinity " can be expressed much more clearly and satisfactorily in music than in verbal formulæ ", and consequently that music is capable of being a vehicle for the presentation of religious truths or philosophic concepts. These are only a few examples, chosen at random, of the possibilities of expression afforded by the art of music, and it would be easy to adduce as many more. And if the foolish question be asked, whether music should be physical, emotional, or intellectual in its appeal, we can only reply that it should be all three ; that the listener who is incapable of appreciating it in all three ways is simply an incomplete musician, and that the work which does not satisfy him in all three ways is not a perfect work, or even a good one. A great work of art should appeal to the whole man, and not merely to a part of him.

The fault, then, of all the various answers we have been examining to the question " What is music ? " is not so much that they are wrong—indeed, each of them contains a particle of truth—as that they are inadequate and mutually exclusive. The fact remains, however, that although there is probably nothing in the whole range of human experience that cannot be expressed in music, there are certain things that it can do better than any other form of art, and other things that it cannot do so well. In other words, although the circumferences of all the arts intersect each other and overlap to a greater or lesser extent, they have each a fixed and immutable centre about which they are described. And however contradictory and irreconcilable all the foregoing theories may appear to be on the surface, one fact at least clearly emerges from a consideration of them all taken together, and it is a very curious thing that it should never have been observed before ; namely, that whenever and wherever the specifically Christian, mediæval, or romantic values—they are all in essence the same thing—are in the ascendant, music is universally regarded as first and foremost among all the arts ; that when the pagan, classical, or eighteenth-century values are uppermost, music is despised or misunderstood, and relegated to the humblest position of all.

It is significant to note, moreover, that this alternate sympathy and hostility manifested towards the art of music by Christian and Pagan, by romantic and classic thinkers respectively, corresponds with the historical and æsthetic conclusions which have been arrived at in the course of the book. We have seen, for example how the establishment of the Christian order brought about the liberation of music from literary shackles, and its triumphant apotheosis ; how it continued to flourish so long as it remained in the service of the Christian ideals ; how about 1600 the momentary acceptance of the Greek ideals entailed its renewed subservience to literature, and the temporary loss of its primacy among the arts ; how the religious revival and the reaction against the Renaissance brought about another great musical wave culminating in Scarlatti, Bach, and Handel ; how the classically-inclined eighteenth century again caused a diminution of its prestige and power, from which it only recovered towards the end of the century ; and how the Romantic Movement resulted in a development and expansion of musical art on a scale hitherto unknown, and was, indeed, first and foremost a musical movement, as I have already shown in the first chapter of my " Survey of Contemporary Music ".

In a word, the conclusion to which we are unescapably drawn, the conclusion to which all the evidence at our disposal unmistakably points, whether we approach the question from the philosophic or from the æsthetic and historical angle, is, that music is the Christian and Romantic art *par excellence*, standing at the very opposite pole to the plastic arts, and to sculpture in particular, which is the art in which the Pagan and Classical values find their most complete and convincing expression. It follows that the æsthetic centre about which the musical circle is described, and the direction in which its greatest strength lies, consists in the expression of emotions rather than of thoughts, in the realization of intangible moods rather than of concrete forms, in the depiction of ideality rather than of reality, and in the appeal to spirit rather than to sense. All these other things music can do, as we have abundantly seen, but nothing so well as these ; these the other arts can do, but nothing like so well as music can. And corollarily, it also follows that the outermost circumference of the musical circle, and the direction in which its greatest weakness lies, consists in the creation of plastic, clearly defined forms, if only because, all *a priori* considerations apart, it is obvious that an art which exists in time instead of in space is unable to present a work simultaneously, and this is a necessary condition for the apprehension of formal beauty. It can only be achieved in music by abstracting the time-element which is the very essence of its nature, and by artificially conceiving the work statically and spread out in space.   In this way, but in this way only, can music succeed in satisfying our sense of purely abstract, formal design, but not so well as it can satisfy any other demands ; this is what the plastic arts, but especially sculpture, can do very much better than music can.   And in the same way that the later work of Rodin, in its endeavour to realize the ideas and conceptions proper to music, represents the farthest outpost of plastic art, so the music of the eighteenth century, generally speaking, in its attempt to achieve the precise and clearly defined forms proper to plastic art, so far from constituting the innermost core of music, as Hanslick and his followers would have it, stands in reality on the ultimate periphery of the musical circle.

In conclusion, then, music is the Christian, Mediæval, and Romantic art, the most characteristic art-expression of our era, and consequently provides a better key than any other to the understanding of the innermost spirit of the modern world and of the History of Civilization.

BIBLIOGRAPHY

A COMPLETE bibliography of musical history would obviously demand a whole volume to itself. The following list only represents a few of the more important and useful authorities in various languages. English translations of foreign works are given, where such exist.

WORKS OF REFERENCE

DE BEKKER (L. J.), Stokes' *Encyclopædia of Music and Musicians* 1910
EITNER (R.), *Biographisches-bibliographisches Quellen-Lexikon* .. 1900–4
FÉTIS (F. J.), *Biographie Universelle des Musiciens* 1878–80
GROVE'S *Dictionary of Music and Musicians* 1927–8
RIEMANN (H.), *Musik-Lexikon* 1922

GENERAL HISTORIES

ADLER (G.), *Handbuch der Musikgeschichte.* 1924
AMBROS (A. W.), *Geschichte der Musik* (With additions by Leichtentritt) 1860–1909
BURNEY (C.), *General History of Music* 1776–89
COMBARIEU (J.), *Histoire de la Musique des origines à la mort de Beethoven* 1913–19
EMMANUEL (M.), *Histoire de la Langue Musicale* 1911
FÉTIS (F. J.), *Histoire Générale de la Musique* 1869–76
HADOW (W. H.), *The Oxford History of Music*, comprising :—.... 1901–5
    WOOLDRIDGE (H. E.), " The Polyphonic Period."
    PARRY, (C. H. H.), "The Music of the Seventeenth Century."
    FULLER MAITLAND (J. A.), " The Age of Bach and Handel."
    HADOW, (W. H.), " The Viennese Period."
    DANNREUTHER (E.), " The Romantic Period."
HAWKINS (J.), *General History of the Science and Practice of Music* 1776
LANGHANS, (W.), *Geschichte der Musik* (continuing the work of Ambros) 1882–7
LAVIGNAC (A.), *Encyclopédie de la Musique* ..,.............. 1914, etc.
NAUMANN (E.), *History of Music* 1898–1900
RIEMANN (H.), *Handbuch der Musikgeschichte* 1919–22
STANFORD (C.), and FORSYTH (C.), *History of Music* 1916

STUDIES OF SEPARATE PERIODS AND COUNTRIES.

(Arranged chronologically so as to correspond roughly with the order of chapters adopted in the present work.)

GASTOUÉ (A.), *L'Art Grégorien* (Les Maîtres de la Musique) 1913
GATARD (A.), *La Musique Grégorienne* 1913
GEVAERT (F. A.), *Les Origines du Chant Liturgique* 1890
POTHIER (J.), *Les Mélodies Grégoriennes* 1880
WAGNER (P.), *Introduction to the Gregorian Melodies* 1910
— *Einführung in die Gregorianischen Melodien* 1895–1921
SCHUBIGER (A.), *Das Liturgische Drama des Mittelalters und seine Musik* 1876
COUSSEMAKER (C.), *Histoire de l'harmonie au Moyen Age* 1852
GASTOUÉ (A.), *Les Primitifs de la Musique française* 1922
AUBRY (P.), *Trouvères et Troubadours* (Les Maîtres de la Musique) 1909
BECK (J. B.), *La Musique des Troubadours* (Les Musiciens célèbres) 1910

FÉTIS (F. J.), *Les Musiciens Belges* 1848
KIESEWETTER (R.), *Die Verdienste der Niederländer um die Tonkunst* 1826
STRAETEN (E. van der), *La Musique aux Pays Bas* 1867–88
SCHERING (A.), *Studien zur Musikgeschichte der Frührenaissance* 1914
DICKENSON (E.), *Music in the History of the Western Church* 1902
TERRY (R. R.), *Catholic Church Music* 1907
TREND (J. B.), *The Music of Spanish History* (Hispanic Notes and Monographs) 1926
VAN DEN BORREN (C.), *Les débuts de la musique à Venise* 1914
WINTERFELD (C. von), *Johannes Gabrieli und sein Zeitalter* 1834
BIAGGI (G.), *La Musica nel secolo XVI* (La vita italiana nel cinquecent) 1894
DAVEY (H.), *History of British Music* 1895
FELLOWES, (E. H.), *The English Madrigal Composers* 1921
VAN DEN BORREN (C.), *The Sources of Keyboard Music in England* 1914
WALKER (E.), *The History of Music in England* 1907
WARLOCK (P.), *The English Ayre* 1926
GOLDSCHMIDT (H.), *Studien zur Geschichte der italienischer Oper* 1901–4
HENDERSON (W. J.), *Some forerunners of Italian Opera* 1911
ROLLAND (R.), *Histoire de l'Opéra en Europe avant Lulli et Scarlatti* 1895
SCHNEIDER (M.), *Die Anfänge des Basso Continuo* 1919
SOLERTI (A.), *Le Origini del Melodramma* 1903
FLORIMO (F.), *La Scuola musicale di Napoli* 1880–2
— *Cenno storico sulla scuolo musicale di Napoli* 1869–71
VILLAROSA (C. A.), *Memorie dei Compositori di Musica del Regno di Napoli* 1840
WIEL (T.), *I teatri musicali veneziani del settecento* 1897
CHOUQUET (G.), *Histoire de la Musique dramatique en France* 1873
ECORCHEVILLE (J.), *De Lulli a Rameau* 1906
NUITTER (C.), and TOINAN (J.), *Les origines de l'opéra français* .. 1886
WESTPHAL (J.), *Das evangelische Kirchenlied* 1918
WINTERFELD (C. von), *Geschichte des evangelischen Kirchengesangs* 1843
LINDNER (E. O.), *Die erste stehende Deutsche Oper* 1855
ARIENZO (N. d'), *Dell opera comica dalle origini a Pergolesi* 1887
BURNEY (C.), *The Present State of Music in France and Italy* 1771
— *The Present State of Music in Germany, the Netherlands and United Provinces* 1773
GOLDSCHMIDT (H.), *Geschichte der Musikästhetik im 18. Jahrhundert* 1915
LEE (VERNON), *Studies of the Eighteenth Century in Italy* 1907
WALTER (F.), *Geschichte des Theaters und der Musik am kurpfälzischen Hofe* 1898
SOUBIES (A.), *Le théâtre italien de 1801 a 1913* 1913
RIESEMANN (O.), *Monographien zur russischen Musik* 1923

HISTORIES OF FORMS AND CATEGORIES

KRETZSCHMAR (H.), *Kleine Handbücher der Musikgeschichte nach Gattungen,* comprising : ....
    SCHERING (A.), " Geschichte des Instrumentalkonzert " 1905
    LEICHTENTRITT (H.), " Geschichte der Motette " 1908
    SCHERING (A.), " Geschichte des Oratoriums " 1911
    KRETZSCHMAR (H.), " Geschichte des Neuen Deutschen Liedes " 1911
    SCHMITZ (E.), " Geschichte der Kantate " 1914
    KRETZSCHMAR (H.), " Geschichte der Oper " 1919
    BOTSTIBER (H.), " Geschichte der Ouvertüre " 1913
    WAGNER (P.), " Geschichte der Messe " 1905
    (other Volumes are in the course of preparation or publication).
BIE (O.), *Die Oper* 1913
SEIFFERT (M.), *Geschichte der Klaviermusik* 1899

SELECTED MONOGRAPHS AND BIOGRAPHIES
(arranged chronologically).

HABERL (X.), *Wilhelm Dufay* 1885
BRENET (M.), *Jean de Ockeghem* 1893
— *Palestrina* (Les Maîtres de la Musique) 1906
BAINI (G.), *Memorie storico-critiche della vita e delle opere di Giovanni Pierluigi da Palestrina* 1828
JEPPESEN (K.), *The Style of Palestrina and the Dissonance* 1926
COLLET (H.), *Victoria* (Les Maîtres de la Musique) 1914
PEDRELL (F.), Tomás Luis de Victoria Abulense.............. 1918
DESTOUCHES (E. von), *Orlando di Lasso* 1894
VAN DEN BORREN (C.), *Orlande de Lassus* 1920
WINTERFELD (C. von), *Johannes Gabrieli und sein Zeitalter* 1834
GRAY (C.) and HESELTINE (P.), *Carlo Gesualdo; Musician and Murderer* 1926
FELLOWES, (E. H.), *William Byrd* 1923
HOWES (F.), *William Byrd* 1928
PRUNIÈRES (H.), *Monteverdi* 1926
SCHNEIDER (J.), *Claudio Monteverdi* 1921
PRUNIÈRES (H.), *Lulli* (Les Musiciens célèbres) 1905
PIRRO (A.), *Schütz* (Les Maîtres de la Musique) 1913
— *Dietrich Buxtehude* 1913
FLOWER (N.), *Georg Frederic Handel* 1923
LEICHTENTRITT (H.), *Handel* 1924
ROLLAND (R.), *Handel* (Library of Music and Musicians) 1916
STREATFIELD (R.), *Handel* (New Library of Music) 1909
PIRRO, (A.), *J. S. Bach* (Les Maîtres de la Musique) 1913
— *L'esthétique de Jean Sebastien Bach* 1907
SCHWEITZER (A.), *J. S. Bach* 1911
LA LAURENCIE (L.), *Rameau* (Les Musiciens célèbres) 1908
LALOY (L.), *Rameau* (Les Maîtres de la Musique) 1908
ABERT (H.), *Niccolo Jommelli als Opernkomponist* 1908
BITTER (C. H.), *C. P. E. und W. F. Bach* 1868
RADICIOTTI (G.), *G. B. Pergolesi* 1910
NEWMAN (E.), *Gluck and the Opera* 1895
TIERSOT (J.), *Gluck* (Les Maîtres de la Musique) 1910
UDINE (J. d'), *Gluck* (Les Musiciens célèbres) 1906
BRENET (M.), *Haydn* (Les Maîtres de la Musique) 1909
BELLAIGUE (C.), *Mozart* (Les Musiciens célèbres) 1907
DENT (E. J.), *Mozart's Operas* 1913
JAHN (O.), *Life of Mozart* 1882
LEITZMANN (A.), *Wolfgang Amadeus Mozart* 1926
SCHIEDEMAIR (L.), *Mozart* 1922
BEKKER (P.), *Beethoven* 1925
INDY (V. d'), *Beethoven* (Les Musiciens célèbres) 1905
THAYER (A. W.), *Life of Beethoven* 1921
TURNER, (W. J.), *Beethoven* 1927
BOURGAULT-DUCOUDRAY (L. A.), *Schubert* (Les Musiciens célèbres) 1908
DAHMS (W.), *Schubert* 1912
BELLASIS (E.), *Cherubini* 1912
HOHENSEMSER (R.), *Luigi Cherubini* 1913
DAURIAC (L.), *Rossini* (Les Musiciens célèbres) 1905
PARENT DE CURZON (H.), *Rossini* (Les Maîtres de la Musique) .. 1920
PIZZETTI (L.), *La Musica di Vincenzo Bellini* 1916
SERVIÈRES (G.), *Weber* (Les Musiciens célèbres) 1907
MUENZER (G.), *Heinrich Marschner* (Berühmte Musiker) 1901
DAURIAC (L.), *Meyerbeer* (Les Maîtres de la Musique) 1913
EYMIEU (H.), *L'oeuvre de Meyerbeer* 1910
BELLAIGUE (C.), *Verdi* (Les Musiciens célèbres) 1911
GLASENAPP (C. F.), *Life of Wagner* 1900-8

NEWMAN (E.), *Wagner as Man and Artist* 1918
NIETZSCHE (F.), *The Case of Wagner* 1914
BOSCHOT (A.), *Hector Berlioz* 1906–11
COQUARD (A.), *Berlioz* 1903
JULLIEN (A.), *Berlioz, sa vie et ses oeuvres* 1889
HUNEKER (J. G.), *Chopin, the Man and his Music* 1903
LISZT (F.), *Life of Chopin* 1877
NIECKS (E.), *Chopin as a Man and a Musician* 1888
KAPP (J.), *Paganini* 1913
PRUD'HOMME (J. G.), *Paganini* (Musiciens célèbres) 1907
CALVOCORESSI (J.), *Liszt* (Les Musiciens célèbres) 1910
CHANTAVOINE (J.), *Liszt* (Les Maîtres de la Musique) 1910
BELLAIGUE (C.), *Mendelssohn* (Les Maîtres de la Musique) 1907
DAHMS (W.), *Mendelssohn* 1919
— *Schumann* 1916
MAUCLAIR (C.), *Schumann* (Les Musiciens célèbres) 1905
FULLER-MAITLAND (J. A.), *Brahms* (New Library of Music) 1911
KALBECK (M.), *Johannes Brahms* 1904–14
DECSEY (E.), *Hugo Wolf* 1919
NEWMAN (E.), *Hugo Wolf* (New Library of Music) 1907
DECSEY (E.), *Bruckner* 1920
KNAPP (A.), *Anton Bruckner* 1921
OREL (A.), *Anton Bruckner* 1925
INDY, (V.d'), *César Franck* 1910
CALVOCORESSI (M. D.), *Glinka* (Les Musiciens célèbres) 1911
HABETS (A.), *Borodin and Liszt* 1895
CALVOCORESSI (M. D.), *Moussorgsky* (Les Maîtres de la Musique) 1916

THE HISTORY OF CIVILIZATION

A COMPLETE HISTORY OF MANKIND FROM
PREHISTORIC TIMES TO THE PRESENT DAY
IN NUMEROUS VOLUMES DESIGNED
TO FORM A COMPLETE
LIBRARY OF SOCIAL
EVOLUTION

Edited by

C. K. OGDEN

of Magdalene College, Cambridge

Published by

KEGAN PAUL, TRENCH, TRUBNER & CO. LTD.
BROADWAY HOUSE: 68-74 CARTER LANE, LONDON
1943

Roy. 8vo.

PREHISTORY AND ANTIQUITY

The Earth Before History: Man's Origin and the Origin of Life. By Edmond Perrier, late Hon. Director of the Natural History Museum of France. With four maps. 16s. 6d.

Prehistoric Man: a General Outline of Prehistory. By Jacques de Morgan, late Director of Antiquities in Egypt. With 190 illustrations and maps. 14s.

Social Organization. By W. H. R. Rivers, LL.D., F.R.S. Edited by W. J. Perry, Reader in Cultural Anthropology in the University of London. With a Preface by Professor G. Elliot Smith. 12s.

Language: a Linguistic Introduction to History. By J. Vendryes, Professor in the University of Paris. 18s.

A Geographical Introduction to History. By Lucien Febvre, Professor in the University of Strasburg. With 7 maps. 18s.

Race and History: an Ethnological Introduction to History. By E. Pittard, Professor of Anthropology in the University of Geneva. With six illustrations and three maps. £1 3s.

The Aryans: a Study of Indo-European Origins. By V. Gordon Childe, B.Litt. With eight plates, 28 text illustrations, and a map. 12s.

From Tribe to Empire: Social Organization among the Primitives and in the Ancient East. By A. Moret, Professor in the University of Paris, and G. Davy, University of Dijon. With 47 illustrations and seven maps. 18s.

Life and Work in Prehistoric Times. By G. Renard, Professor at the College of France. With 25 illustrations. 14s.

EARLY EMPIRES

The Ægean Civilization. By G. Glotz, Professor of Greek History in the University of Paris. With four plates, 87 illustrations and three maps. 18s.

The Nile and Egyptian Civilization. By A. Moret, Professor at the Collège de France. With 24 plates, 82 illustrations and three maps. £1 7s. 6d.

Minoans, Philistines and Greeks: 1400-900 B.C. By Andrew Robert Burn. With sixteen plates. 16s. 6d.

Israel, from its Beginnings to the Middle of the Eighth Century. By A. Lods, Professor at the Sorbonne. With 16 plates, three maps, and 38 text illustrations. £1 7s. 6d.

The Prophets and the Rise of Judaism. By A. Lods, Professor at the Sorbonne. With eight plates. £1 7s. 6d.

The World of Hesiod. By Andrew Robert Burn. 14s.

GREECE

The Formation of the Greek People. By A. Jardé, Professor of History at the Lycée Lakanal. With seven maps. 18s.

Art in Greece. By A. de Ridder, Curator at the Louvre Museum, and W. Deonna, Director of the Geneva Museum. With 24 plates and 66 text illustrations. £1 3s.

Macedonian Imperialism, and the Hellenization of the East. By Pierre Jouguet, Professor at the University of Paris. With seven plates and four maps and plans. £1 3s.

The Greek City, and its Institutions. By G. Glotz, Professor of Greek History in the University of Paris. 18s.

ROME

Primitive Italy, and the Beginnings of Roman Imperialism. By Leon Homo, Professor in the University of Lyons. With 13 maps and plans. 18s.

The Roman Spirit in Religion, Thought and Art. By A. Grenier, Professor in the University of Strasburg. With 16 plates, and 16 text illustrations. 18s.

Rome the Law-Giver. By J. Declareuil, Professor in the University of Toulouse. 18s.

Ancient Rome at Work : an Economic History from the Origins to the Empire. By Paul Louis. With four plates and six maps. 18s.

The Roman World. By Victor Chapot, Professor at the École des Beaux-Arts With two plates and twelve maps. 18s.

Roman Political Institutions, from City to State. By Leon Homo, Professor in the University of Lyons. 18s.

The Economic Life of the Ancient World. By J. Toutain, Director at L'École des Hautes Études. With six maps, 18s.

The Rise of the Celts. By H. Hubert. With 47 illustrations and 12 maps. 18s.

Greatness and Decline of the Celts. By H. Hubert. With three maps. 18s.

BEYOND THE ROMAN EMPIRE

Chinese Civilization. By Marcel Granet, Professor at the School of Oriental Languages, Paris. With 12 plates and 5 maps. £1 7s. 6d.

The Life of Buddha, as Legend and History. By E. J. Thomas, D.Litt., Under Librarian in the University Library, Cambridge. With four plates and a map. 14s.

A History of Buddhist Thought. By E. J. Thomas, D.Litt. With four plates. 16s. 6d.

The Heroic Age of India. By N. K. Sidhanta, Professor of English at Lucknow University. 14s.

Caste and Race in India. By Dr. G. S. Ghurye. 12s.

Ancient India and Indian Civilization. By P. Masson-Oursel, H. de Willman-Grabowska, and P. Stern. With five maps, 16 plates and 24 black and white illustrations. £1 3s.

CHRISTIANITY AND THE MIDDLE AGES

The History and Literature of Christianity : from Tertullian to Boethius. By Pierre de Labriolle, Professor of Literature at the University of Poitiers. With a foreword by Cardinal Gasquet. £1 7s. 6d.

Life and Work in Medieval Europe, V-XV Century. By P. Boissonnade, Professor in the University of Poitiers. Introduction by Eileen Power, D.Litt. With eight plates. 18s.

Life and Work in Modern Europe, XV-XVIII Century. By G. Renard, Professor at the College of France, and G. Weulersse, Professor at the Lycée Carnot. Introduction by Eileen Power, D.Litt. With eight plates. 18s.

Travel and Travellers of the Middle Ages. Edited by A. P. Newton, Rhodes Professor of Imperial History in the University of London. With eight plates and maps, 14s.

Chivalry : its Historical Significance and Civilizing Influence. Edited by Edgar Prestage, Camõens Professor in the University of London. With 24 plates. 16s. 6d.

The Court of Burgundy. By Otto Cartellieri. With 25 plates. £1 3s.

The End of the Ancient World, and the Beginnings of the Middle Ages. By Ferdinand Lot, Professor in the University of Paris. With 3 plates and 3 maps. £1 3s.

Jesus. By Charles Guignebert, Professor of the History of Christianity at the Sorbonne. Illustrated. £1 7s. 6d.

The Feudal Monarchy in France and England from the Tenth to the Thirteenth Century. By Ch. Petit-Dutaillis, Member of L'Institut de France. With 2 maps. 18s.

The Jewish World in the Time of Jesus. By Charles Guignebert, Professor of the History of Christianity at the Sorbonne. £1 3s.

MODERN TIMES

London Life in the XVIIIth Century. By M. Dorothy George. With eight illustrations from contemporary prints. £1 3s.

SUBJECT HISTORIES

The History of Medicine, from the time of the Pharaohs to the end of the Eighteenth Century. By C. G. Cumston, M.D., Lecturer on History of Medicine in the University of Geneva. With an Introduction by F. G. Crookshank, M.D., F.R.C.P. With 24 plates. 18s.

The History of Music. By Cecil Gray. 14s.

HISTORICAL ETHNOLOGY

The Threshold of the Pacific : an Account of the Social Organization, Magic, and Religion, of the People of San Cristoval in the Solomon Islands. By Dr. C. E. Fox. With a Preface by Professor G. Elliot Smith. With fourteen plates, 39 illustrations in the text, and map. 20s.

The Peoples of Asia. By L. H. Dudley Buxton, M.A., F.S.A., Lecturer in Physical Anthropology, University of Oxford. With eight plates. 14s.

The Civilization of the South American Indians, with special reference to their Magic and Religion. By Rafael Karsten, Professor of Moral Philosophy, University of Finland, Helsingfors. Preface by Professor E. Westermarck. £1 7s. 6d.

The American Indian Frontier. By William Christie Macleod, Assistant Professor in the University of Pennsylvania. With 13 maps. £1 7s. 6d.

Death Customs : an Analytical Study of Burial Rites. By E. Bendann, Ph.B., A.M. 14s.